A HORSE
A HUSBAND
AND
CANCER

For Penny - and Family - whose kindness and friendship knows no borders, it is a joy to be among you.

xx

A HORSE
A HUSBAND
AND
CANCER

by Elaine Kirsch Edsall
with Mark Edsall

Lilith House Press
Estes Park, Colorado

ISBN 978-1-7369673-0-0 (print)
ISBN 978-1-7369673-1-7 (ebook)

Cover Design: Jane Dixon Smith/ jdsmith-design.com
Cover photo: Mark Edsall
Editing: Anna Blake with Maxie Jane Frazier

Lilith House Press

CONTENTS

INTRODUCTION

This is not a book about horses; nor is it a book about husbands, and it is certainly not a book solely about cancer.

Though that condition is the core reason for this work, it does not make this some sort of self-help book for those suffering from this illness or yet another set of pages condoning positive thinking and attitudes to try to overcome despair and fear.

Elaine was my wife for the last twenty-five years and six days of her life, in all we were together for some thirty years. One year into our (then illicit) relationship she discovered the first cancer; little did we realise then that it was going to be a recurring theme for the rest of her life, neither did we know the extent of the struggle to come or the battlefield our lives were to turn into.

This book leads you through one woman's fight to stay a step ahead of the silent assassin within. Armaments for this battle consisted of more than just the medical procedures and treatments she had to endure. Elaine dug deep within to find her allies and always refused any hint of sympathy from others.

Her story of how she tried, not always successfully, to make sense of the path her life had taken and where it ultimately was going to lead. Her deep-seated and dark sense of humour, her even deeper love for me and for her friends and horses helped her to prevail, against the odds, for so long. She was bruised and battered in mind, spirit and body so many times, yet a two fingered salute was all the ground she would give to the cancer.

A short time ago she started the online blog from which this book gets its title. She wrote about her shrinking world with observations from within and without, and proved that living with a terminal illness can be accomplished with style and humour.

Her words are honest, straightforward and from the heart; she doesn't pull punches to spare herself. Indeed, she leaves herself at the mercy of her readers on more than one occasion.

After her death, I continued her blog to complete her story and to try and make sense of where I stood. I am deeply honoured that the first thirteen of those blogs have been included to complete this book. I think Elaine would be pleased too.

So, if you have an interest in horses, husbands or cancer there is something here for you to chew over; but if you want to hear of the unrelenting human spirit even knowing the fight is unwinnable, then read on, there is a feast before you.

MARK EDSALL
August 2021

PROLOGUE

THE IRISH COLT

Southern Ireland is famous for the craic, the Guinness, and the rainfall but even by Irish standards, the spring of 1994 was unseasonably wet and cold. In a field where coastline meets countryside, and horizontal shards of rain drive straight from the sea, the foal was born on a moonless May night. He was a large foal and although his mother had produced many before him, this one came at great cost to her elderly body. She was too weak to lick her newborn, let alone encourage him to suckle, and they lay together in the wet grass until daybreak, when the farmer found them on his early morning rounds.

Cussing that his inattention could cost him dearly, he hoisted the foal up onto his shoulders, and with the mare following, took them to a waiting barn where old straw was piled up high to make a warm bed. What the bed lacked in freshness it gained in depth. He twisted straw into a rope, and then into a pad and roughly massaged the mother and foal. As warmth returned to the mare's body so did maternal instinct, and she began to wash her foal. The farmer sat back on his haunches in the straw to have a closer look at his ill-advised 'investment'.

The standing foal wobbled and fell and wobbled again before finding his mother's udder. He suckled noisily, his feather-duster of a tail bobbing up and down as he grabbed greedily for milk. As the farmer noted his handsome head with a bright white star shining like a beacon, his soft pink muzzle surrounded by a web of spidery whiskers, huge shoulder sloping like an anvil, disproportionately large backend and four white socks. He mentally ran through the ancient adage "one white sock, keep him all your life, two white socks, give him to your wife, three white socks give him to your man, four white socks sell him if you can."

Well, that was the plan; the mare's value was in her foal, fathered by a local Irish Draught stallion, and she had the graceful thoroughbred bloodlines to soften any plain traits passed down with the sire's strength. Pleased with the look of this foal, the farmer almost allowed himself to pet the mare for her effort. He wasn't a cruel man, just ignorant; he had bought the broodmare cheaply at the sales, wanting to make as much money as he could with as little effort as possible.

The mare and foal spent the rest of that summer alone in the boggy paddock. Without a helping human hand to provide extra food, the mother struggled to produce milk and neither of them thrived. The mother could barely look after herself, let alone teach her foal valuable life lessons, and the foal hung back, absorbing her anxiety instead of pushing boundaries in what should have been a confidence-building new world full of wonder. He was always hungry.

As late autumn headed towards winter, the cold wind blew in from the coast and the old mare lost what little bodyweight remained. The farmer slipped a halter over her scraggy head, led her into the same barn (with the same bedding) and the foal followed at a cautious distance. Once the foal was inside the barn, the mare was quickly pulled away, the door boarded up and the foal left alone in the dark to scream and holler. The mare was led into the waiting lorry and taken to the hunt kennels. By lunchtime she was dead, leaving hounds complaining about their sparse rations. In her youth, she'd won many races, and as she aged, she'd bred many fine foals. She'd done her job, and the circle of life was complete.

In the dark stable the foal begged for his mother, begged for comfort, begged for milk and vainly flapped his lips together . . . a habit that would last a lifetime.

After his traumatic weaning, the black colt retreated within himself, alone in the paddock for two long winters. When the farmer and a companion visited one morning, he registered little interest and continued grazing at a distance. Giving himself time to watch the farmer whom he dismissed with disdain, he noted that the companion trod with the ease of someone totally in charge and spoke softly as if he had something interesting to say. The colt flicked one ear forward and momentarily stopped eating. He felt a primeval need for a safe leader surge through his body, rippling his thin coat and making him shiver with anticipation.

The man spoke to him so quietly, the colt had to move alongside to hear the tone, and he stood calmly as the quiet man ran the palm of his hand softly down his neck. It reminded him of how his mother had licked him, and he liked it. As he stood, he noticed the man's coat smelt of nice things, and he liked that too. The dealer's hands felt his legs, his rump and his ribcage, and the colt felt warm and secure.

Suddenly, the farmer waved his arms and shouted, and slapped the colt to make him run away. Bucking and kicking, he galloped to the far end of the field, wheeled round in a large arc and trotted back to the dealer man, who smiled and nodded, and breathed out slowly in answer to the colt's anxious breath. A rapid exchange of words passed between the two men, concluding with a wad of notes being pressed into the farmer's hand. The farmer brought the mare's old halter from the barn, and before the colt knew what was happening, he was manhandled into a trailer and driven away from a life he never quite forgot.

After traveling for about an hour, the Land Rover and trailer turned through metal gates and parked in a large, well-fenced field. The colt was loose inside the trailer, and the ramp was barely down before he fled its confines. The grass under his feet was long, lush, and green. He put his head down and ate, great tufts of goodness torn nervously and devoured greedily. He continued eating as five field-mates cantered towards him, bucking, leaping and running amok like a bunch of carefree hooligans. They squealed to a halt at the fence line before wheeling round in unison and trotted towards the shade of the trees. Four of the colts began to graze with apparent nonchalance, but the fifth, a stocky bay who was large in stature if not in size, walked towards the black colt with the swagger of a born leader and barged straight into him.

The black colt's teeth were momentarily separated from the grass. A challenge was annoying enough, but any interruption that stopped him eating was far more irksome. The two colts faced each other. The black colt had no confidence, no experience of other horses and no social skills but he had greed, and great strength comes with any kind of greed, so he promptly turned his back on the bay colt and let fly with both back legs powered by his disproportionately large backend. The bay reeled in indignation and pain as a flying hoof made contact with his shoulder but came straight back to do battle. Refusing to be side-tracked, the black colt waved a back leg with threatening intent and flattened his ears flat against his head and continued eating. The bay had no option but to rejoin his friends and no one bothered the black colt again. He didn't play, he didn't enjoy mutual grooming, he didn't help swish flies or gallop with the wind in his tail, didn't bite and nip and test the pecking order or look for imaginary monsters. He just ate.

The black colt lived among but not 'with' the others for two more winters. They were all gelded together, returning to the field somewhat more subdued and the black felt the most pain and took longest to recover. He remembered his mother and flapped his lips for comfort. All six boys had daily lessons learning how to walk in-hand, carry a saddle and wear a bridle. The girl grooms leant across their backs, and they were long-reined with sacks tied to the saddle. The farrier trimmed their feet and they became accustomed to cars and tractors. The black horse was eager to please, very quick to learn, and more compliant than his classmates, and the girls loved him. He liked being petted and he liked to have someone in charge but most of all he liked to eat. He didn't like being scolded or having his thin coat brushed with rough brushes, and he didn't like being shut in a stable.

Appraising his crop of youngsters in the summer of their fourth year, Ned Mahoney smiled with satisfaction at a job well done. They had grown fat and sleek. The young black cob was the pick of the bunch and looked outstanding with his arched neck, deep body, broad chest, strong loins and hugely powerful backside. His mother's thoroughbred breeding showed in his clean featherless legs and elegant head, silky coat and well-set tail, but most of her characteristics had channeled themselves into his temperament. With some trepidation, Ned recognised that this middleweight cob was more like a thoroughbred than many racehorses he'd known and wondered what life would be like for one so sensitive. With the Irish showing season about to begin, he moved the black horse, the bay, and a nicely marked piebald into a field alongside the road where he'd replaced the high hedge with a post and rail fence. Three fine youngsters for sale to suit all tastes, and he believed in giving prospective purchasers a roadside view.

In the early morning mist, Hilary Marson loaded her two show horses into the lorry, closed the ramp and hoisted herself into the cab. Another showing season, another batch of young horses for training and selling, and hopefully enough money earned to pay for a long-awaited roof repair on her house. Having done a day's work before the sun came up, she contemplated the competition ahead and thought ruefully of her comfy bed and assorted dogs still sleeping there. Taking the top road out of the village, she had just enough time to drive past Ned's farm and see what was in the viewing field.

You had to be quick with Ned. His sales patter might always

begin with the line "I'd have kept this 'un if only I had the room . . ." but as a middleman able to see potential in a gangly youngster, he had the best horses for miles around, flourishing (he said) on fields fed by holy wells. Whatever his secret, many champions had come from his farm. Gently shifting the lorry's gears in order not to jolt her precious cargo, Hilary reached the field and saw two horses snoozing side by side; a nice bay, somewhat light of bone for her taste and a piebald with a pony-ish head. She had her foot back on the gas ready to drive on when she noticed the black horse grazing slightly away from the others, head down, tucking into a dewy breakfast. She turned the steering wheel and headed the lorry up the farm drive.

The deal was sealed within thirty minutes. As the black horse was loaded into Hilary's lorry, he flapped his lips with anxiety but didn't call out. The two horses already standing tied in the lorry flared their noses in greeting and remembered the morning they too had come from the same field. Hilary named the black cob Ned after the dealer, but with his flapping lips, he was registered in his passport as 'Look Who's Talking'.

Ned thrived with Hilary and her dedicated team. He over-came his fear of being stabled but at the first sign of anything stressful he would rasp the walls with his teeth creating great gashes across the wood panelling. He loved the grooming massages with soft brushes, and his silky coat shone beneath the groom's powerful hands. He had a season's hunting with Hilary's head girl who found him excitable but controllable, and with his sensitive mouth, there was no need for a strong bit to give extra brakes. He took to jumping like a duck to water, and as long as his jockey gave clear instructions he would face any obstacle with confidence, leaping hedges and rails, gates and ditches like an old-timer with athleticism that belied his stocky frame!

Hilary taught him balance and cadence and delighted in the lightness of foot his schoolwork brought. His barrel body became toned and honed, his neck increased its magnificent arch and his bottom developed a deep cleavage. Measuring

15.3hh he was perfectly proportioned for a maxi cob, echoing the judges from yesteryear who decreed a show cob should have "the face of a duchess and the backside of a cook."

His manners were impeccable. He automatically stood square, galloped like a seasoned hunter and won every cob class he entered, charming judges and spectators alike by flapping his lips with perfect comic timing at the prize-giving. Throughout the year Hilary turned down many requests to buy Ned, but as he left the ring at Dublin Show decked in his winning ribbons, the deal offered by the Englishman could not be bettered. She put Ned's saddle back in the lorry and watched with great sadness as he was led away. As she began her journey back to her quiet village, the black cob began his journey to his new life in England.

The huge transporter truck carried a cargo of nine Irish horses, and the journey to England by road and sea was long. Loaded in order of geographical drop-off, Ned was flanked by a grey heavyweight cob also acquired by his new owner, who ran a classy hunter dealing yard in affluent Oxfordshire. They were loaded first and would be the last consignment delivered. A nervous young thoroughbred had trouble keeping his balance in the confined partition space and thrashed about with each rolling turn. Fretting at the distress, Ned was unable to relieve tension with teeth rasping, so he gently swayed from one foot to another. In the time it took to cross the Irish Sea, he had taught himself another calming technique.

Two girl grooms wearing smart green sweatshirts with an entwined 'FFK' logo were waiting as the transporter drove through the ornate iron gates of Frank Fyford-Knox's dealing yard. They quietly untied Ned and the grey horse, spoke some soft words between them, and led the horses down the ramp of the empty lorry. The horses blinked in the evening sunlight, bodies wobbling as their legs adjusted to terra firma, and the girls let them stand a moment to re-balance, before walking across the immaculate courtyard to a block of Victorian stables with hayloft and clock tower above. Timeworn cobbles formed an apron in front of the stables, swept clean without a wisp of hay to be seen. A Victorian water trough, overflowing with brightly coloured flowers was the only concession to frivolity in an otherwise mellow colour scheme. Frank Fyford-Knox personally sourced horses for money-rich-time-poor clients and charged them handsomely for the privilege. His reputation was impeccable, his client list always full, and his staff of experienced grooms and younger working pupils provided the highest standards of turnout and professionalism. At the back of the farm there was a field for landing helicopters, and the elegant manor house dining hall hosted lavish lunches for prospective buyers.

The two new horses were led into large looseboxes where rubber-matted floors had deep beds of shavings. Plump haynets and automatic drinkers were in one corner and the back windows looked out to paddocks beyond. As their headcollars were removed, both horses sank to the ground grunting and rolling to relieve the stresses of their journey. Then, rising in unison and shaking vigorously, they walked to their water and drank deeply before tucking into nets of sweet haylage. The grooms left them alone to settle for the night. Early next morning they found the grey asleep and snoring, and the black cob, having re-decorated the walls of his box with rasping teeth marks, calmly shredding the front of his cotton stable rug into thin strips.

After two days grazing together in the paddock, Frank's head lad rode both horses in the Olympic-sized arena and jumped them over some stout fences. He felt the black cob was a little sensitive in the mouth for a novice rider to hunt, but as opinions didn't please his boss, he kept his thoughts to himself. Later that week after trying their mounts and being wined and dined, the prospective owners paid the full asking prices subject to positive vetting. Both horses passed the vet tests with flying colours, and when the grey left the field to travel to his new home, Bruce continued grazing, viewing the expanse of grass he could now eat without interruption. It was a yard custom for the grooms to name their charges, and the black cob was now called Bruce. Next morning Bruce flapped his lips as he journeyed south to his new hunting home in Dorset. It was his fourth move and he was six years old.

Neither he nor I had any idea of the other's existence, and it would be some years before our paths crossed, and our lives entwined.

PART ONE

FIRST HORSE FIRST HUSBAND FIRST CANCER

Nana lived with us and knew that horses were my world. She bequeathed an item of precious family jewellery to each of my cousins, but left me the most precious gift of all: one hundred pounds to buy a pony. A pony!! A pony of my own!!

1 FIRST HORSE

Horses are the cord that has laced my life together; my chapters are woven around equines that share those ties. From the beginning, books and ponies were my entire life. I read every book I could find on how to look after ponies, ride ponies and train ponies, and every storybook about girls who had ponies. In the garden at home, my imaginary pony was Black Beauty's friend Merrylegs. Merrylegs and I flowed through our paces with effortless movement, schooling over jumps made of twigs. We were as one, and I could effortlessly see a stride. With small hands holding the reins and, a silver trophy and the biggest rosette imaginable, we cantered our winner's lap of honour around the garden; physically and mentally moving as one being. I dismounted and put my arms around my pony, thanked him for being the best, and led him, prancing, and dancing, to the make-believe stable. We squeezed through the narrow gap between two trees, and I re-arranged the bracken bedding and settled him for the night. After feeding him a 'bucket' of mash from a flowerpot, I went indoors for my dinner.

Donkey was grey, and had an unusually broad brown Jerusalem cross, reaching from tail to withers, with crossbars that ended below his knees. Such vivid markings made him a church favourite at Easter and Christmas, and although he was not heady with fame, he certainly knew his own mind. Donkey lived at the pig farm where my school friend Maureen kept her pony. I helped her in the evenings, and the farmer lent me Donkey so we could ride together. I found riding Donkey a mixed blessing, but he was real, and a huge improvement on imaginary predecessors.

I put the grooming kit I'd bought especially for him in my bicycle basket, and cycled twenty minutes to the farm, lifted his felt saddle-pad and bridle from the hook in the barn and carried it out to the field. Wherever Donkey was standing in the field was where I brushed and dressed him, because I quickly learnt it was pointless to suggest somewhere different, no matter how many times I told him he was handsome and good. The first time I put his bridle on I thought he was going to die; as I slipped the headpiece over his ears he began to splutter and heave, with huge internal bellows pumping overtime. I stood back thinking his sides would explode, until he turned his head towards me, and uttered one huge monotone out-breath bray, which was loud enough to split the atom. He did this at every bridling, moving closer and closer to my own ears, which seemed to amuse him. Once mounted, we trotted round the perimeter of his field three and a half times. He was intransigent about the pace, direction and number of laps, and it was a while before I questioned his authority . . .

One morning I decided we would like to go for a walk outside his field. He decided we wouldn't. As we walked through the gate, he planted three hooves on the ground and one front hoof directly on my foot. Half in and half out, I was trying to hold him, hold the gate which swung towards us, and move him off my foot. No matter how much I pulled, pushed, cajoled, or chastised, he remained motionless and stood with his ears pricked and eyes fixed on me. I can clearly remember his look, and I swear he was smiling. The pig farmer walked past us, with a sow on its way to the slaughterhouse, and nodded in our direction. Not wanting to lose face, I pretended I was petting Donkey, and standing mid-gate was a predetermined destination. Sometime later, the farmer walked back, and didn't seem surprised we were still 'petting'. Without saying a word, he took hold of the gate so I could move my aching arm, and made a hissing noise at Donkey, who swished his tail, turned round and walked back into his field. I un-tacked him, hung everything back in the barn and placed his grooming kit next to the saddle pad. I limped to my bike and pedaled slowly home.

Elizabeth was horse-mad too, so she was my best friend at school. When we turned eleven, our parents agreed we could have riding lessons every other Saturday with Miss Bush. We lived and breathed for those Saturday lessons. Built like a tiny sparrow, with weatherbeaten features and curls of soft white hair, Miss Bush was a dynamo of wiry energy. Born into a wealthy family, the Victorian family house and stables became hers when her parents died, but there was little money for upkeep. Everything had an air of neglected grandeur, but she was a local legend, and her teaching was superb. Along with a string of patent-safety ponies, she kept three chestnut thoroughbreds stabled in the old cobblestoned coach house. We girlies worshiped the big horses, and if we rode particularly well in our lessons, our reward was to groom them. It was joy beyond words to touch that velvet skin, and brush the silken tail of a proper horse, like the ones who showjumped on television. I saw Miss Bush again years later, shortly before she died, and she didn't look any different to that first day in 1966. She was eighty-seven, and she died wearing her riding boots just as she wished.

My grandmother died when I was twelve. Nana lived with us and knew that horses were my world. She bequeathed an item of precious family jewellery to each of my cousins, but left me the most precious gift of all: one hundred pounds to buy a pony. A pony!! A pony of my own!! None of my family is, or ever was, in the least bit horsey. Mum used to take me to the saddler so I could spend my savings on a brush, or halter, or saddle soap in readiness for my own pony. But when I began to look at local ponies for sale, Elizabeth and I cycled to see them on our pushbikes. We rode the pony and asked pertinent questions, but most suitable ponies were above my budget. On the cycle ride back home, we discussed the pros and cons, and as soon as I was indoors, I wrote concise details in my Pony Book. Sitting and writing that book at the dining room table was a hidden memory that came floating back, as I type this on the laptop.

The advert for Jimmy appeared in the Saturday edition of our local evening paper: 13.2 dark bay New Forest pony gelding for sale, 7 years old. Good with traffic, farrier etc. £75.00 including tack. I phoned the seller and arranged to see him the following morning. Elizabeth was going to church, so I cycled there alone. Something intangible connected me to Jimmy the first moment I saw him, and it gave me a sharp rush of adrenaline. None of my pony books had mentioned this happening. It's a pattern that's been repeated with all my best horses, leading to logic being chucked on the muck heap, and the famous words "I'll have him" being blurted without forethought. Jimmy was a neat stamp of pony, true to type for his New Forest breeding. He had a small white star and mealy coloured muzzle, and of course, he had the sweetest breath and kindest eyes ever bestowed on any pony. The woman selling him saddled up her own horse and took me for a ride to try him out. His steering was very wobbly, his balance ungainly, and I fell off as soon as we started cantering. (I later discovered he was actually rising five and just broken). But I adored him, and he was within my budget so I got back on and said I would have him, and next day Mum wrote the cheque. My life was just about to begin because I owned my very own pony. I found a field and stable to rent for him, and a week later we rode the eight miles to his new home, with mum following in her car. Today, the very thought of riding a four-year-old just-broken pony with no steering, along those busy roads makes me cringe, but back then belief triumphed over everything, and no harm came to us.

Life with a pony settled into the routine I had meticulously planned in my dreams. Every evening after school, I cycled my favourite journey to Jimmy's field, because everyone would know that a bucket balanced on the handlebars, and saddle strapped gardeners.

—————————

wholesaler.

Postcode	: BH21 1PL
EAN	: 9781444006360 X 1 (£ 6.99)
Title	: The One Dollar Horse
Author	: St.John, Lauren
Dues Record	: Yes
Customer Ref	: .2
Line Ref	: allenbourn

**** CUSTOMER QTY RECEIVED ON THIS DELIVERY: 28
**** CUSTOMER NOTIFIED OF ARRIVAL BY EMAIL
Comments   :

Customer Order: 27

Name	: Allenbourn Middle School
Address	: East Borough
	: Wimborne
	:
	:
Postcode	: BH21 1PL
EAN	: 9780571299508 X 1 (£ 6.99)
Title	: Champion Horse
Author	: Smiley, Jane
Dues Record	: Yes
Customer Ref	: .2
Line Ref	: allenbourn

**** CUSTOMER QTY RECEIVED ON THIS DELIVERY:
**** CUSTOMER NOTIFIED OF ARRIVAL BY EMAIL
Comments   :

to the back of my bike meant I had a pony. I fed and groomed him and loved him more than anything in the world. At the weekends, we went riding on the heath and that was where my fantasy abruptly ended. In reality, riding Jimmy scared the daylights out of me. Loving a pony doesn't stop you falling off, and nothing had prepared me for riding an uncouth, unschooled bundle of nervous energy. Time after time I lay winded in the heather, watching him gallop home and gradually I realised he would never be Merrylegs. Sadly, his sweet breath and mealy muzzle didn't make that realisation hurt any less.

With un-horsey parents and nobody on hand to help, I took him to a Pony Club rally hoping for tuition. I bathed and brushed him and trimmed his hairy bits. Despite having a new white school shirt to wear with my jodhpurs and shoes, we were still the scruffiest among a field of expensive show ponies, immaculately dressed little girls and matching mothers. Nobody picked us to join their teams, and none of the instructors sensed my problems, so we never went again. Instead, I decided we had to work this out ourselves. We ignored all the pony books and made it up as we went along, spending rides instinctively doing what felt right for us. Eventually, I learnt to sit and he learnt balance; more of an achievement than I knew. We taught each other to jump which wasn't pretty, but like everything else it worked for us and that was what mattered. Jimmy never became Merrylegs but he became something so much more, and the only dreams that became reality were that we moved as one.

In 1976 I wanted to travel abroad, so my friend Sheila took Jimmy to use in her riding school. He became a firm favourite with the school clients, and forged a lifelong friendship with Mickey, a lookalike New Forest pony. When I came home from my year in Canada I used to visit and ride Jimmy regularly, and Sheila gave me the job of taking out experienced clients on a 'fast ride' while she accompanied the beginner walkers. No matter how many other people rode Jimmy, we never lost our bond or our own intuitive way of doing things, and the self-judgment of 'proper' riding never replaced the joy of free-wheeling. Jimmy died when he was thirty-four, shortly after Mickey.

2 FIRST HUSBAND

Depending on whether I wore a blindfold or rose-tinted spectacles, the 1990s was either a very good or very bad decade. The only certainty was that it was life changing. After years of dithering about starting a family because 'the time was never right', nature made the decision for me and I began the decade pregnant. My brain immediately went into scrambled-egg-mode and my hormones ran a gamut of emotions which changed hourly; if I wasn't terrified, I was ecstatic. I spent a lot of time writing lists, and by twelve weeks, I realised how much I wanted this baby. My husband didn't say much at all, which I took as a good sign.

I was leading the horses out to their field one morning when a crippling cramp in my abdomen made me scream out loud and double-over in pain. The horses stood politely while I recovered, and then we continued as if nothing had happened. But I knew it had. That night I sat on the cold bathroom floor propped against the side of the bath, pain etched on my face. In my hand I held the tiniest most translucent creature I have ever seen, curled like a tiny leaf. Intuitively I knew he was a boy, and as I bent to murmur how loved he was, a tear fell on his tiny head. This was my baby. In the quiet of the night, I wrapped him in toilet tissue and placed him gently in a matchbox. With numb mind and body, I fumbled for boots and a coat and slipped out the back door, walking noiselessly down to the river that ran alongside our house. On the bank I paused, and then placed the matchbox in the river. It bobbed along, bathed in moonlight and love, and I watched until it filled with water and sank out of sight. Slowly I returned home and climbed back into bed, shivering.

"Have a good cry," said my husband waking briefly from deep sleep. "You'll feel better in the morning." That was the night he lost me forever.

Up until that moment I thought I was invincible, and the blow felled me like nothing before. I was on my knees with a pain so guttural it consumed every moment whether awake or asleep, and profound grief was exacerbated by being told I'd get over it and could always try again. My hair fell out, I couldn't eat and didn't know how to assuage the unbearable yearning. There was no one to tell. My husband showed little emotion or support and I couldn't shake off the feeling of deep and irretrievable loss, not just for my baby, but for the overwhelming flaw in my marriage that I'd tried to ignore for so long.

Dennis was fifteen years older than me, had been married twice before, and had grown-up children. We began our marriage at opposite ends of the emotional scale. While I was tactile and showed my feelings, he was impassive, and hugs were an alien concept. I knew I was condemning myself to an unresponsive partnership, but I loved him. Over the years I buried my vivacious personality to become the dutiful wife he wanted, I unpinned my heart from my sleeve and shrouded it so no one would know how I felt, not even me. I lived as the weight to Den's ideas, and when I really needed him he was unable to respond. With hindsight, I'd repeated a familial pattern and married my father, but I didn't have my mother's humility to smother the person I really was.

3 ASTRA

I had bought a young Arab mare to train when Den and I were first married. Den became interested in horses, so I showed him how to do everyday tasks and he began taking riding lessons at the local school. My mare was a stunning 14.2 Arab cross. She looked like a dapple-grey rocking horse with fine features and elegant limbs, long flowing mane and tail, but she had a quirky personality. As her training increased, so did her Jekyll-and-Hyde behaviour and I didn't deal well with her problems. She became aggressive around food, running at me with her ears flat back as I fed breakfast, so I would get out the stable as quickly as I could, closely followed by splinters of wood as her hooves double-barrelled the door. Mareish? I gave her the benefit of the doubt. I was grooming her outside while she dozed in the sunshine, and as I turned to brush dust from her quarter, a searing pain tore through my shoulder; she had bitten me hard for no apparent reason, ripping my tee-shirt and my skin. I tied her shorter to prevent further accidents, but she began to cow kick with vengeance, and she had perfect aim with a deceptively long range. Each time something happened, I made another excuse; that she was in season, ticklish, or maybe the flies were worrying her. One afternoon we were lunging in the arena when she stopped, looked me in the eye, turned and galloped straight at me. I threw my arms in the air and waved the lunge whip at her, but she kept coming. I jumped out of the way just in time. Afterwards, she stood calmly while I gathered the lunge line, and walked back to the stable as if nothing had occurred. I even began to doubt it myself, until the same thing happened when I went to catch her in the field.

After a thorough workout, the physiotherapist pronounced Astra 'as sound as a pound'. The vet found nothing wrong with her teeth or eyes, and gave her an internal exam. She behaved impeccably for both people, and I suspected they thought I was exaggerating, so I carried on pretending her outbursts were normal because I didn't know what else to do. If I shouted at her, she reared up and boxed at me with her front legs. The one time I smacked her, she reacted like Satan's child, and I never did it again. In the end, I just tried to keep out of the danger zone, because when she was good, she was fantastic. She was quick to learn and absorbed her training without batting a long-lashed eyelid.

Astra worked diligently and muscled-up into an absolute showstopper but as she gained confidence in her body, her powerful outbursts worsened again, and being bitten and kicked became normal. I felt like an abuse victim. Needing a professional opinion, I chose a well-recommended schooling yard, where the owner agreed to take her for an assessment month. She went to Rosemarie's with a danger warning!

Two weeks into Astra's training, I made a pre-arranged visit to the yard, and found everyone praising her progress. Rosemarie suggested I bring the mare out of her stable and pop over a couple of jumps in the arena. The moment I entered the stable alone, Astra turned her back on me and fired a warning kick that made sharp contact with my knee, and I doubled-up in pain, stifling a scream. Why did she hate me so much? Trying not to wince, I led the mare to the mounting block and as I slowly swung myself into the saddle, Astra hunched her back, turned and snapped at my leg. Rosemarie saw the snap, shouted loudly, and Astra went straight upon her hind legs. Luckily, I had both feet in the stirrups, and I clung to her mane until she was back on the ground.

Rosemarie raised an eyebrow, and held the mare's bridle while I steadied myself. "She's done that a couple of times since she's been here," she said with a grimace, "but I thought we'd sorted it."

As we warmed-up, Astra's floaty paces felt more elastic and balanced, and she trotted over a row of ground poles without missing a beat. She popped over a couple of rustic uprights like a pro, and Rosemarie pointed towards a spread fence, which stood about three feet high. As I turned my waist to see the jump properly, Astra gathered herself together and transitioned smoothly into a powerful canter. She approached the jump with perfect ease, and cleared it without breaking rhythm. I had a childhood flashback to jumping Merrylegs in the garden and grinned from ear to ear.

"Crumbs," I said. "She's good!"

Rosemarie smiled, nodded, and held Astra as I dismounted. "I'd say she could go far. I can sell her if you want, but she's the best horse you'll ever have. Why not give it a bit more thought?"

I felt such indescribable elation riding her that I did as suggested and gave it more thought. I wanted to feel that connection again and again. Unfortunately, rhetoric painted a rosier future than reality could create; within a year I became so frightened of her behaviour that when an experienced friend offered to take her on loan, I readily agreed. Sarah knew her full history, and wanted to expand her jumping potential. Before she went to Sarah, I had the farrier fit a new set of shoes. Astra was in season and being particularly difficult, and none of us were in a good mood.

"I've got a client with a nice thoroughbred gelding for sale," said Clive, wiping sweat from his brow. He took a break as I poured coffee from a thermos. "Older horse, placid chap, would suit you to a tee."

"I've got that one," I replied, waving my coffee mug in Astra's direction. "For better or worse." We both laughed which eased the tension.

"And it all seems to be for worse with her, doesn't it?" said Clive.

"Buying another horse wouldn't go down very well at the moment," I replied and I think my face must've clouded over because he gave me a big smile.

"Ach," he said with a wink. "You'd get your way if you wanted. As I said, he's a good horse. And cheap." He wrote a phone number on a piece of paper, wrote BARNEY TB GELDING next to it, and then he underlined it.

Astra showed no signs of aggression with Sarah until she suddenly lunged forward and bit a chunk out of Sarah's head when she bent down to clean the mare's feet. Sarah was rushed to hospital and her husband phoned to ask me to come and fetch her. I hitched the trailer to the Range Rover and drove to Sarah's home, in absolute turmoil about Astra's future. Her size and looks made her a perfect child's pony and her jumping ability had enormous potential, but her dangerous temperament meant I wouldn't sell her in case she injured someone. I dreaded having her back. My only option was to find her a companion and keep her in the field.

There was no one home at Sarah's, but her husband had left the mare in her stable, and her tack and rugs neatly stacked in the feed room. I slipped a bridle over her headcollar and led her into the trailer. She was quiet and compliant and stood while I removed her bridle, and tied her up and gave her a haynet. So far so good. I closed the ramp and set off for home. The moment the trailer moved forward Astra began kicking. I stopped and checked but she was eating hay and seemed unconcerned.

She kicked the ramp for the next six miles, then began kicking the side of the trailer. At the crossroad traffic-lights we were delayed in road works. The thud-thud was constant even while we were stationary, before it changed from banging to splintering and in the wing mirror, I saw a hoof come through the trailer side. It was that hoof that sealed her fate. Once we were clear of the road works, I made a split-second decision and gripping the steering wheel until my knuckles were white, I turned left instead of going home, and drove to Burden's Abbatoir in the nearby market town. With a heavy heart I pulled into the yard, parked outside the office and walked in.

The man at the desk looked up and moved his cigarette to the corner of his mouth with a twitch of his lips. It bobbed up and down as he spoke. "Yes miss, what can we do for you?"

"Can you . . . can you put a horse down, please." The words were out, I'd said it.

"Yes," he replied, "we can do that." As he spoke the bobbing cigarette ash dripped onto his jacket and joined a silver trail of older spillage, meandering down towards the hem. "When would you bring the horse over?"

"Now," I said. "She's outside in the trailer now. You'll need someone to unload her because I don't want to go in there."

He looked at me quizzically, opened the office door and saw the trailer with a gaping hole, rocking from side to side as Astra released her vehemence. "Ah, I see," he said, nodding his head and discarding the cigarette. "I'll get someone." He trod the burnt-out stub with his heel and shouted "Alf! 'Ere, in the yard. Now!"

A burly red-faced man wearing a flat cap and clean overalls walked across the tarmac and joined us watching the trailer rock. He moved his hat further back on his head and rubbed his face with a calloused hand, before going to the front of the trailer and cautiously opening the groom's door. He shut it again quickly and said "I'm not unloading that. You sure you want this done?"

I nodded.

"You go in the office and do the paperwork. I'll get the bolt-gun and do her in the trailer, not s'posed to but probably better for her. And us. And quicker. Give me your keys and I'll drive her round the back."

I did as I was told, and I must've looked more upset than I realised because the man made me a cup of tea before lighting another cigarette. When I went back out Astra had gone, her empty headcollar hung forlornly on its tie-ring, and the trailer was hosed clean. It was a silent drive home and it took me a long time to forgive myself.

Back then I couldn't help her, or manage the problem because I didn't know what I didn't know. The thing she did teach me was the importance of consistency. Horses like an easy life and being directed to do something avoids a lifetime of niggling correction. It's no good imposing boundaries if you disregard them on 'the days you can't be bothered.' She also taught me the obvious symptoms of gastric ulcers.

4 ACCIDENT-WAITING-TO-HAPPEN.

By the time Barney came into my life, Den and I had moved and converted an old dairy building at the front of our cottage into stables. Barney was a nicely built bay thoroughbred who'd been a point-to-point racing schoolmaster, and at the age of fifteen, was looking for an easier job. Straightforward and amiable, his only quirk was panicking when tied up, but you could halter him and tie an imaginary rope, and he would stand quietly until "untied". One evening I "tied" him to groom, remembered I had to put our dinner in the oven and went back to the house, got side-tracked rescuing a mouse from the cat, and when I came back out to the stables an hour later, he was still standing by the wall, sound asleep and resting a hind leg. He was such a kindly, simple soul and after being around him for a while, Dennis said he wanted a horse of his own.

As we began looking for a suitable horse for Den, I discovered the word 'suitable' means different things to different people. I envisioned a good steady cob, a real been-there-done-everything sort who wouldn't be bothered by a novice rider. My husband wanted a thoroughbred, and he wanted a big thoroughbred. Dennis bought his thoroughbred ex-racehorse against all advice. Paddy was bright chestnut the colour of newly shone copper and stood just under 17hh. Every aspect of his head was sharply defined and poised in alertness, searching for danger before it even happened. His muscular neck had a natural crest, accentuated by his deeply sloping shoulder. Paddy's problems were legendary; physically, all his lower leg tendons were blown, knees were broken, hocks full of arthritis and he had a jumper's bump (sacroiliac joint injury) behind the saddle the size of a ski-slope. He wind-sucked, cribbed, and weaved like a demon. Mentally, he had an aversion to almost everything, expressed by spinning in circles or running backward. When ridden in traffic he kicked out at cars and jogging or galloping were his only speeds. It was so obvious to everybody except Den that he was not a horse for a novice, but to say it again here would be a waste of breath. I wish I'd known the history that caused such turmoil, because Paddy had a huge heart that never stopped trying, and once you'd glimpsed the horse inside the train wreck, he got under your skin despite all the problems. Den adored him, Barney worshiped him, and I tried to hold it all together.

The accident-that-was-waiting-to-happen happened on one of those perfect English summer mornings that you read about in stories. Den and I were riding over the heathland behind our cottage, and Paddy tripped while galloping, turned a somer-sault and landed on top of Den. I heard a loud crack as bones snapped, and Dennis lay motionless in the heather with his left leg splayed at an acute angle. I jumped off Barney, caught Paddy, quickly checked him for injuries, and told Den to stay as still as possible. He mumbled, "What else can I do?"

The nearest house was a mile across the heath, so riding Barney and leading Paddy we set off at a fast pace and quickly reached our destination, where the man of the house was sitting on the upstairs balcony drinking coffee. Still in his pyjamas and understandably shocked to see us clattering up his driveway, he stood up and shouted "Mind the lawn! Don't let the horses on the lawn!"

"My husband's had an accident" I shouted, looking up at him from Barney's back. "He's had an accident up on the heath at Crooked Withies Pond, broken leg, can't get up." I slid off Barney who was heaving from the unaccustomed gallop, and yanked Paddy's reins to try and stop him eating the immaculately manicured lawn. Unfortunately, the excitement got to him and he started to run backward onto the grass, and the more I pulled the faster he went backward. With my arms fully outstretched trying to hold the two horses, Barney obediently followed me across the lawn as I hung on to Paddy. The man came down from the balcony and watched in sheer horror as his lawn turned into divots, and divots into craters.

"If, you could, do your best," he said in short sharp gasps of speech "to remove, your horses, from my lawn, I will phone an ambulance."

I turned Paddy around, brought Barney alongside him and backed them both off the lawn and onto the gravel drive, where Paddy spun in circles until he was all spun out, and then stood chewing Barney's stirrup leather.

Pyjama man returned with a blanket and shook his head in disbelief at the churned driveway. "The ambulance is on its way." He held out the blanket and mumbled "for your husband, he'll be cold." He proffered the blanket again, shaking it at me, his eyes pleading for me to take it and go.

"Thank you, thank you so much" I said. "I'm so sorry about your lawn, and the drive, I'll come back and make amends and bring the blanket. I promise."

"No," he said as I struggled to get up onto Barney from the ground. "No, please don't come back. It will be fine, I'm sure. Keep the blanket. No need to ever come back. The ambulance will come to you, go quickly."

I slung the blanket over the front of the saddle and retraced my way back to Dennis. The horses were in a muck sweat, and feeling my shirt sticking to my back, I knew I was too. Den was cold and pale on the ground. The horses were tired and stood quietly as I wrapped the blanket round Den and cradled his head on my lap. As we waited in the heather for the ambulance, it was the last time we would feel a bond of togetherness. The accident totally changed the dynamic of our marriage; perhaps the situation had been waiting for a catalyst and this was it. I sat with my husband and listened, as the skylarks soared above and sang our lament.

Paddy heard the ambulance siren first, and picking up the horse's reins, I walked them up to the roadside to wave the ambulance in. Thankfully, the driver turned-off the siren when he saw the horses, and the paramedic quickly made Den more comfortable with painkillers, immobilised his broken leg, and they stretchered him into the ambulance.

I walked the horses back home, following the blue flashing light until it disappeared in the distance. Once the horses were in their stables eating hay, I saw Barney was resting a front leg and Paddy had a cut running the length of his face and another from his knee to hoof. Suddenly I felt exhausted, like I'd hit a brick wall of spent emotion. Adrenaline was subsiding but the day was far from over, and I didn't dare allow myself to stop and think about what had happened. I put cooling paste on Barney's leg and antiseptic on Paddy's cuts and went into the house to shower and change and drive to the hospital. It was a journey I got to know well.

After three weeks in hospital, with metal rods inserted to stabilise his smashed knee and thighbone. Den was in a plaster-cast from hip to ankle and fretting badly about Paddy. Whether it was the pain or the drugs, he convinced himself the horse was either badly injured or I'd had him euthanized, so I came up with a madcap plan for Paddy to visit. There was a carpark at the back of the hospital where I could pull-in with the horsebox, and the nurses agreed to wheel Den's bed to the window the following day at four o'clock.

I groomed the horse as diligently as if he were going to a show, loaded him into the lorry and drove to the hospital at the agreed hour. Manoeuvring between parked cars was tight but we found a double space to unload, and Paddy jogged down the ramp, surrounded by a group of interested people; I guess a horse doesn't arrive in a hospital car park very often. As Paddy flared his nostrils, grew even taller, and spun around in circles, I looked up at the fourth-floor hospital window to see not only Den watching, but patients and nurses watching from all the other windows too. Someone started clapping, and Paddy took this as a cue for more action, adding bunny hops and semi rears to the spin. Everything about the horse shone and rippled, his eyes were bright, and while it was probably borne of fear, he came alive like never before. Maybe a public performance reminded him of racing. The crowd was getting bigger and louder, so I decided it was time to go home. I made a little farewell bow as I waved up at Den, and along with the rest of the hospital, he waved back. I touched Paddy's neck and turned him back to the lorry ramp, but he was having far too much fun, and I felt my shoulder jar as he pulled back and spun round.

"Don't mess about Paddy," I said quietly. "It's time to go home now, come on." I faced him at the ramp three more times, but each time he got more excited and I got more worried. I cursed I hadn't brought a feed bucket for bribery, and he showed no interest in his haynet. The group of people were offering suggestions which ranged from picking him up and carrying him in, to tethering him on the grass verge and coming back tomorrow, and I was smiling through gritted teeth, wishing a big hole would open up and swallowed us both. Why did I ever come up with this stupid idea?

As I straightened Paddy up for the fourth attempt, a quiet voice by my left elbow said, "I have horses, let me help you." My saviour was a well-dressed woman in immaculately fitting office clothes, high heels and sleekly bobbed hair. Someone in the crowd wolf-whistled as she took Paddy's leadrope, and wiggled her tight pencil skirt up the ramp, while I went behind the horse and persuaded him to keep walking forwards. Knowing the game was up, he walked into the lorry like butter wouldn't melt in his mouth. A huge cheer went up and everyone dispersed. When I looked around to give the woman heartfelt thanks, she had disappeared.

Den's injuries wouldn't heal and he spent months in and out of hospital. As he struggled with his physical incapacity his moods swung between utter despair and reckless abandon, and I was left to run our business while trying to look after him and the horses with minimum help. I was utterly exhausted. While he was recuperating from a bone graft, he decided to expand our business and move to larger premises. I felt it was an ill-timed decision; already staggering under my workload and with signs of economic decline looming, my instinct was to consolidate and weather the storm, but what hurt most was being told the plan, and not asked. Our marriage bore the brunt of his injury and my exhaustion: a period best left buried in the grave of lost harmony with only husband and wife privy to the grief. Suffice to say it was agonising. I shut down because there was no point in speaking, and I didn't tell him I was having major panic attacks because I couldn't cope anymore. I kept thinking about his accident, my baby and what might happen next. Calm and capable me, the multi-tasker, the workaholic who kept smiling, was reduced to a trembling wreck rocking back and forth on the bathroom floor. And I hadn't even peeled the potatoes for dinner.

Together with our marital disparity, the global recession and Den's prolonged absence from work, our business lost its foothold. We were on shaky ground and needed to drastically cull expenses, so I sold the horsebox and my Range Rover. Our house would be next. As everything at work was pared to a bare minimum I wondered if the bumpy ride ahead would be an incentive to pull our marriage back together. It wasn't.

5 YOU'RE THE PAINTER?

Looking back, I think I fell in love with Mark the day he came to paint our house. It was so unexpected, I'm still in awe it really happened. After thirty years, I still can't find the words to describe how or why. It was just meant to be. Before we presented our cottage for sale it needed decorating. I did the inside, but the exterior painting was a professional job, and through a chance of fate, Mark came to do the work. Early on Tuesday morning when I came back from riding Paddy, there was a car parked in the front drive with the tailgate open, and as I dismounted, a figure appeared from behind the car carrying tins of paint.

"Hi," I said, looking up at the man standing opposite me. "I'm Elaine. You're the painter?"

He laughed, raised the paint tins in his hands and replied "Yes, can't deny it."

He was tall, with that slight stoop that people have when they talk to someone smaller than themselves. I looked up at him and as he bent his head, I saw he had the deepest brown eyes, and dark hair that fell forward covering them, I think he would've brushed it back if he'd had a free hand.

"Would you like a cup of coffee?" I said. "I'll just put Paddy out and then I'll make some."

"That would be nice," he said.

I slid Paddy's saddle off and propped it against the mounting block, and he bent to stir an open tin of paint. As I led the horse towards the paddock he looked up and said quietly, "By the way, my name's Mark."

Turning to face him again I said "Hello, Mark." He rested the stick against the side of the tin and proffered his hand. It was large and open, and my fingers fitted quite snugly in his as we formally shook hands.

I brought out two mugs of coffee and, as I mucked-out, he leant against the stable door. I was aware I was being watched. We chatted about the painting, which he estimated would take two weeks. One of the cats came to meet and greet him and had lots of fuss, by which time I'd finished my coffee and the stable. "Right," I said, "now I must get on to work. Dennis will be home early this afternoon but I've left you a door key. Help yourself to more coffee and there's another cat asleep somewhere who'll want fuss." I smiled as he moved from the doorway so I could wheel the barrow past.

"Thanks for coffee," he said, rinsing the cups under the outside water tap.

"You're welcome," I replied, "thanks for washing-up."

Over early morning coffees, we continued talking. We talked a lot and then we talked some more. And more. I couldn't remember a time I'd had the freedom to just talk or had someone who listened. We talked about everything and nothing and we laughed at life and other people, and ourselves and, as we talked and laughed, somehow we fell in love. I can't explain it any better than that. We both knew something was going to happen, but it wasn't a rampant torrent of illicit passion, more an understanding of having found our other halves. The day Mark finished painting was my afternoon off work, so I arrived home early, just as he was just packing up. We looked at each other awkwardly, not sure what we were supposed to do. He broke the silence first.

"Do you fancy a cup of tea back at mine?" he said. It was a simple enough question, but I was aware the answer would change the course of my life. "I could drop you back home afterwards," he added as I hesitated.

"Could we go for walk?" I replied. Somehow a walk didn't seem as dangerous as a cup of tea.

"Where would you like to walk?" he replied gently, instantly understanding my hesitation.

"By water, a river?" I felt an overwhelming need to walk by water.

"Eye Bridge, down at Cowgrove," he said. "You ever been there before?"

"No but it sounds perfect."

He opened the car door for me and moved his tool bag off the front seat. "Jump in then, Eye Bridge it is."

We walked along the riverbank in silence because we didn't know what to say, and then we held hands without looking at each other. And then we stopped under a willow tree and kissed. It was the easiest and most difficult thing, and still I remember every moment of that first kiss. I loved my husband. I was very married, and someone like me didn't do something like this. I planned and took measured steps, not great leaps into the unknown, and I was very bad at telling lies, especially to people I love. I knew an affair meant lot of lies. But this felt so right in its overwhelming wrongness that I had to take a chance no matter where it led. I'm glad I did. For thirty years we've walked along the riverbank on the anniversary of that day. The willow tree fell in a storm and re-grew again and we still kiss under its branches. We've never stopped talking, never stopped laughing and we've never stopped being in love. And I still can't believe it happened.

6 FIRST CANCER

Easter, 1991

On Good Friday evening, any plans I was formulating to leave Den came to an abrupt halt. I lay in the bath, trying not to fall asleep while I worked out the staff rota for the week ahead. Because of mum's cancer history, I'd always followed self-examination instructions when I washed, and now I'd hit the jackpot; on my left breast I found a large lump. There was the lump I'd been looking for, alien yet familiar, and a strange calmness washed over me as I greeted my destiny. I'd been worrying about what might happen next, and now it had happened. It was Easter weekend, there was nothing I could do about it and there was no point in telling anyone so they worried, too. I gave the lump a good prod although I didn't know what I was expecting it to do, took one of Den's sleeping pills and went to bed early. On Tuesday morning I saw the doctor. He agreed it needed further investigation but told me not to worry. As an afterthought, he added most breast lumps are benign and I was far too young to have breast cancer. I was 36 years old and so naïve I had to look-up 'benign' in the dictionary.

Days and weeks of worry followed. The thought of cancer invaded everything, like an unpleasant smell tainting thoughts and actions with the whiff of 'what if'. Two separate needle biopsies proved inconclusive, so I had surgery to take a tumour sample. The nurses told me most breast lumps are benign and I was far too young to have cancer. Six days later, I sat alone in the consultant's office armed only with my customary smile. The consultant had a kindly face, but he didn't return the smile, and without preamble or emotion he said "Your biopsy was positive. You have breast cancer. Would you like a lumpectomy along with axilla clearance, or a mastectomy?"

I didn't know what a lumpectomy was, and I didn't know axilla meant underarm, but I knew about mastectomies because mum had one twenty years earlier. Having seen hers, a little voice in my head was shouting "Save the breast, save the breast," so I replied, "A lumpectomy please." He gave me a hospital date for the surgery and said I might need radiotherapy afterwards. I didn't know what radiotherapy was either, and the consultant was so aloof it was obvious you didn't ask him questions. If cancer could smile it would be grinning from ear-to-ear. Another victim signed-up to the exclusive club, lifetime membership guaranteed.

I went home and phoned the doctor's surgery asking for any information on breast cancer. The receptionist went and had a look through the waiting-room leaflets, came back on the phone and said there's nothing. I told my husband what the consultant said. He had no idea what a lumpectomy entailed, nor what axilla clearance or radiotherapy were, but he asked if I felt okay. Next morning I told Mark, and then I went to work. Business as normal.

The lumpectomy left a crater-like dent in the side of my breast. Axilla clearance involved removing a selection of underarm lymph nodes, and the severed nerve-endings sent electric shocks up-and-down my arm as they searched for their other-halves, like Cathy and Heathcliff vainly trying to re-unite. The wound wouldn't drain properly so I stayed in hospital for five nights, which gave much needed time to think. I was far too young to have breast cancer. A meeting worthy of romantic fiction had led to finding unexpected love with Mark. My marriage was in pieces, we were going to lose our home and probably our business. I needed to try and sort everything out before I left, because I owed that to my husband. But I was quickly learning life was too short not to follow my heart.

After the first groggy post-surgery day I was desperate for fresh air, so one morning I wedged the underarm drain bottle and its attached tube into my jacket pocket, slipped past the duty nurse and out of hospital. The smell of summer filled me and sunshine bathed my face as I tottered along the pavements stopping only to catch my breath and re-adjust the secreted drain. It's an old cliché, but it felt so good to be alive that morning, and have everything carry on as normal when my life was anything but. People went about their daily doings while all I managed to do was shuffle through mental fug and uncertainty. Walking was surprisingly tiring, how did ninety minutes pass so quickly? I turned and headed back to hospital hoping I could slip back to the ward unseen, but my absence had been noticed and I was read the riot act. I climbed into bed. Exhaustion was the price of my folly, but the sunshine and the respite had been worth it. I slept until the afternoon tea trolley arrived, and woke up smiling.

Five days after hospital discharge, I found another lump under my arm. I was alone in the house. Panicking, I phoned the doctor, and the receptionist said Dr Hathaway would visit on his morning rounds. When I heard the dog barking by the front gate, I went out to meet the doctor who greeted me with a stony stare. Walking back to the house I told him what happened.

"House calls are for patients who really need them," he said, without stepping further than the front door.

"Sorry?" I stuttered in disbelief.

"You're up and walking." He looked back over his shoulder to the car parked in the drive. "House calls are for patients who can't get to the surgery."

My heart was pounding with anger, hot breath stuck in my throat. Verging on hysterical, tears were streaming down my face and my whole body shook as the fear and upset I'd been controlling these past weeks erupted. "I can't drive. I'm five days out of hospital." I spat out the words like bullets. "I'm here on my own. I'm walking because I'm . . . I'm fucking walking because I'm not fucking dead. I've got cancer and I've found another lump. Exactly how ill do I have to be? If you don't want to see me then fine. Fuck off right now. Go on. Go see someone who really needs a doctor because I clearly don't!"

Dr Hathaway turned without hesitation and walked briskly back down the drive. It took an hour before I was calm enough to phone the doctor's receptionist and tell her what happened. I heard her shocked gasp, and then a silence while she composed herself. She promised to send another doctor immediately. The lump turned out to be a harmless knot of scar tissue, but what Dr Hathaway did that day was unforgivable.

Unfortunately, the lymph nodes also tested positive for cancer, showing it wasn't only contained within the tumour. Six weeks of debilitating daily radiotherapy were needed once the incisions had healed. My husband voiced his concern to the consultant that I'd lost weight and hadn't even begun treatment.

The consultant suggested I might be worried. Not knowing what to expect, I went to my 'marking' appointment thinking it would be questions and answers. I found myself laying propped-up on a cold flat table, wearing a thin hospital gown while uniformed radiologists discussed me like I wasn't there. In many ways I wasn't. I was measured and prodded and had my arms moved for me as small tattooed dots were applied to my breast and underarm, to guide the radiotherapy beam. Little purple pinpricks looking like the shape of The Plough in the night sky. I felt violated, like I was a statistic, not a person. It dawned on me the treatment was going to be harder to bear than the cancer. And this was only the beginning.

I drove to hospital each afternoon after work, changed into my gown and sat with the other patients until my number was called. I walked through the double-doors to the radiotherapy room, was placed on the treatment table laying slightly on my right side with blocks under my back, and had my arm moved into position over my head, while the beams were lined-up corresponding with the tattooed dots. The radiologists left the room and I had to stay perfectly still while the machine did its work. It was all over in minutes, then the table was lowered and I scrambled down. By the time the course ended, my breast was burnt and swollen, and I was utterly exhausted. Driving to the hospital each day for treatment, trying to work, manage the horses and home and see Mark had taken its toll. The oncologist prescribed ointment for my breast and explained radiotherapy effects would build up during the next ten days, and I would feel more tired (was that possible?) but afterwards I could start to get back to normal. He suggested a nice holiday would be the perfect tonic.

That night over dinner I told Dennis about Dr Goode's suggestion of a nice holiday, and he asked me where I'll go. I was determined to go somewhere, but where could I go on my own that was relaxing, pampering, and I would be brave enough to take myself?

7 HEALTH FARM

Sunnyside Hall Health Farm was an elegant Victorian mansion set in its own extensive grounds just outside the affluent market town of Marlborough in Wiltshire. The brochure looked so inviting that when Dennis saw it, he said he'd come with me. But still hurting from his initial reply, I told him I was going alone. He could stay home and look after the dogs and horses. On Friday morning I packed my bag, had a major panic attack and unpacked it, told myself how stupid I was being, chucked everything back in the bag and ran out of the house while my legs were still working. I got lost twice on the drive there and went miles out of my way, and by the time I arrived for my long weekend break I was exhausted and gasping for a cup of tea. But I'd made it this far, and at least that was a start. I parked the car, unloaded my little carry case and walked across the scrunchy gravel to the imposing front door, which was opened by a uniformed nurse. I suddenly felt hopelessly out of my depth. The nurse ushered me upstairs to a small white bedroom over-looking manicured lawns, showed me how the TV, radio and luxury shower worked, and instructed me to change into my robe and follow the signs back downstairs for my assessment. I asked if I could have a cup of tea and she replied I'd need an assessment first.

The Assessment Manager took my medical details, I was weighed and measured, and it was clear to see she couldn't figure out why I was at a Health Farm, so I explained I didn't know where else to go on my own. She asked if I'd like my introductory peat bath now, and I asked if I could have a cup up of tea first. Unfortunately, I couldn't, I'd missed lunchtime, and it wasn't teatime until four o'clock.

Sitting in a deep roll-top bath, full of tepid brown peat water that smelt like compost is not an experience I would previously have considered paying for. The assistant suggested I try to relax. I asked if I could have a cup of tea while I soaked.

My complimentary massage followed swiftly. Of course, we know now that deep massages are not recommended for people with recently active cancer, and Jacuzzis and saunas can cause swelling when lymph nodes have been removed. Most modern spas won't treat cancer patients until they are five years clear, but this was thirty years ago. It was the first time I'd gone 'public' with my misshapen breast and disfiguring scars, and as I grabbed the fluffy white towel close to my skin, the masseuse suggested I try to relax. I'd never had a massage before and didn't know what to expect, and like the peat bath, I didn't find it relaxing. I just wanted a cup of tea but during my massage, teatime had been and gone. I was shown the comfy loungers in the conservatory and left to 'relax.'

The lady reclining on the wickerwork lounger next to mine looked up from reading Vogue and asked politely, "Do you play bridge?"

"No" I said, snuggling into my fluffy robe and wishing I could disappear.

"Golf?"

"No." She went back to reading Vogue. I ask if she knew how one would get a cup of tea, but she didn't look up again.

Dinner is at six o'clock. I shower to rid myself of the peaty whiff, and change into newly bought leggings and ballet pumps. I un-pin my hair which falls in layers of soft curls, I run my fingers through it, and activated by the shower steam, the loose curls tighten into their customary corkscrews. After all these years I still hadn't learnt to love them. I sprayed some perfume, took a deep breath and walked down to the dining room.

The bridge/golf lady was already seated at a table-for-two by the window and beckoned me over to share. We had little in common and after stilted pleasantries, looked out the window and ate our meagre rations in silence. I quickly cleared my plate and asked the waitress if I could have another helping of the vegetable loaf, which was delicious. The dining room fell silent. I noticed people had paused with food mid-way to their mouths, and with all eyes on me and the waitress, I felt like Oliver Twist innocently asking for more gruel. No one had told me about Health Farm etiquette. The waitress ran to the kitchen to fetch the Assessment Manager, and my dining companion continued staring out of the window, trying to pretend she wasn't seated opposite me.

The AM sighed when she saw it was me. "We don't recommend eating above the set portions," she said, standing by the side of the table. "All the meals here are healthy, portion controlled and calorie counted."

"But I'm starving," I replied. "And the vegetable loaf was delicious. And I missed out on lunch. And tea."

"Och, gi her seconds for ony sake," said a man in a broad Scottish accent, seated at the table behind me. "Canna you see the wee size of the lassie?"

A ripple of laughter went round the room that made me blush bright red. The Assessment Manager nodded approval to the waitress, but her eyes glared at me and I knew I'd been branded a troublemaker. I thought to hell with it and asked if I could also have a cup of tea.

On the way back to my room after dinner, I saw the kitchen door was wide open. I looked inside and saw chef singing to himself while wiping down worktops. Primed by my success with second helpings, I smiled my best smile and said, "Excuse me chef, I hope you don't mind me asking but . . ."

He put down his cloth and smiled back.

"Would it be possible to have some toast? I know it's not allowed, and dinner was lovely but there wasn't very much of it . . . of course I wouldn't tell anyone and I'd eat it in my room."

The chef roared with laughter. He made me three rounds of wholemeal toast, spread thickly with deep golden butter. And jam. And he made me a cup of tea with real milk.

I climbed into bed with my tea and toast, and left the window and curtains open. As the sky turned from evening to night, I fell asleep. Later, I woke in the strange dark room trying to remember where I was, and why. A breeze blew through the open window, scented with cut hay and honeysuckle. Suddenly I found myself crying like never before, smothering my mouth in the pillow to stifle the racking sobs. I wept for my marriage, my breast, my pain, my guilt, my baby, my utter loneliness, and the total despair that's deepest at three in the morning. I cried myself empty. Eventually I cried myself back to sleep and slept right through breakfast.

I'd booked a weekend of swimming lessons, clay-pigeon shooting lessons, aqua-robics, guided walks, and yoga. Saunas and Jacuzzi filled the gaps, contraband toast filled my tummy. While out walking I met the man with the Scottish accent, and discovered he wasn't Scottish at all, but a famous stage actor who couldn't resist playing a part. We giggled conspiratorially and I introduced him to the chef, who laughed at our story, and shared his breakfast bacon sandwich. The actor ran upstairs to his room to eat it, and the chef ran after him with a bottle of ketchup, while I stood at the bottom of the stairs feeling life was good. Sunnyside Hall Health Farm had provided some unexpectedly uplifting moments.

After an early Monday morning yoga session, I had my leaving consultation. The Leaving Manager asked how I had enjoyed my stay, whether I thought I would return, and how I planned to continue my 'new healthy regime.' The yoga must have left me in a Zen state of mind because I answered very tactfully. The journey back was uneventful and gave me time to think about the experience, I was smiling as I drove, and singing along to the radio. I stopped off to see Mark before going home. We talked and laughed as I told him all about the chef and the 'Scottish' actor, and although the health farm wasn't what I'd expected, it was what I needed. I felt stronger, empowered by a weekend of re-discovering the confidence lost when my body failed itself. I felt I'd be able to get our business back on an even keel, explain everything to Dennis and leave my home and husband without pain and recrimination. Of course, I was still in that Zen state of mind, it was all wishful thinking and real life didn't run that smoothly.

8 TEDDY

I remember the first time I saw a special horse the way other women remember the first time they saw the man who would become their lover. And so it was with Teddy. Seventeen hands of bright bay Belgium Warmblood, with an old-fashioned carriage horse body rather than the leggy ballerinas favoured for dressage. He stood watching my actions from the back of his stable with a serene expression on his over-long face, and as I entered the stable, he dipped his head until our eyes were level. For brief seconds we stood face-by-face, until an imperceptible movement of his poll signified a nod of approval, and he stepped forward.

"Do you mind riding him today?" said Adele. "He's still doing getting fit walking but he's comfortable enough. If you go down through the woods and come back up the road he'll get some hill work, but you'll need to make sure he works, there's a lot of him to get going."

"Whose is he?" I replied, ducking under his neck because I couldn't see her over his back.

"Belongs to new client Piers Archer. Good rider who wants to go eventing, bought this one from Fred Welch as a hunter. Supposed to be fantastic over jumps and started out as a showjumper, great with height but couldn't make the Grade-A spreads. Piers paid a lot for him, his paces look good, workmanlike but cracking power once he uses himself."

Adele was an old friend who ran high-class livery and teaching stable. She'd invited me to ride with her so we could have a gossipy catch-up, but when I arrived, she was expecting a prospective pupil and asked if I'd mind riding alone. I was a bit peeved . . . until I saw Teddy. I tacked-up the big horse and climbed aboard. His large heavy head hung on the end of a very long neck, and he fell contentedly onto his forehand, leaning heavily on the bit to save the effort of holding his front-end up. I immediately understood why Adele had suggested wearing spurs, and by the time an hour passed I wished I'd taken her advice. I was exhausted. At walk, Teddy definitely spent no more energy than necessary, but he felt so comfortingly solid, so dependable, and I hoped I might be asked to ride again. Three months later I got my wish.

Adele's mount was a showy little Anglo-Arab dressage horse. Teddy made him look like a child's pony, but they matched strides and we chatted easily as we rode, re-connecting with our thoughts and mutual friends. I'd missed her company. I craved Adele's horse knowledge, absorbing the information that littered her conversation even though I didn't agree with all her methods. She'd lost friends and clients with her straight-talking lack of flattery, but she'd fought to get the highest teaching qualifications while running a solo business and she'd earned my admiration. We turned off the gravel track into an open field and Adele suggested we have a canter across the old turf, warning there was a post-and-rail fence at the end which I was welcome to jump, although she would use the gate. Leaning slightly forward in her dressage-cut saddle she set off at a perfectly collected canter, and I felt Teddy shorten underneath me as he tucked his chin into his chest and launched into a rocking-horse gait that went up and down more than it did forward. I softened my hands on the reins and felt him relax, and as he did, his bounce turned into powerful ground-covering strides that quickly overtook Adele. She waved me on, shouting "hunter coming through!" and as I passed laughing with excitement, the fence ahead came into view. Teddy's ears shot forward, his impulsion increased as his speed slowed and I counted-down the strides, trying to hold him with my tummy muscles rather than the reins. He soared into the air without any assistance from me, landed without missing a beat and only slowed because I asked him to wait for Adele as she opened and shut the gate with perfectly executed pirouettes. I've never felt exhilaration like it. What a horse. Boy what a horse!

A week after I got home from the Health Farm, Adele phoned. We'd not spoken since the previous winter. "You know that big warmblood you rode," she said without pre-amble, as if it was only days ago.

"Yes, Teddy. How could I forget him?"

"Well, he turned out to be a whistler. He's had Hobday surgery so it's best for him to keep some fitness until he's needed for hunting, Piers asked if I knew anyone who'd like him on loan for a few months . . . and I thought of you, I heard your old horse has been lame since Den's accident."

I knew whistling was caused by a paralysed larynx nerve, and affected horses doing fast work because they couldn't inhale enough air. The Hobday operation removed tissue to streamline the airway.

"Yes, poor old Barney, he tore a collateral ligament galloping for help, Paddy turned a somersault and was unscathed. There's no fairness is there? Ummm, this new horse, I'd love him, but you know I've not been well. . ."

"Oh, yes. Sorry, I should've phoned, you know what it's like, everything gets so busy there's never enough time. If you don't want him, I can always find someone else. How are you now?"

"I'm fine now," I said. "When would he go back?"

"September probably, so you'd have enough time for some fun, and not have to worry about keeping him through the winter."

"I'd love to have him," I said, thinking quickly that if things changed at home, he could go back to his owner and if it was only short-term, I should be able to find the extra money for feed and shoes.

"Want him at the weekend? Piers can bring him over in the lorry. I'll make sure his tack and rugs come too."

"Errr . . . yes! Yes, that's fine, Sunday morning would be good. I'd better go and get his stable ready! Thanks Adele, thanks for thinking of me."

"I often think about you," she replied, and I thought for a moment she was going to say more but she didn't. "Bye, Elaine."

"Bye, Adele."

I told Dennis what had happened. I was really happy, and he didn't say much, which I took as a good sign.

Teddy's size dwarfed my tiny frame, but he was the most honest horse I've ever known. He was a superb jumper and never put a foot wrong, despite having me as a rider. I took him showjumping and cross-country, where he carried me every step of the way. All I had to do was allow enough time to trot up hills when he ran out of breath cantering and sit quite still while he negotiated the jumps that scared the daylights out of me (which was most of them). He was rock-steady to ride, a dream to do in his stable and he quite literally stole my heart. I kept waiting for Piers to ask for him back, but no call came until November.

Unknown to Dennis, I'd taken independent financial advice on the viability of saving our business, and the answer was an overwhelming no. I told Den that it was time to call in the liquidators, that our rescue attempts were too little too late, and damage limitation was the best we could hope for. He didn't argue, I think he was secretly relieved. I made phone calls to the relevant people and waited for the shit to hit the fan.

Dennis understandably fell into a huge depression, the culmination of his accident, our marriage problems, losing his business and imminently his home. I wished I could've found time to help him, but I was working two cleaning jobs, and had taken space in my friend Jimmy's shop so I could re-start my antique selling business. Money was not tight, it was non-existent, so when Piers said he was buying two eventers and selling

Teddy, his offer of first refusal couldn't have come at a worse time. Pride had long gone, so I candidly explained the situation to Piers. How could I possibly buy another horse? His reply was as generous as his horse.

"I paid three thousand pounds for Teddy, and that's what I want back. So long as you send me some money every month, I don't mind how long you take to pay it off. You keep a tally and let me know when he's yours." How could I refuse?

PART TWO

FAMILY

Uncle Lionel was in hospital trying to die. For the past forty-five years, he and my father had been sparring partners and friendly rivals. Never wanting Lionel to beat him at anything, dad unexpectedly died first, and my mum lost her brother and husband in the same week. Uncle Lionel was a respected and pious member of Jewish society, and my father an esteemed figure in financial circles, so it was jaw-dropping when their deaths revealed Uncle Lionel's secret second family and dad's insolvency hidden in a labyrinth of maxed-out credit cards. Mum and I stood firm in the aftermath and faced the apocalypse together

9 DROPPING THE BATON

Two weeks before Christmas, Dennis discovered my relationship with Mark. At first, he couldn't believe it was possible I'd been so spontaneous and done something without first making a plan, and then the hurt and pain came out. I couldn't deny I'd fallen in love with somebody else, I tried to explain but we were too far apart to listen to each other. I said I would leave and he replied I had to take my cats with me. The next morning, I told him unemotionally that the sensible thing to do was have Paddy and Barney put down. They were inseparable, both old and lame and it would be impossible for either of us to look after them. I said if he went out, I would deal with it all, and then I would leave. Dennis didn't argue.

Later that day I held them one after the other while they stuck their heads into a bucket of feed, and the knackerman expertly did his job. I watched as they were winched into the trailer, then I hosed the concrete, cleared their stables, went indoors and sobbed my heart out. What a hard heart I had grown.

That evening I left my husband, my home and my dogs. Teddy was in the trailer hitched behind the truck, the cats were in a basket on the passenger seat, and we drove out the gate leaving behind a life that looked so perfect. I lodged with a friend, the cats stayed with Mark, and Teddy lived in luxury at livery stables. I worked flat-out trying to keep a stabled horse on a shoestring budget; there were times when he ate and I did not. To say it wasn't an easy time would be a major understatement, I felt like an alien in this new environment unsure who I was, what my capabilities were or what the future held.

New thoughts, released from years of curtailed emotion were challenging. My relationship with Mark was bedrock in the shifting soil, but new dynamics caused some angst as I explored different ways to make my life work. I was offered a live-in nanny job with top three-day event rider Lucinda Green, and as I excitedly recounted the news to Mark, I completely misjudged his reaction, which was shock-horror about me being away all week. "I've just got you, and now you're leaving again?" he said, and I wasn't sure if I wanted to be got.

The livery yard Teddy was in was the only one I could find with vacancies so close to Christmas. It was expensive, and I knew he wasn't happy, but he was safe. He had a habit of jumping out of field to go visit with other horses, which wasn't appreciated by the other horses, so his grazing time was limited to one hour, one day in three. It was far from ideal. I desperately needed to see him after work each day, but one evening Mark's car broke down and he asked me to tow him home. Help Mark or see Teddy? It shouldn't have been such a hard decision. should it? By the time I reached the livery stables, everything was shut and bolted for the night. I stood outside holding the gate and talking to Teddy to tell him I'd come, and then I just stood holding the gate in silence. I hope he knew.

My divorce drama ran concurrently with business bankruptcy proceedings and my brother celebrating his mid-life crisis by hooking-up with an anorexic waif from Alabama (whose family were KKK), becoming a born-again hippie and fleeing to Nepal to find himself. All he found was a lot of dust and camel shit and he eventually lost the waif.

Dad had the last of many heart attacks followed by triple-by-pass surgery, while I was also in hospital having a complicated guided-wire operation to biopsy a breast lump. Mum was awaiting a hospital appointment for a breast lump biopsy of her own, which she'd put off to care for dad and hadn't mentioned to anyone because she "thought we were all a bit busy with other things." And then dad died.

Burying dad was a drama like no other. The Jewish religion is very male-orientated, and the Rabbi made it obvious he would prefer dealing with the son than the daughter. Unfortunately for us both, that wasn't possible. Mum and I prepared the end-of-life rituals, while Mark ran errands, collecting the low Shiva chairs and prayer books from the synagogue, and looking after us as best he knew how. Mark isn't Jewish so all this was new to him, and pretty much a baptism of fire. A Jewish funeral needs to take place within forty-eight hours and Dad was in arrears with his annual synagogue payments; the rabbi said he couldn't be buried until the balance was paid. With their joint bank account frozen, I ran round borrowing money from everyone I knew, and as the mourning party gathered in the prayer-house to bury my father, I presented the Rabbi with a plastic bag of banknotes and loose change. He had the good grace not to check it was correct.

As prayers were said at the graveside, mum and I stood tearless until a respected member of the congregation stepped forward and picked up a black bin-bag from a pile behind the rabbi and lowered it into dad's grave, followed by another and another.

I lurched forward in a panic and screamed "STOP!!" Mum grabbed my arm but I didn't feel it. "STOP! You can't put the rubbish in there, that's my dad!" The Rabbi and the Cantor standing opposite me suddenly found themselves extremely short-sighted, and moved their prayer books up in front of their faces. Swaying in unison, they silently mouthed the prayers they were reading, determined not to look up. If I'd turned and looked at the mourners behind, I might have seen a few amused faces, but by this time I was teetering on the edge of dad's grave, peering down at the bags and thinking about pulling them out. Mum's grip tightened on my arm. By now I was crying, and that made mum cry, two more bags went in, and no one seemed concerned.

My cousin stepped forward, stood next to me and said in

a low voice "They're prayer books, Elaine. Used prayer books. It's a great honour to have them placed with the coffin. Prayer books."

I blushed bright red, drained deathly white and went hot-and-cold in the space of five seconds. "Prayer books?"

"Yes, prayer books. It's an honour."

"Not bags of rubbish?"

"No, bags of prayer books."

Mum released her grip on my arm and her hand moved down and held mine tightly, in solidarity. The Rabbi recited the Mourners Kaddish, we all put some dirt on top of the bags, nobody looked at me, and dad was gone.

Back at her home, mum and I sat Shiva for a week which is intended to help mourners through the first intense days of grief. Relatives came and went, tut-tutting my brother's absence like we hadn't noticed he wasn't there. Friends came offering food, condolences and their recollections of dad, which were quite different to my own. Ten men gathered each evening for a prayer Minyan, and mum and I talked long into the night before snuggling into her bed together and dreaming horrible dreams.

One night while mum slept, I went through dad's paperwork. It dawned on me that his finances were in such disarray that in his eyes, he had no alternative but to die. He was a proud man so needful of creating a successful impression, and he knew he would have to face his financial failures. I had to break the news to my mother she had a mortgage to pay, and dad had no life insurance. I wasn't sure I could cope with being the grown-up.

Mum couldn't attend her brother Lionel's funeral because she was in hospital having her breast biopsy. She'd had a radical mastectomy for cancer twenty-five years earlier, and thankfully this time the lump was benign. The day after her surgery my beloved cat Peedles died and that was when everything hit me. I unashamedly mourned the loss of that cat more than I did my father.

My dad didn't believe that simply being good at something

was good enough, you had to be the best. Oh, how I must have disappointed him. Childhood me failed to stay cute, failed exams, failed to grow into a demure young lady. Adult-me failed a first marriage, failed to provide grandchildren, failed to live conventionally, even failed to stay solvent. But I hit my stride when I got invasive breast cancer, with the highest-grade tumour for starters. The treatment choices on offer were a mastectomy, or lumpectomy and radiotherapy. I quite liked my breast, so I chose the latter; the cancer returned within four years, so that choice was probably a failure too.

A dervish-like approach to coping overshadowed any fear of cancer. Everything I could possibly control was micro-managed and governed with an iron fist. I became the Dictator of my own mind, certain that mental discipline was the key to survival, and my default setting was being best at fighting cancer. It was an interesting approach, and a coping mechanism that worked at the time. With hindsight we learn the tighter the grip, the harder the lesson. Life doesn't necessarily obey your will, however much you crave a parental pat on the back.

Dad died in circumstances that showed his whole ethos was less 'do as I do' and more 'do as I say'. His fear of failure led him to his grave and from there, he reached out and passed me the baton of his impossibly high standards. Being a control freak brings many benefits; namely burying the real picture in minutiae of managing detail. I called it 'dealing with cancer', called myself a 'workaholic' and carried on regardless. The day of reckoning came in the form of a mental breakdown, and true to form, it was spectacular; the best implosion I could possibly manage.

Psychotherapy, talking therapy, medication, holistic therapy, horses, husband and friends pulled me through. I am very lucky. One momentous day, I shed my armoured coat and walked in my own skin. It was a shaky start, and I admit I wasn't very good at it, but not being good felt okay and the world didn't stop turning.

Of course, I'm not the first to realise this. It is summed up perfectly in the famous quote by C. JoyBell C.: "It's the hard things that break, soft things don't break."

I've found the key to staying soft is noticing when I'm not. I can manipulate and forcefully manage if I choose, but I notice it doesn't really work; other people don't follow your expectations, life often doesn't go the way you want, and horses have their own agenda.

There's more to be had from gaining knowledge to better cope with a situation and make informed choices that stack the odds in your favour. Inevitable change stays inevitable however many barricades you build. I still don't like things that happen to me (who would?), but by managing myself, I feel more in control than I ever was before, and at the moment I feel the best I can possibly feel. Sorry, Dad; I failed to carry your baton, but it was the best failure I ever made.

10 KITCHEN TABLE PROPOSAL

I really like my husband. It goes without saying that I love him more than anyone else on earth, but I also genuinely like him. I don't agree with all his views, his politics, or his taste in food, but we've come to a tacit agreement that he voices his opinions, I certainly voice mine, and if contentment means sometimes cooking two separate dinners, then so be it. I wouldn't call him my best friend because I have friends who are that; we have a unique bond that is part spouse, teammate, partner-in-crime, lover and friend. We've both concluded that somewhere back in time we'd been together before, and this was just another chapter in the same book. Even so, it took him a while to say he loved me. This man treads slowly.

The slow tread took me a long time to respect because I dash everywhere, on foot and in my head. Mark does something properly the first time, while I return repeatedly to stick patches on a rushed job. I walk quickly while he sees where he is going and doesn't fall over the kerb. Mark is also completely true to himself, which I admire and envy. He never alters his persona to fit a situation, and his job has never defined him. My personality and my status are contained in what I do and without my job, I'm lost. Mark is simply himself and work is a means to money, not self-recognition.

Mark proposed very romantically as we sat eating fish and chips at the kitchen table. He got down on one knee. I accepted immediately and then we finished our chips! My only proviso was that he put some heating in our freezing cold house.

My first cancer arrived too soon into a fledgling love affair, but when would have been a good time? We survived it side by side but separately and continued finding our togetherness. The second cancer diagnosis was definitely ill-timed and the hardest to bear; ten days before our wedding I find a tiny lump smaller than a pea, just above the top of my breast. Immediately I know it is cancer. The biopsy is physically straightforward and mentally hellish, I can't get beyond thinking this is retribution for sins of the past and need to know the results before Mark makes his vows. On the eve of our wedding, we get an appointment late in the evening. Once again, we sit with the consultant, and I notice a little sadness fluttering around his eyes. When he falters reading the results, it's obvious our pre-nup will be more Sickness than Health.

"I'm afraid the biopsy is positive," he says, putting words to what we already knew. "It's a Grade 1 tumour, so I must recommend a mastectomy followed by six months chemotherapy."

"Should we cancel the honeymoon?" says Mark, with a voice stronger than I had expected.

"No," replied the consultant. "Have your three nights away. I've scheduled surgery for the first week in January. Meanwhile, enjoy your wedding, Christmas and New Year as best you can." We all stood and he shook hands with Mark, put his hand on my elbow and as we instinctively hugged, he said quietly "You're amazing. You'll get through this."

"I'll save you a piece of wedding cake," I replied with the biggest smile I could muster.

I want my wedding day to be as special as possible and refuse to let anything ruin it. I don't want people feeling sorry for me and saying, "Oh doesn't she look lovely but . . ." and I don't want my mum to know, not yet. So, Mark and I decide to each tell just one person. I tell my friend and witness who swears loudly and hugs me. Mark tells his best man who swears loudly and pours him a large drink, which he continues to do all day.

Our ceremony is in the local Registry Office; there's snow on the ground and it's below freezing. I designed my outfit and had a fashion design student make up for me, a tight blue velvet Edwardian hobble skirt and short fitted peplum jacket with plunging neckline. It was going to be my dream outfit but instead of a sexy lace push-up bra, I wore a white high neck sweater to hide the biopsy dressing, which made the jacket too tight to move my arms. As armour against the cold, I had thermal long-johns under the skirt, which didn't help the hobble effect.

The reception for sixty is an afternoon tea party at home, with the rooms swathed in boughs of holly and ivy, red berries and mistletoe. On an incredibly tight budget, I baked my wedding cake and then I baked my wedding reception, with scones and clotted cream and jam, and enough cake to feed an army. Dainty canapes are *so* not me. With all the emotion my wedding brought, following a recipe in the kitchen became my ten-step programme to calm. I regained my composure with the rhythmic ritual of beating air into eggs and sifting my flour.

The day didn't start well. In between making sandwich fillings, I fiddle with the wedding cake icing and knock the cake off the turntable. It hits the floor with a sickening thud, and lays mocking the occasion with bruised contempt. I gingerly scrape it back onto its cake board and apply liberal blobs of apricot jam to stick the jigsaw of icing shards back together. I wonder if its crazed appearance would be an apt reflection on this marriage but decide to hide the cracks and phone the florist who promises to rustle up a garland to cover the top, with leaves to wind around the cracked edges.

The Christmas tree stood floor to ceiling in the corner of the sitting room, dripping with twinkling lights, decorations and baubles. For a reason known only to his feline brain, Jimmy the cat woke from sedentary slumber and decided it would be the perfect moment to investigate the fairy at the top of the tree. In the middle of cake mending, sandwich making and scone buttering, I heard a loud crash followed by softer echoes of breaking glass. The tree lay strewn across the floor.

By the time the hairdresser arrived to do my hair, the tree is back in place, hastily redecorated and securely fixed to the ceiling. The hairdresser rolls a large joint and hands it to me, begins styling . . . and the rest is history. Well, it would be history if I could remember anything other than having a fit of giggles when we arrived at the Register Office to find the ceremony delayed due to a backlog of people needing to register deaths.

Our official photographer is mum's elderly neighbour. In younger days he'd been a stalwart member of the local Camera Club and he was happy to take our pictures free of charge. He snapped away happily all afternoon on an ancient Bolex camera, changing lenses and filters, organising group shots and capturing hilariously off-guard moments. Ten days after the wedding we opened the photo packs with great expectations and found our poignant wedding pictures blurred and misty, it was like peering at the day through a shaking, veiled curtain. I asked mum if she knew James had Parkinson's?

"Well dear, he does have some sort of disease, but I know it's not catching. . ."

11 THE LEFT BREAST FAREWELL TOUR

We begin The Left Breast Farewell Tour the following morning. As I drive our trusty (and rusty) pickup truck to our Devon honeymoon, Mark sleeps soundly in the passenger seat, ashen grey and suffering from the solace he found trying to forget the circumstances of our wedding day. My wedding posy sits on the dashboard reminding me to be happy and full of excitement marrying the man I love, but our honeymoon will also be my breast-leaving-party, and everything feels tainted with loss. Our honeymoon B&B lies deep in the Devon countryside. Our host smiles at my wedding posy and places it in a beautiful vase on the dressing table. Mark and I feel slightly awkward, shy, and sit on the bed pretending to read magazines. We make love tenderly, and afterwards I want to cry silently into the plump feather pillow, but there are no tears left. No feelings, just a great ache of nothingness. It's a relief to stop smiling.

On New Year's Eve we drive across the swirling mists of Dartmoor to dinner at the Widdecome Inn, singing disconnected verses of Uncle Tom Cobbley. In front of a roaring log fire, we bravely toast the New Year and smile for each other, for better or for worse. On the way home the mist is so thick I drive off the road, narrowly missing a herd of sheep. I repeat the old saying "ninety-nine ways for a sheep to die and only one way to live" in reference to the sheep but at exactly the same time we both realise the irony of the words and start laughing. We're still laughing when we get back to the cottage and climb into bed.

On New Year's Day we take a long wintery walk, inadvertently trespassing into the grounds of Castle Drogo, and marvel at the magnificent building, a tribute to a dead son, rising above the leafless trees. We lunch in Drewstainton one of the smallest pubs in England and have a generous evening meal with our hosts. We spend the night talking, holding, loving. On the journey back home, reality hits very hard and the laughing stops. We return to face surgery and chemotherapy.

My 41st birthday tries to be a cause for celebration but fails miserably. In honour of their last hours together, I grant my breasts a final day of unfettered freedom. I could have easily burnt my bra, and everything else along with it. We arrive at the hospital at midday for the mastectomy surgery. My op was last on the list, so the nurse says she'll collect me from the ward and take me to theatre around five o'clock. Sitting quietly on the hospital bed reliving the drama of the past few weeks, I got steadily more anxious about everything that had happened and what the outcome might be. At four o'clock, the nurse gave me a pre-op sedative, and I drifted into deep sleep. Three hours later I woke and drowsily told Mark I had no pain at all. He replied the surgeon was delayed. I hadn't had the surgery yet.

Due to complications caused by removing more underarm lymph nodes, the drains wouldn't stop draining and I spend a week in hospital, surprised a mastectomy doesn't hurt more. I feel quite buoyant and receive so many flowers they overflow out of my room and into the corridor. I had so many visitors I was exhausted being a captive audience. Those who know me offer practical comfort, speaking openly and plainly. Others talk in slightly hushed tones, either airing their own cancer fears or regaling me with uplifting stories about friends-of-friends who made miraculous recoveries. An acquaintance asks how they could do the surgery if your breast goes flat when you lay down, and my ex-sister-in-law says she'd have the other one cut off to match. I remind myself to concentrate on what people mean to say rather than the drivel that actually comes out.

The day the dressing is removed, I stand in front of the bathroom mirror for the inaugural unveiling. Mr. Rowe-Jones, the breast surgeon, had left me with a neat horizontal scar on pancake flat skin. The scar is quite high, red enough to be sore, but not angry. It's a neat, fine line cut and stitched with care, which contrasted sharply to my mum's mastectomy scar in 1968 (she was also 41). She was hacked from shoulder to waist and while such radical removal undoubtedly saved her life, yet she was literally scarred for life both physically and mentally and died aged 77 without ever looking at it again. I write a thank you letter to the surgeon; it was the least I could do. "My mother's mastectomy resembled a giant motorway hewn without regard across the surrounding countryside. In comparison, my incision looks like a purposeful track neatly landscaped into a site of outstanding natural beauty."

Concerned about Mark's reaction, I reveal the damage when he visits that evening. I slipped off my top and stood with my back to the basin in the privacy of the hospital bathroom. He had his back to the door, and I watched his face as I carefully took down the bandages; he stood unflinching, his eyes fixed on mine before flicking down to my breast.

"That doesn't look bad at all. It's very neat. Are you okay with it?" He smiled and kissed me.

"I think I'm fine," I replied through the tears. "I'm fine now you've seen it."

Mark wrapped his arms tightly round me (narrowly avoiding the drain tubes) and we stood for a long time together in the bathroom. In later years he told me it seemed very weird, like it was me but not me, and although he'd tried to prepare himself, he was still unprepared when he saw it. He knew he had to show no emotion. He came home and had several very stiff drinks.

I left hospital with a wad of tissues stuffed into my bra and got on with life as best as I could under the cloud of imminent chemotherapy. I started riding my horse again, but found the underarm surgery restricted movement, and got upset thinking it would be permanent. Being back home seems strange. I try to do ordinary, mundane things and feel exhausted. Defiantly I make myself a "this one" badge with an arrow so visitors don't need to peer quite so indiscreetly at my lopsided chest. The breast-care nurse visits to check the wound, fits me with a temporary, light-weight prosthesis and says she'll make me a clinic appointment to be fitted with proper silicone look-alike prosthesis.

On a bleak midwinter day when I was feeling at my lowest ebb, the appointment arrived. I couldn't pretend this insult to my body was okay, as if making my outward appearance 'normal' somehow mended the inside. I postponed the date and then postponed it again. When the dreaded day eventually arrived, I wanted someone to accompany me, but I also wanted to go alone and wallow in the misery of my situation. Sitting having a cup of tea until it's time to leave for the clinic, I think back about my boobs, and the morning mum suggested we go and buy a bra, for me. I hadn't noticed I needed one, but when I looked through my white nylon school shirt, I could certainly see her point. Or two. It was a short bus ride to Cox's, the local ladies-wear shop, where Mrs. Cox showed me to the fitting room, and busied herself measuring my budding breasts. Mum and I left the store with two soft triangular cups of blue check gingham called a Berelei Beginner.

By the time my teens arrived, baby breasts had transformed into a pair of pendulous knockers, and dainty blue gingham had given way to matronly white lace, with staunch straps and three hook back fastening. I'd obviously bypassed the rosebud stage and gone straight to full bloom. It was the early seventies, and I embraced hippiedom with the desperation of a teen trying to belong somewhere other than where she was. Free-falling hair worn with a headband was a heaven-sent style for me, and I flowed ethereally, draped in patchwork and velvet.

Aspiring to be a feminist, I read Cosmopolitan Magazine, but stumbled at the first hurdle of liberating myself from my bra.

One sunny afternoon, as I bounced along Bournemouth's Old Christchurch Road wearing frayed Levis and an antique blue silk kimono, I noticed the bus I wanted to catch was about to pass me. I made a run for the bus stop at the top of the road, but as I began to sprint, my liberated breasts ricocheted their way out of the kimono. All the builders working on an adjacent site downed tools and cheered, cars slowed, people turned to watch, and as the bus passed, I saw open-mouthed passengers staring at me as I desperately tried to run, whilst stuffing two heaving watermelons back into a thin wisp of silk. Red faced (probably red breasted too) I clamped my arms firmly across my chest and made a sharp left turn down a side road, heading straight back home. My breasts were deposited back in the security of their formidable Cross-Your-Heart custodian, never to bounce freely again.

I'm short and slight, and by the time I met my first husband in my early twenties, my breasts were a full double-D cup size. They used to arrive in a room a good few seconds ahead of me, but my husband wasn't complaining so I packed them away as firmly as I could each day and risked a black eye if I turned quickly in bed at night. Big-breasted girls were not yet fashionable; I think Gossard were the first company to produce a larger size underwire bra in colours other than black, white or beige. I remember buying a plum coloured one in the wonderful lingerie shop 'Just Jane' in Salisbury, where the strippers and fetish-wearers shopped. For the first time since blue gingham days, my boobs felt special, and they looked glamorous too!

The Breast Prosthesis Department was actually a Portakabin in a car park. I rang the doorbell, and an immaculate woman in a starched white hospital coat ushered me in and directed me to a seat in her windowless office. She sat on one side of the desk, and I sat on the other. Her hair was an impossibly uniform shade of auburn, and sat on her head like a metallic helmet, accentuating her thickly powdered and rouged face, arched eyebrows, and vermilion lips.

"Today we're going to fit you with a breast prosthesis" she said, gesturing vermilion-painted nails towards stacks of boxes on shelving that ran the entire length of the room. "But first I need to take some notes."

I sat glumly, answering questions about operation and treatment dates, and size and shape of my remaining breast before she asked me to remove my top garments. After recording my measurements, she surveyed my remaining breast from different angles, and gave me advice about buying a non-underwire bra to better support the new prosthesis. She then walked to the shelves and returned with three identical boxes, and as she laid them on the floor by my feet, I had a sudden vision of buying new shoes in a shoe shop. I desperately tried to suppress a giggle, which came out sounding like a giant gurgle, but she didn't bat a thickly mascaraed eyelid. She removed the protective cardboard from around the first box, revealing a small black patent carry case. Inside, quivering in a nest of black satin, sat a beige coloured, breast-shaped, silicone filled prosthesis, looking remarkably like a large chicken fillet. I was surprised at its weightiness as she slipped it into my bra cup and re-fastened the back hooks.

I stood, turned and bent as instructed, before she shook her head. "That's really not good enough. Let's try the next one." She put the fillet back in its case and read the name on the second box. "Ah yes, this is the Doreen; it'll be a better shape for your small back." I thought I might be expected to shake hands with Doreen as she was hoisted from her box and dug my nails into my palms to remain sane. Alas, Doreen didn't fit, neither did the Elizabeth nor the April, and by the time we got to the June, I was ready to stay flat-chested.

"I think we're going to have to consider a Special," she said, frowning at the boxes on the floor. "You're quite deceiving, but we must get it right. . ." She moved a stepstool towards the shelves and reached boxes from the top shelf. The Special case looked identical to the others but had a red satin lining. I half expected a trumpet fanfare as Special Marguerite was uncased and fitted and declared an outstanding success. TaDa!

I was issued with a 'How to Wash Your Silicone Prosthesis' leaflet and two cotton prosthesis covers, and left the Portakabin carrying Marguerite in her red-lined case. Later that night in my sleep, I heard the most guttural, heart-wrenching sob. I woke with a start, and in the depths of solitary darkness, realised the cry was mine. I got out of bed and quietly felt my way across the bedroom to where Marguerite's box sat on the dressing table. Opening the cupboard door, I silently buried her in the furthest, darkest corner, underneath seldom-used suitcases. I climbed back into bed and snuggled into Mark's back. As I listened to his steady breathing, I tried to forget everything about Marguerite, and all the fear she brought with her.

12 LIKE ACID ON VELVET

I'm loathe to describe chemotherapy lest I scare someone who is about to experience it, but it affects people differently and I can only tell you how it affected me. Should you need to experience it, you'll probably sail through without a hitch. I do hope so.

Mark and I are sitting in the chemotherapy waiting room, deep in the bowels of the hospital. Various attempts at conversation have failed, but the silence between us is companionable, and not a measure of distance. The oncologist calls my name twice and does a double take as I walk towards him "I didn't recognise you without your curls!" he says. I'd had my hair cut short in readiness.

"No, neither do I." I reply glumly.

The chemotherapy suite is furnished with grey and pink comfy chairs, patterned curtains and brightly framed floral prints. The grey and pink upholstery perfectly matches the pallor of the patients sitting in them. Most of the patients are connected to mobile drips, and some look up encouragingly as we walk in. In the weeks to come I also contribute to the wave of empathy as a newbie innocently enters hell. A cheerful nurse shows me to a basin in the cloakroom where she wets my hair and smothers it in conditioner. I've chosen to wear a Cooling Cap which will literally freeze my head, reducing the amount of chemotherapy drug reaching my hair follicles and minimise hair loss. The conditioner aids connection twixt the cap and my scalp. It's now been twenty-five years since that first chemotherapy, and I still cringe at the feel of hair conditioner.

I'm seated in the chair flanked by the oncologist, two nurses, Mark and the mobile drip when the drugs arrive; flouracil epiubicin, and cyclophosphamide a trio which go by the rather apt name of FEC. One of them is the colour of Cherryaid. The oncologist deftly finds a vein in my lower right arm flushes it through with saline solution, and then the drugs enter, intravenously flowing to every cell in my body in order to carry out their carnage. My mouth fills with a disgustingly druggy taste, and the nurse offers mint humbugs to suck. I flush violently hot and feel like I've wet myself. The oncologist smiles gently "it's just the drugs" he says softly. The Cooling Cap pulses and freezes, my head feels like it's being forcibly shrunk, the throbbing is almost unbearable, and my forehead is screaming for release. All of me is screaming for release. I sit in my comfy chair hooked up to a trio of steadily dripping poison and I realise the screaming is silent. I look at the other people and wonder if they're screaming too.

After an hour I'm unhooked, un-capped and unceremoniously blow-dried, issued with an appointment card and a batch of anti-sickness ampoules to be kept in the fridge and administered by the district nurse if vomiting persists. Mark and I walk slowly up the hospital stairs until we reach daylight and look at each other expectantly.

"You okay?" he says?

"Yup. You?"

"Yup."

Neither of us believes the other, and we hold hands tightly until we reach the car where we continue the conversation.

"You okay?"

"Yup. You?"

"Yup."

We sit and wait, expecting something to happen but it doesn't so we drive home, stopping on the way to give Teddy his feed and settle him for the night, and once back home people phone, speaking in low voices, asking how I am. I don't know how I am; I can't put words to it. My brain feels thick, and my body feels full of something it doesn't like. My mum phones and I try to speak brightly, dismissing any side effects because, for her, I can't be ill. She seems re-assured. And then I go to bed. Light turns to dark and light again. I crawl to the bathroom and dry retch through cracked, ulcer-covered lips. My skin is yellow, eyes black-lined red. Some people suffer no ill effects from chemotherapy but alas I'm not one of them. My teeth ache, my hair aches, my fingernails ache, everything aches, and I have thrush in every orifice. And then a 'friend' phones to re-assure me if I stay positive, the chemotherapy won't have any ill effect.

After two days I rise like Lazarus from the dead. Mark goes to work. I go back to bed. At some point, probably evening, Mark comes home.

"You okay?"

"Yup. You?"

"Yup."

I can eat cold stewed apple and ice cream. I can talk and walk and laugh when the Get Well cards arrive urging me to *Be Positive*.

"You okay?"

"Yup. You?"

"Yup."

Dark thoughts crowd in, mocking my lucid moments with increasing regularity, like football hooligans running riot with banners proclaiming YOU'RE GOING TO DIE A SLOW ROTTING CANCER-RIDDEN DEATH. I phone Cancer Backup helpline. "I've got cancer. I'm not being positive."

"Oh, I think you are," replies a soothing voice, "otherwise why would you be phoning?"

I go back to work. The shop is cold so I can't even look like death warmed up; I just look like death. My workmates joke a bit and then they feel very sorry for me. I stay for an hour and drive home. Exhausted doesn't even begin to describe it.

My chemotherapy is six cycles at three-weekly intervals. The day before treatment I have blood tests and the veins become scarcer and less co-operative as I become weaker and less tolerant. A student nurse, panicking after the fourth attempt to find a vein, suggests using the finger-prick method, and makes so many attempts to gather drops it looks like my fingerprints have been erased. After that, I look for the older nurses because they have more experience coaxing blood from a stone. I feel trashed.

I've been having acupuncture each week after chemotherapy because it helps restore my stamina before the next onslaught. Even I see the irony in yet more needles. The acupuncturist asks how I am and I can't answer. I simply sit and sob. He moves his chair next to mine and holds my hand in an act of human kindness which stays alongside me for years to come. Mark busies himself building a patio at the top of the garden. Each chemotherapy cycle sees more earth dug, levelled and removed, more stones laid, cemented. I watch from the bathroom window, standing on tiptoe swathed in blankets. Life goes on and the pattern of weeks and months becomes familiar. Friday afternoon poison, home to bed for three days. Pick up and carry on as best as I can for two weeks, working when energy and side-effects allow. Wake-up on the final Monday morning to begin the countdown of dread.

On Treatment number four I refuse to go. Mark physically picks me up and puts me in the car.

"You okay?"

"No, I'm fucking not."

On Treatment number five I beg the oncologist to let it end. Please. I can't do any more. He puts his hand on my arm and says this will be the last, five out of six cycles was sufficient and we could finish. I want to be pleased but I can't find the strength. I had worn the same set of clothes for each treatment and after that final cycle, I made a bonfire and burnt them all. I didn't want to see, feel or smell them ever again. I vow never, ever to have chemotherapy again. And then I put the smile back in place and get on with my life.

Looking back, I realise how much is thankfully forgotten and how much remains tightly wrapped, stashed in the darkest corner of hell. I still can't put into words how those months of chemotherapy affected me, and how it burnt through to my soul like acid on velvet.

13 RECONSTRUCTION

By the time summer arrived, things began to return to how they were; I went back to work full time, and back to riding regularly. I got used to my new appearance and the missing breast didn't feel strange, but the remaining one looked odd and isolated without a partner. Eventually I exhumed Marguerite from the cupboard. She was quite weighty to wear; I hadn't realised how voluminous a breast can be. Despite the cotton cover, the silicone became very hot and sweaty, so I tried a bra with pockets to house her, but the weight dragged the bra forward. One glorious sunny morning, I was mucking-out Teddy's stable and vigorously sweeping the yard, dressed in shorts and a vest top, when Marguerite flew out of my bra, swooshed across the concrete and landed in a wobbly heap by the water bucket. Teddy shot to the back of his stable, snorting at the alien missile, and I didn't know whether to laugh or cry. As I stuffed her back in my bra, Farmer Jim (who owned the stables) walked round the corner, looked at my hasty re-alignment, looked at my face, turned round and walked back again. I saw him every day for many years afterwards, and he never mentioned it. A few weeks later, I was at the osteopath, and as I bent forward for him to check my pelvis, she slipped out again, landing with a quivering plop in front of us. There was a moment of stunned silence before I began to giggle, and I was comfortable enough with the osteopath to enjoy the 'shared moment', but I knew it was time to think seriously about breast reconstruction.

By the age of forty I'd had breast cancer twice, and a generous helping of the side dishes that came with it. I felt I'd done enough to appease the gods of unlucky statistics and would live the rest of my life in boring equilibrium. Ha! Once again, the hand of shite reached down and pointed at my breast. While washing in the shower, I found a lump on my right breast. Rather than waiting for a doctor's referral I phoned the oncologist's office directly and was admitted to hospital where guiding wires were inserted in my breast under ultrasound, and the lump removed with local anaesthetic. The procedure was every bit as unpleasant as it sounds! A week later, when the oncologist gave us fab news that it was a benign cyst, I asked him the chances of cancer occurring in my remaining breast. He replied the chances were twenty-five percent.

"Well, you know you offered me breast reconstruction" I said, sitting up straight because I felt I had to sell the idea, "I've been thinking if have reconstruction done, they'll have to operate on the other breast to level it up, or else one will be pert, and the other pendulous." I paused, and Dr Goode nodded. I took a deep breath before continuing, trying to make what I was saying sound like a request and not a question. "As there's a high possibility of still getting breast cancer, could you take the other one off and reconstruct them both at the same time." This was seventeen years before Angelina Jolie made preventative mastectomy fashionable, and genetic screening made the reasons more obvious, and my request was breaking new territory. Dr Goode wrote some notes in my file, and said he thought a woman in Bournemouth had recently had a prophylactic double mastectomy, and he would raise the issue at the next oncology meeting. I knew I could trust Dr Goode to do his best for me, and three weeks later, I got an appointment to see Mr Hobby the plastic surgeon.

The plastic surgeon cupped my remaining 34DD breast in his hand and asked me what size I would like to be.

"A perfect 34C please" I replied, and he nodded approvingly.

He explained the lengthy procedure, which took pads of

latissimus dorsi muscle from the shoulders and swiveled them around to the front, to give support for the breast implants while maintaining the blood supply. They would remove triangles of skin from the centre of my back to shape the breasts, and graft nipples from skin on my inner thigh, for an authentically coloured areola. He said he would insert the implants slightly above the breast line, allowing them to drop into their correct position. I was worried about silicone leakage and toxicity, and we had a lengthy discussion about my decision to have saline-filled implants; my biggest concern was falling off my horse and rupturing them. He said he didn't have another patient who rode after reconstruction, but reluctantly agreed with my reasoning. He must have been both baffled and amused by my priorities.

On December 29th Mark and I celebrated our first wedding anniversary with overflowing glasses of champagne and wry smiles; some year, eh? If we were still laughing after that first year, we would conquer anything, and two days later, I was booking into hospital for six hours of breast surgery; Mr Rowe-Jones would do the mastectomy, then pass my body to Mr. Hobby the plastic surgeon for reconstruction. New Year's Eve was the only free date in their schedules, and the nurse recounted later how they both arrived and left wearing their black dinner suits, ready to celebrate New Year's Eve. Two suave surgeons, dressed in formal attire for my surgery!

A nurse with a kindly face held my hand tightly in the freezing cold pre-theatre room, as the anaesthetist pushed the plunger on his syringe. It felt cold inside my veins. And then the next moment, Mark was standing over me as I woke-up in the recovery room. There was a white pony wandering between the beds, which nobody had noticed, and I told Mark to catch him *quickly*! Mark walked to the next bed, slipped an imaginary halter on an imaginary pony and turned to me with a look of real-life confusion.

"Tie him up to the end of the bed!" I said with exasperation. "What is it with everybody here?"

I remember feeling excruciating pain as they tried to move me from the hospital trolley to my bed. In a dreamy far-off land, I heard bloodcurdling screams and someone swearing vehemently. Nurses darted about holding tubes, moving wires and issuing commands, as they slid me in ungainly style onto the cold white sheets. Exhausted from pain, I couldn't catch my breath with the oxygen mask covering my mouth, and was uncertain who or where I was (or even if I still was?) I saw Mark on my right side, jostling for space between the equipment and the nurses; he looked terrified. The nurse showed me how to press a button on the morphine drip for pain relief, then Mark showed me, then the nurses showed me again. "Press the button, Elaine" was all I could hear, but I couldn't understand it. What button? Then nurse Christine with the kind face took charge, and as I pressed the button, she winked at me. I wished her Happy New Year before pressing the button again and slipping into cloudy oblivion.

I spent my birthday in hospital and shared the 'celebration' with my new breasts, which were one week old. I was napping on the bed when a nurse woke me. I'd barely opened my eyes when all the nurses came into the room, carrying a pink iced birthday cake with blazing pink candles, and sang happy birthday. Such a lovely gesture and I was deeply touched by their kindness, but I hated it; I was feeling grumpy and emotional and not in the least like being the centre of attention. I thanked everyone profusely and cut half the cake for them to take to the nurse's station, but all I wanted was to curl-up and stop trying to be strong. I knew I should celebrate every day, but it was such hard work, and cancer clouded so much. I wanted to ride my horse, and breathe into his soft neck and feel alive again, but here I was, in hospital, on my birthday. It was one of the few times I've felt total, wretched despair, and I didn't know how to climb out of it.

The despair got worse when the surgical dressings came off, exposing skin as pink as the birthday cake. The right breast reconstruction was neatly shaped, but the left implant sat extremely high, with a weird lopsided overhang at the top. The doctor explained again that the implant would gradually settle into the correct placing, but in later months it became clear this wasn't going to happen. Eventually, the consultant opined radiotherapy and surgery had compromised breast tissue quality, and the implant was unable to move. I knew things weren't going to look perfect, but I wish I'd known about encapsulation, so I could've been prepared. It was my first big lesson that you don't get answers if you don't know the right questions to ask; a lesson that set me in good stead for the future.

My daily excursion around the hospital corridors had progressed from a hunched, protective-mode shuffle to a brisk walk, made easier once the drains came out, and the bottles didn't bounce around in my pockets. The incision and the skin graft on my back were numb, which meant sleep was more comfortable, and the elasticated bandage that bound my breasts would stay on for another three weeks; I felt an uncanny empathy with Frankenstein's monster. Pain meds made no impact on the hundred small knives stabbing my insides when I moved my arms, picked anything up, or tried to push down. I imagined all the severed nerves irrevocably parted to front and back, frantically waving and calling in vain for their Other Ends. Eventually, they ceased calling. With strict instructions to rest, I was discharged from hospital ten days after surgery. Pain was a compelling threshold to cross, and I did too much too soon. I still haven't mastered the fact that recuperation takes time.

14 WATERLEAKGATE

In the spring of 1998, a friend was staying with us, and we were happily sitting around the supper table, laughing, eating and drinking, when for some reason I looked down at my bosom and saw only one breast. With an overwhelming sense of panic, I made an excuse, dashed to the bathroom, and tore off my clothes. My left breast was intact, still perched high above my bra but my right breast was just a fold of loose skin with no filling; the implant had ruptured. I phoned the hospital, but it was 'out of hours' and there was nothing they could do except confirm I must have leaked and tell me to call again in the morning. There was no pain, and the saline would just disperse into my body, but I felt so angry this had happened to me. For some reason, I also felt embarrassed. I clamped my arm firmly across my chest, returned to the table and drank several large glasses of wine. Next day at the hospital, the plastic surgeon looked aghast. Yes, the saline implant had leaked, and a pair of fresh implants would need fitting; he was adamant he'd use silicone, and I couldn't really argue.

If only it had been that easy. Breast reconstruction following mastectomy is now a standard option with cancer treatment, but back then, it was a fairly new procedure, and the NHS were reticent to replace the implants. The implant supplier discovered a batch of implants had leaky valves, which meant the saline wasn't completely sealed; if I wanted, I could sue them but litigation would take some time. I needed something done quickly, so I went on the warpath and phoned the hospital plastic surgeon daily. I made allies of the medical secretaries who were tremendously sympathetic and helpful, and got the implant suppliers to reimburse the NHS. A month after Waterleakgate, I got an operation date, and spent four nights in hospital for what is now a day-case procedure. My stay was unmemorable except for the nurse who attempted to remove my drain without first removing the holding stitches; that pain was worse than all my surgery! I left the hospital with a new set of scars, but on the positive side, I had two evenly placed silicone boobs.

At my next routine check-up, I ask the oncologist the Baby Question. "Now I haven't got any breasts, so my risk of cancer is lower, is it safe to go ahead and try for a baby?"

The oncologist takes an ominously deep sigh and I wonder if they practise doing them at med school. "I think you'll find your age and chemotherapy have lessened your ability to conceive, and we can't give you fertility drugs without the risk of causing more cancer. The recommendation is staying five years cancer-free before trying for a baby."

"But I'll be ancient in five years," I protest. "So, I'm never going to have a baby?"

"Of course, we'll support whatever decision you make, but it's not as simple as just removing breasts because the cancer can return anywhere. We've lowered the chances significantly, but because you've already had cancer twice it's a huge risk to take."

Mark is adamant that he won't risk my life for a baby, and in some insane way I would. I can't stop the visions of him as a dad, me as a mum, but unwillingly I've joined the silent band of women who were almost mothers. Chemotherapy, mastectomies and debilitating surgeries are a fair way to test the strength of any marriage but being unable to have children was the blow that felled me; my husband would've become a wonderful father. He didn't say much about it at the time, just that he understood my distress. We got used to it together, and over the years I found carrying the loss alongside was easier than wearing it as a physical burden. And then girlfriends had daughters who got married, which was something else I could never share, and without warning the original feelings returned in a torrent of unresolved loss as fresh as the day they were first felt. Then the grandchildren started to arrive.

Mark and I continued trying to live life alongside our foe, and not let it live life for us. The years passed in the way day-to-day living only sneaks up on you in memories. We became complacent in our cancer cares, finding odd places to leave cancer behind, and mostly we succeeded. Twice was enough for anyone and each year clear surely meant it was gone, but it always sat on my shoulder as I tried to live my life with happiness, and then I'd forget to turn slowly avoiding the harbinger of doom, and we'd meet head on. Face to face. Smack, straight between the eyes. I can't really tell you how Mark treads the balance of living with death, because having dealt him that blow, I feel too guilty to look deeply. We deal with practicalities as a team and employ the Humour of Doom to lessen the bitterness of unpalatable topics. I notice that sometimes the whisky bottle empties quicker, and I know when he lays awake at night. We both think we're good at hiding things from each other, but we're not. We just hang on by our fingernails to what we have, trying to ignore the fact cancer is hanging there with us.

We used to be more adventurous; I wonder if these days we cling to our routine and comforts to lessen the effects of things we can't control, or whether it's a natural progression for two aging earth signs? I'm just grateful for evenings spent on the sofa, reading our books, with the cats asleep in front of the woodburner. I have no hankering to see the Seven Wonders when I have domestic bliss under my nose. The price I pay for staying alive is living with cancer.

15 MUM'S WEDDING

After ten years as a widow, my mum had re-built her life as best she could. It was rocky, but she made it through. Passionate about Old Time Dancing, she also became passionate with the gentleman who ran the dance sessions in the local church hall. He'd had two wives and didn't want a third, so she settled for what made him happy. She had spent her whole life settling for what made other people happy. Then she got bowel cancer and while he helped nurse her, he realised what he might lose and changed his mind. They bought a house together and set the wedding date.

I'd organised a small reception lunch at a smart hotel and baked her wedding cake, but she didn't know what colour she'd wear, so I couldn't decorate it or plan her bouquet. After a lengthy wardrobe trying-on session, we decided on an apricot dress and coat with pearl jewellery, and almond shoes and bag. She stood in her wedding finery and agreed it fitted the occasion, but she looked every inch of her seventy-seven years. I put her lack of sparkle down to pre-wedding nerves, but it struck me how swollen her ankles looked in the low court shoes. Later that day I covered the cake in apricot fondant and ordered apricot and cream roses for her bouquet.

Four days before the wedding I was mucking out Teddy's stable early and was halfway to the muckheap with wheelbarrow piled high, when mum's partner, Leslie, rang my mobile phone. It wasn't like him to be up so early.

"Hello Elaine!" he shouted, in the way older people often

do on the phone. "I just wanted you to know your mum's not feeling very well."

"Oh, I'm sorry," I replied. "What's the problem, what can I do?

"She had a heart attack. She's in the ambulance outside the house. Could you meet her at the hospital? I'm waiting to have the freezer delivered so I'll come along after that."

I sat on the wet ground in the middle of the stable yard as the blood drained from my body. "She's *what*?" I shouted back, matching his volume "she's had *what*?"

"She's had a heart attack," he repeated. "She felt funny and was sick and dizzy and I said I'd phone the doctor, but she said no, dial 999 for an ambulance. She didn't look very well at all. They treated her in the bedroom for ages, and then outside in the ambulance, and then they drove off." He told me again about the fridge-freezer.

"Okay, okay," I stammered. "It's okay, I'll go straight to the hospital. Thank you, Leslie."

"And what shall I do about the freezer?" he asks, in a tone that made me want to weep.

"Come to the hospital after the delivery?" I suggested, at a loss to think of another solution. "I'll phone you from the hospital and let you know what's happening. Don't worry, I'm sure she'll be alright. I expect its last-minute nerves. I'm on my way."

Dropping everything and running to the car, I tried to process this calamitous news. I phoned Mark, who said he'd meet me at the hospital, and my friend Colleen, who said she'd look after Teddy. The drive to the hospital was mercifully quick, and my prayer for a vacant parking space was answered. I bought an all-day ticket and rushed up the hospital steps just as mum was being unloaded from the ambulance.

"Mum!" I shouted, hurrying to the trolley. The paramedics slowed very slightly, and I glimpsed her pale, near-death face. "I'm here mum, we're here, it's okay" I squeezed her hand and from the look on her face, I didn't believe it would be okay at all. Mark arrived and we sat in silence, unaware of the hospital hustle and bustle all around. A nurse showed us the coffee machine and said the doctor knew we were waiting. So, we waited. And waited. Leslie arrived in a flurry of confusion, uncharacteristically wearing a mismatched suit with tie and hair awry.

We hugged and took turns trying to convince each other (and ourselves) everything would be okay. As he told us how difficult it was manoeuvring the large freezer into a small kitchen without scratching the paintwork, I understood the solace in mundane and meaningless conversation.

Around one o'clock the nurse led us into a small windowless office where the doctor was perched on a desk facing us. He looked about twelve years old and for a ridiculous moment, I thought it was Bring Your Child to Work Day, and glanced past him, looking for a responsible parent. There were no chairs, so we shuffled into a straight line in front of him. "Sorry to keep you waiting. I'm Doctor Jim," he said in a very grown-up manner. Uncertain where to direct the conversation, he looked at each of us in turn. "And you are . . .?"

"I'm Elaine, Fay's daughter," I replied, standing a little straighter. "This is my husband Mark, and mum's fiancée Leslie."

"We're getting married on Monday!" shouted Leslie brightly, smoothing both his hair and tie.

"Err . . . I don't think Monday will be possible," said Dr Jim gently to Leslie, before turning to me.

"Your mother is in a very serious condition. She is in ICU; she's had clot-busting drugs to give her the best possible chance. The heart attack caused major damage and she needs cardiac surgery. We're waiting to transfer her to Southampton as soon as a specialist bed is available. Do you have any other family?"

"My brother, in Brighton," I said, realising the implication of the question.

"You should contact him sooner than later."

Mark took my left hand tightly in his while Leslie gripped

my right hand with equal force. For a second it felt like we were about to take an absurd theatrical curtain call and a giggle of panic rose in my throat. I bit my tongue so hard warm salty blood filled my mouth, providing the necessary distraction. With mouth semi-closed, I mumbled, "we need to see her." It was a statement, not a question.

"Just two of you then, for no more than ten minutes."

"Thank you," we all said in unison.

Leslie and I spent our ten precious minutes with mum, as Mark waited in the family room. Mum's tiny body was engulfed in tubes and machines; I'd expected machines, but not this many. The Intensive Care Nurse brought two chairs and motioned us to sit. The machines hummed, the air was cool and the ward had a chilling atmosphere of imminent danger while mum, oblivious to everything drifted in and out of consciousness. I wish the way she looked in ICU was a blank memory, but her ashen, terrified features were haunting, and knowing she was sedated was scant consolation.

16 CHANGE OF PLANS

Leslie came home with us, and I made lunch which no one of ate. I phoned my brother "Hi, it's Elaine."

"Hello darling, how are you?"

"It's not good news, I'm afraid. Mum had a heart attack this morning. We've just got back from hospital." Silence. "I'm so sorry Colin." There was no way to make this any easier for him.

"Wh . . . what . . . where . . ."

"She's in Poole Hospital Coronary Care Unit. Visiting is from two 'til eight. She's in and out of consciousness, which they said was normal at this stage, but . . . but you need to come."

"What, now?"

"Yes now."

"But we're coming on Monday for the wedding . . ." he tailed off.

"I know, but there's no wedding now. She had a heart attack instead."

"I can't come right now, I need to wait a bit and then I'll come."

"When will that be?"

"I don't know . . . soon."

"Okay, call me when you leave. We'll go back later but they only allow two visitors."

"Yes. Yes, I will. She'll be alright, won't she?"

"No Colin, I don't think she will." What was I supposed to say?

Leslie, Mark, and I sat on the sofa watching old black-and-white movies on TV, drinking tea and looking at each other in silence. At six o'clock I re-hashed the lunchtime sandwiches, and we all made an effort to eat one. Back at the hospital mum was still asleep. I left Leslie holding her hand and had a word with the matron who told me I could phone at any time, and by tomorrow they should've removed some of the tubes and monitors. She put a compassionate hand on my elbow; enough to show concern, but not enough to make me cry. Colin arrived, and I felt so sad for what he was about to face. We hugged, exchanged brief words, and I left him to fall down the rabbit hole alone.

The days settled into a routine of hospital visits, tending Teddy, and trying to concentrate on work. I cancelled the wedding reception (they kept the deposit!) removed the icing from the cake I'd so proudly decorated and gave it to our local old-folks home.

Mum was tough and had much to live for, and as soon as she was sitting up, she became the darling of the ward. Leslie phoned friends with the good news, and I phoned family. Her wedding day was horribly sad, and not the best day to have a urine catheter fitted. I sat holding her hand and feeling her pain. She hated hospital food, so each lunchtime I took her a flask of homemade chicken broth and a little plate of sliced fruit. After a week of stressing about the delay getting to the specialist heart unit, she phoned in a panic early one morning to say the ambulance was arriving for her transfer.

"I won't know any of the nurses. I won't like Southampton," she said anxiously.

"I'll be straight down, we'll talk it through," I said, once again abandoning Teddy's muck barrow in the middle of the yard. I arrived at the ward outside visiting times, buzzed the doorbell and explained the situation to the nurse who smiled, put her finger to her lips to indicate quietness and let me in. I whispered reassurances to mum. Yes, the nurse would pack her bag when the ambulance arrived, and I wrote her name across the top so the new nurse would know it was hers.

The paramedic would be with her throughout the journey because I wasn't allowed to come with, and they were unlikely to use the blue light. I didn't mention she'd be in a general mixed ward until her surgery. She asked me to trim her hair, so I borrowed the nurse's scissors and we giggled at the impromptu salon. With a great deal of love, I gave her a bed bath, and fought back tears feeling the frail body beneath my hands. We hugged and kissed, and she promised to phone when she arrived because she wanted to get settled before having visitors the next day.

Afternoon parking at Southampton Hospital was non-existent. We left the car in a side street half a mile away and walked. Smartly dressed in his best suit and tie, with a raincoat neatly folded over his arm, Leslie strode out ahead while Mark and I trotted to keep up with him. We found mum in bed, anxious and upset. She blurted out how they'd lost her bag, weren't expecting her arrival, and all she got to eat was a cheese sandwich. Doctors had woken her during the night for blood tests, the adjacent patient snored, and the menu was fried food, spicy food or sandwiches. There was no natural yoghurt. She couldn't work the phone and she couldn't understand the foreign nurses. As Leslie sat on the visitor chair and gently recounted the minutiae of his day, she visibly relaxed and played with his hand on the bedcover. Mark connected the pre-pay patient TV and phone, and I found the lost bag in her bedside locker. Making an excuse to buy biscuits from the hospital shop, we tactfully left them to share their world together, uninterrupted.

For some inexplicable reason when we left her, we didn't hug. I turned at the door and waved, we blew kisses and went. Mum's heart op was booked for eight a.m. next morning and she didn't want me at to the hospital before her surgery. At eight-thirty, swaddled in blankets and comfortably sedated, she had a second, massive heart attack as the trolley entered the operating theatre. To my eternal shame I wasn't with her. I was with my horse trying to pretend none of this was happening.

At lunchtime, the surgeon phoned to tell me the news. "We still performed the surgery and have put her in an induced coma to aid recovery." I held the phone in a vice like grip and prayed silently.

Standing by her bedside that afternoon, I prayed again. Laying immobile in a sterile sea of white, with tubes supporting every function, was a swollen face barely recognisable as my mother, her chest rising and falling to the ventilator tune. Leslie leaned over the maze of tubes to kiss her, and her blue-tinged lips puckered in a weak smile. Then her heart stopped, literally. They shocked her back to 'life' and the machines stopped screaming murder. At the bottom of the bed her foot peeped out from under a blanket, and I noticed it was just like mine with big toe shorter than second toe. I concentrated on that revelation because it was easier to understand than anything else.

Visitors were discouraged in the high dependency unit, and family allowed briefly, no more than two at a time. I yearned to sit alone with mum, hold her like she'd held me and tell her stuff, and I felt so envious because everyone else was getting their chance to be with my mum, but circumstances conspired against me. I spent a long week watching her die and supporting everyone else. She stayed in the coma for five days, machines providing life support while her body began its own process of shutting down. Her kidneys were failing, her heart was failing, and the machines continued to mercilessly invade her frail body because death was not an option. On Saturday evening, Leslie and I consulted with her doctor, and I asked the hardest question of all. "Can't we simply unhook everything, and let her go, in peace. She's not going to recover is she, so can't we release her from this living death?" I never thought I'd ask for my mother's death.

"No" he replied, with textbook compassion, "we cannot. She can still recover. We can dialyse her kidneys; she'll be in a wheelchair and need extensive therapy to get her back walking, and of course she'll need twenty-four-hour care but there should be quality of life." I realised quality of life has a personal definition. I drove Leslie home and without a hint of embarrassment, he sat in the passenger seat and cried his heart out. When he finished, he blew his nose loudly and muttered "must've had something in my eye." Without taking my eyes off the traffic, I moved my hand to the gear stick, and he rested his on top.

In mum's final hour, they shocked her heart into re-starting as many times as protocol allowed. At seven o'clock she was declared brain-dead, and everything switched off. She didn't have the death she deserved, but she probably didn't have the life she deserved either.

The phone call came at seven o'clock on Sunday morning. Mark and I sat bolt upright in bed. I answered the call with dread. "Hello, Elaine? It's the CCU nurse from Southampton Hospital." How many times must she have spoken those words to a daughter like me?

"Earlier this morning, your mum went into cardiac arrest. The crash team treated her immediately with defibrillation and drugs, and she stabilised, but then unfortunately crashed again. They worked on her but couldn't save her. The monitor still shows very minor brain activity, but she is clinically dead."

"Brain activity?" I said, emphasising the word activity. "So, she is not dead yet? If we came straight away . . ."

"No" replied the nurse with the gentleness of experience. "Come when you are ready but don't rush. She has died."

"Please can you just stay with her until the activity stops? Just stay by her side, instead of me. Tell her we love her and its okay to go but go back and stay with her. Please."

"Of course," said the nurse "I'll do that now. I'm on duty until this evening, I'll be here when you arrive."

To this day I don't know if mum fought to die or fought to stay alive. That death-defined Sunday morning was surreal. We got out of bed, opened the curtains and faced each other in naked grief. She was the last of our parents to die. We dressed, Mark made tea, and I had an irresistible urge to vacuum the house.

Forty-five minutes later, we were on our way to Southampton hospital for the final time. The weak sun-bathed trees in a rising mist as we drove through the New Forest National Park. The mist drifted across the road in random clumps, like groups of ghostly figures hurrying to the other side. I shivered and leaned forward to turn up the heater and blessed my seatbelt as Mark suddenly hit the brakes. In front of us a crashed delivery van laid across the road, while the driver stood stunned, surveying the vegetables that spilled out the buckled doors.

Mark opened the car window. "You all right mate?" He asked.

The driver nodded his head and leant against the car door. "Yeh, I think so. A deer ran out, didn't stand a chance. It's dead under the van somewhere. Tried to stop but the whole thing went over.

"Dunno how I got out but here I am!"

"Can we help? Can we phone anyone?"

"Nah, police are on their way. My boss is gonna be livid, it was a brand-new van." Two police cars and an ambulance arrived, so we said our goodbyes and drove carefully around the van, squelching vegetables in our path.

"If we hadn't delayed at home, that coulda been us . . ." I said as we continued our journey.

"It doesn't bear thinking about, does it?" interrupted Mark.

17 SHIVA FOR MUM

At the hospital, the nurse greeted us with coffee, explained again what happened, and what to expect next. Then she showed us to mum's bed. Unhooked from her electrical empire, mum was peacefully pale, her body tucked under fresh bedcovers. We sat on the bed, held her cold hands, and thanked her for everything. I brushed her hair and swept it back from her closed eyes. We'd picked a posy of garden snowdrops and laid them on the pillow by her cheek. We loved her and hadn't wanted her to go but were so relieved she had. Then I gathered my courage around me like a cloak and walked slowly to the nurse's office to phone Leslie.

He answered on the third ring. "Leslie darling, it's Elaine. We got a call from the hospital at seven this morning. We're here now. I'm so sorry to have to tell you mum has died."

"You'll never be as sorry as I am, my dear," he answered sadly.

"We're leaving the hospital now, can we come straight to you?"

"Of course, you can," he whispered. "Drive carefully."

That was when the pain hit. It would be pointless to say I wasn't prepared for the pain because who could be? It was indescribable. It had no colour, no scale, no sell-by date. It just was. If you've felt it, you'd know, and if you haven't then you don't want to know. I sunk into the chair, wracked with guilt as the memories surfaced, and just as the what-ifs began, my dead mother appeared by my side like she'd been waiting for the pause between breaths.

"Hi mum," I said as I patted her bony arm. "How are you?"

"How are you?" she replied, neatly avoiding the obvious answer, that she was dead.

"Oh, you know . . ."

"Yes, I know," she said quietly, moving her hand over mine. Two seconds later she'd gone, and I couldn't tell you how she looked or what she was wearing, but her Chanel scent lingered in the air and lingered on me.

Mark and I blew kisses towards mum's room. The nurse told us to phone if we had any questions, and we left.

Leslie made a large pot of tea and placed it on the table alongside mum's framed photo. Freshly showered and shaved, he'd dressed in a blue suit with pink shirt and tie, which was mum's favourite, and he wore tartan slippers that made me smile. We sat, formally sipping from bone china cups, while the smiling face that was no more sat opposite. "What happens next?" he asked.

"The nurse said there'd be a post-mortem, to confirm hospital procedures were followed," I replied, taking solace in practicalities. "They'll collect Mum today and once the coroner gives the say-so, we can do the funeral. It should all be straightforward."

"You'll want to bury her quickly for your religion?" His steady voice reflected his shared solace in practicalities.

"Yes. I'll contact the synagogue office when we get home and start arrangements. First, I must phone Colin. Could I do it from here, now?" Mark told Leslie about the accident on the motorway while I made the phone call; it wasn't a conversation I ever want to repeat.

In the following days, I wished I'd never said 'it should all be straightforward.' Mum was raised orthodox Jewish, and I needed to do right by her beliefs. Somewhere between the hospital and morgue autopsy, the coroner's department had lost mum's body. They documented her hospital collection, but farcically "couldn't pinpoint her current location." The coroner and I agreed this was not good, as she required a quick burial.

The Jewish faith isn't great at celebrating women's strength and the Rabbi made it quite clear he'd have preferred it if my brother was in charge of arrangements. I would've preferred that too, but my brother always avoided anything unpleasant, and mum's death was more than he could comprehend, let alone organise. Through gritted teeth I Googled the necessary details and correct protocol, while my orthodox cousins phoned each day to remind me mum should've been buried by now. I stopped answering their calls and emailed the completed plan to the synagogue secretary. Sometimes the closer people think they are to God the further they are from humanity.

Finally, the tide turned. The coroner's secretary saved the day. "She's here with us!" she said excitedly on the phone. "I'm looking after her personally to avoid any more misadventures. We'll express the post-mortem today and I'll phone you directly with the result." The coroner quickly cleared mum for burial and Mark drove to Southampton to speed the process by collecting her death certificate. We set the funeral date, and my cousins insisted on attending to say prayers, but as I wasn't kosher enough for their dietary requirements, they'd be unable to come back to my house afterwards. I said their presence was unnecessary and left it at that.

With the help of mum's address book, I contacted my second-cousin Bernard, a London market trader and the black sheep of his family. He told me exactly how to proceed with the funeral and offered to speak with the rabbi. He also told me some very inappropriate jokes, and I laughed at the jokes and laughed because I couldn't remember the last time I laughed. My ex-sister-in-law visited. Our sister-ship hadn't always been straightforward, but her support and offer of help with the funeral food was gratefully received. Leslie arranged the newspaper announcements and notified his friends and family. We made provisions for about thirty at the cemetery, with maybe twenty people coming back to house for refreshments.

Leslie didn't want to see mum at the funeral home, so

Mark took me, but at the last minute I was afraid to go in. On Valentine's Day, Leslie had given mum a funny Purple Ronnie card that played a tune when pressed. At the time, she'd been annoyed not to receive something romantic, but I thought she'd like to take the card with her, along with some family photos, so Mark slipped the envelope into her coffin, as a pillow behind her head.

After a week of threatened snow, it fell heavily on the morning of mum's funeral. I cleaned my grandmother's silver Shabbat candlesticks, covered the mirrors in my house, borrowed prayer books and low Shiva chairs from the synagogue, bought kosher smoked salmon, round challah rolls and cheesecake from the Jewish deli and boiled the traditional hardboiled eggs for the Meal of Consolation. Plastic crockery and cutlery was on hand in case the Orthodox Ones made an appearance. Then I dressed in my daughter-of-the-bride wedding clothes and tore the appropriate amount of cloth on the left side of my funeral outfit to show my pain and sorrow.

I sat numbly through the service supported by my ex-sister-in-law. I couldn't follow the Hebrew readings and prayers. Mark stood opposite side with my brother, men on one side of the Oel, women on the other as tradition decreed. The Rabbi stood at the front of the little congregation, singing in the most out-of-tune voice I had ever heard, and we stifled grimaces as the dull flat notes bounced from the ceiling and broke against the end wall. Mum would have seen the irony in it. As the coffin was wheeled from prayer chamber to grave to be buried alongside my dad, I led the way while Colin waited for his wife. Prayers at the graveside followed, mum's coffin was lowered into the void and as it tipped slightly headward, I heard Purple Ronnie playing his tune from her pillow. Leslie, my brother, and I held hands and as the snow began to fall, I turned my head to heaven and watched as my mummy sent wondrous white flakes to cover the heaped earth.

Stuck in snowbound traffic on the M25 my Orthodox cousins

never made it to the service. They arrived just as everybody was leaving, hastily said the necessary prayers and declined my invitation to join us at home because the plastic cutlery and crockery weren't in sealed wrappers. Our sad little party, having laid our loved one to rest, returned home. I knew we wouldn't have a Minion for prayers that evening or any other, but it was okay. I sat on the low Shiva chair, because traditionally, immediate family sat and mourned for a week, while visitors came to pay respects and talk about the dead person. Sonia served the food, and we decided to go to Shul that evening for one last time, to hear mum's name read into the register of the dead. Her husband Bob drove us through the darkening snow-covered roads to Bournemouth.

In Shul, Sonia and I sat tightly side by side in the downstairs women's section while the men prayed together in the centre seats. With our heads covered by shawls, we held hands and prayer books and became totally immersed in the familiar smell, sound, and prayers of our religious childhood. It eroded all the years of liberalism. Briefly, our mothers were with us again, but we would never become them. Sonia and I had been at infant school together. Friends, hippies, rebels, sisters-in-law, confidantes and saviours; we had both been part of the many people we became along the way. In later years we fell apart. My most precious memory is our solidarity that evening.

A few weeks later Leslie asked me to clear mum's things from their house. I cringed at his haste. For me, it was too soon. The smell and significance of mum's hanging-on-to-the-past mementos was overwhelming; letters I didn't know she'd kept, boxes of our baby clothes, a mountain of photographs and every brought-home souvenir from every trip we'd made. I made piles to keep, piles to . . . keep . . . and piles to keep. Smelling Chanel perfume on her clothes as they slipped seamlessly from wardrobe hangers into charity shop bags, provided no catharsis, and I panicked because I couldn't remember her voice. I tried to feel relief about 'moving on' but it never came.

Life lurched on because it had to. People told me how lucky I was to have had such a good mum, which made it worse instead of better, and then the irony hit me, that after she'd gone, I actually had spare time to spend with her. I felt bad for relishing time alone, that I should've been with her, and then I felt bad for all the bad-daughter stuff, but sometimes she'd been an unholy pain in the arse. (I probably ought to wash my mouth with soap for daring to say that, let alone write it). After the bad-daughter stuff came the where-do-I-put-my-love stuff. In a fleeting moment of clarity, I understood the role of children, but I not having the sweet skin of a babe to bury my head in, I made do with burying it in the sand.

People started to act differently towards me, not in an 'avoiding the bereaved at all costs' kind of way. They either thought I was mum, or else thought I should become her. My brother wanted unconditional praise, my cousins a sympathetic ear, my aunt hinted about money to 'tide her over' (aka her gambling habit). Leslie arranged weekly lunch dates and mum's pen-friends wrote to me in lieu of her. A matriarch badge was up for grabs, but I didn't want it. I was never going to be the saint she was, and they'd have to find someone else to make them feel good about themselves. But I accepted Leslie's lunch dates because who wouldn't enjoy being wined and dined by a dapper elderly gentleman who nearly became their father?

When mum died, the smothering emotion clung and crowded like pondweed in stagnant water, and the only way I could cope was by clearing out the whole stinking mass and starting again. Naively, I waded into the algae not knowing it would take years to reach the other side, but when the water eventually cleared, I realised what a powerful woman my mother had been. Since dad died, I'd been the adult and dutifully guided her through day-to-day practicalities and later, the pitfalls of dating. I was her first call for any problems and when she had cancer, I bore the reality and her care, because as my brother so succinctly said (before disappearing off the scene)

"You know what people with cancer want," and he was right. People who have had cancer want nothing more to do with it, and they definitely don't want to sit watching someone else undergo tortuous chemotherapy. My problem was I still craved a parent because I was mourning dad and all I'd thought he was and battling my own crises together with cancer. Mum said she could cope with anything except me being unhappy or ill, and as unhappiness and illness were the mainstays of my life most of that time, it made things very difficult. It's an honour to be so loved by a parent, but pedestals are shaky places to live.

Mum was constrained by her upbringing, religion, and my father. She served those she loved and bathed in the glow of giving. The only thing that made her feel good was putting others first, and by always doing that, she taught them to put her last. Mum always needed to be happy, and have everyone around her happy, which made little room for expressing true feelings. I came to realise that she needed an atmosphere of continual happiness because she couldn't bear the alternative. She created her own anti-depressant without the need of pharmaceuticals.

She carried guilt that she'd 'given' me breast cancer, and that she hadn't looked after her adored sister enough to prevent her dying.

18 A GLUT OF DEATH

While my mum was making wedding plans, Mark's sister was having scopes and biopsies to locate the cause of her sudden jaundice; it turned out to be pancreatic cancer with a very poor prognosis and she died shortly after mum. Mark got more than his fair share of pain. To lose a sibling is devastating. It didn't transfer, it just doubled up. Mum was seventy-seven and Sue was fifty-one. Christmas that year wasn't much fun, nor was life. I suggested we get a dog, but the words didn't come out quite how I had intended, and the idea fell on stony ground. It must have sounded like lose a sister and gain a dog. In hindsight, I'm ashamed I said such a thing.

As if they were queuing for their turn, more people died. Relations, friends, animals. Some died too soon, some were expected. One died on Christmas morning, and one died by his own hand. People dropped like flies and funerals become our default entertainment. There's a lot to be said about a good interment, and over tea, we compared sandwich fillings eulogies and choice of music. We could've got jobs as roving funeral-critics. At one service Mark went to, a newly ordained African minister, wearing fluorescent trainers beneath his funeral robes, conducted the send-off of an extremely bigoted acquaintance. It renewed our faith in Karma.

The most memorable funeral was when we were directed to the wrong hotel for the wake; the receptionist looked aghast as eighty mourners trooped through the door. Unable to remember the name of the hotel he booked, the nephew-organiser was inconsolable at the loss of dozens of pre-paid sandwiches, curling on their platters at a mystery venue. Like a scene from a comedy sketch, the hotel staff sprang into action, rustled-up hastily defrosted sausage rolls, and lunchtime leftovers liberally garnished and re-named canapés. They opened the bar, and served tea with yesterday's cake, sliced and dusted with sugar. It was the best ad-hoc meal I've eaten, but by then I'd my fill of funerals. I didn't want to go to anymore, not even my own.

While my mum and Mark's sister were going through their own radical events, Teddy had a freak accident. We were out riding and as we went to trot he just dropped, skidded along the stone pathway with his front legs buckled under him, and broke both knees and tore his fetlocks open. I jumped off and helped him back up, and we made the painful walk home. The vet met us at the stable, sedated him and stitched the wounds, and put his legs in immobilising splints. It was horrific, but Teddy was an absolute gentleman. He spent six weeks mending in his stable, and after a further month walking-out slowly in-hand, we made plans for his return to normality. The day we turned him out in the field, he expressed his pleasure with an explosive rodeo display, and caught his hind leg in the wire fence. With a deep gouge sliced all around the hoof, he was swiftly back in his stable, where the vet recommended he stay for another six weeks. To ensure correct alignment, the vet dressed the foot on raised wedges, which quickly aggravated a longstanding hip problem.

For some unknown reason, horses are prone to producing Proud Flesh on lower leg wounds, and as a final blow, the granulation tissue grew around Teddy's cut foot, preventing healing. The vet visited daily to cut it away, and each time he surgically re-dressed the foot, we argued daily about the wedges. Despite daily treatment, Teddy's injury wouldn't heal. I learnt Tellington Touch from a picture guide and followed the movements, hoping it might help him. Sadie gave him massages, Sue gave him Reiki and Sherry the physiotherapist attempted to relieve his elevated hip discomfort, and in her plain-speaking manner told me I needed to take more care of myself. I arranged a session with a horse communicator, who communicated some very interesting things about Teddy and also reiterated what Sherry had said to me. Looking down from his great height, Teddy viewed everything, bar the communicator whom he took very seriously, with mild amusement. Over the weeks, his continual discomfort became crippling pain. He couldn't stand in a stable forever, nor could he be painfully lame for the remainder of his days, and he seemed to be having more bad days than good. Teddy stayed with me as long as he could and now, he said it was time to go.

On the last morning we stood together in his stable, linked in the giving and receiving of a final grooming session. Memories of each passing year embellished the gentle brush strokes as I reassured him about what was going to happen, just as I'd always tried to reassure him in times of uncertainty. I loved this horse with all my heart and carrying that burden, I made the decision to end his life. His ears flicked towards me in recognition of unsaid words, and he momentarily rested his big beautiful head against my arm. How can you describe on paper the love of a free-thinking creature who slips his soul inside your soul, carries you safely through the flames of your fears, and reads your innermost thoughts? With my face against his shoulder, I breathed him one last time. I heard the knackerman's Land Rover and trailer arrive outside, and as I gagged on the inward scream, Teddy turned to face me.

Teddy limped out to meet his death. With his beautiful head in a bucket of feed, I held him for the last time, the shot sounded, and he was down. The rocks of my life had crumbled in an avalanche of death and to this day, I still question my decision.

Deeply mourning mum's tragic death, desperately missing the magical bond of my horse, reeling from my sister-in-law's diagnosis of terminal cancer, my girlfriend battling leukaemia,

I kidded myself that I could cope. I did everything I could to fill the vast void Teddy's huge presence had left, and the aching hole in my soul, but I was bewildered and crippled with grief, so submerged in sorrow my mind shut down. And just when I thought I'd reached the bottom of the hole, I felt the familiar bolt of panic in the shower. There was a small lump under my left arm. I tried to dismiss it with contempt, but neither the lump nor the panic went away. I had no emotion left to feel when I sat on the edge of the hospital examination bed with my arms in the air. The Consultant prodded and poked; my left armpit was a web of scar tissue and she had to press hard to feel what she was searching for. Arms out horizontally. Neck and thorax breathe in deeply, down to abdomen and pelvis. I replaced my clothes and joined her in the consulting room.

"I'm afraid," she began to say in her professionally clinical voice before she acknowledged it was me seated the other side of the desk and changed tone to something less formal. "Elaine, it feels like cancerous tumour. I don't want to wait for a biopsy result, because I'm guessing you want it out, and as soon as possible?"

"You guessed right," I replied.

"I can do surgery quickly," she said to herself as she scanned her diary list. "Yes, surgery at the end of the week. Reception desk will give you all the details. If it's cancerous I'd advise radiotherapy afterwards, but I suspect it's in the middle of the site you had treated in 1991, and we can't treat the same place twice. I'm going to prescribe a five-year course of Tamoxifen, it's the standard drug for oestrogen positive breast cancer in pre-menopausal women, but it'll bring on early menopause." She raised an eyebrow expecting a reply.

"Early menopause is probably the least of my worries." What else did she want me to say?

"Well, you've coped admirably with everything so far, and this is the first recurrence since 1995 so that's a very good sign."

"I'd have said no recurrence would be a good sign?"

She didn't look up again, but she let out a sigh and snapped her diary shut. "I am sorry Elaine, it's not what any of us wanted."

"I know," I replied. "I know. See you on Friday."

She walked me to the door and hesitated. "Nine years clear is a good sign," she tried to re-assure me, " it means it's very slow growing."

I nodded because there was nothing more to say. Surgery went smoothly. The lump was cancerous, and pathology showed the diseased margins were larger than the surgeon expected, so she operated again to remove more tissue. Mark and I were at our lowest ebb, trying to support each other with whatever shreds of care we could muster. I began taking Tamoxifen to try and prevent another recurrence, but three days after the first dose I became red and itchy, with big red welts covering my arms and body. The elderly locum doctor I saw at the surgery was wonderfully sympathetic.

"I've seen this on a few occasions over the years. I think it could be a rare reaction to Tamoxifen. Give it another couple of days to see if it settles." The next morning my entire body was covered in burning red blotches, and I'd turned my body inside-out vomiting. Mark phoned the doctor and he said stop taking Tamoxifen. I spent a week in bed unable to eat or sleep and wondering how much worse hell could get.

Gradually we climbed out of the hole, and I tried to embrace the future without my mum, and for the first time in fifty years, without a horse of my own. Having clean fingernails, extra money and not fretting about mum was a completely new experience which brought a strange and guilty freedom. By the end of that year, the glut of death faded, and we relished the gift of grief-free air, like soldiers home from a war zone. Sometimes we carried the dead in our hearts, sometimes we simply left them where they were.

19 FALLEN DOWN A HOLE

You've fallen down a hole so deep, you're standing at rock bottom. That's assuming, of course, that you are still standing. You tried to climb out, but scaling the sides seems impossible from such a low standpoint, and each superhuman effort barely makes a foothold before sliding back again. You continue trying to scale the walls, getting more frustrated and more demoralised until you give up trying and instead, find diversions that stop you noticing where you are. Each time the walls come into peripheral vision you think about 'something nice'. Then you cry, because the nice somethings are just thoughts; they aren't tangible, and they don't last.

Doing the same thing repeatedly is comforting. You don't have to face a new set of problems because you're stuck in the ones you already have, but Rational You knows it's pointless; you never get a different answer. If you cared to think (which at this moment you cannot) you would realise doing the same thing repeatedly is what tripped you up. Nothing used to faze you. You were so busy being strong for your family, strong for your animals, and strong for the entire human race because strong women are strong and busy. So busy, you never noticed the straw that broke the camel's back until it broke yours too. Did the hole open up and swallow you both, in one massive gulp, belching out the camel as you tumbled free-fall down its steep sides? Has the weight of the camel landed on top of you? He's a heavy beast to shift, and an unwilling participant in anything that involves action. But you've probably already discovered that.

Perhaps the slippery slope got so slippery your footing simply disappeared; you didn't have a chance to stay upright, did you? Down you went like a luge in a speed competition, and yes, you won! Congratulations; you beat the camel by a mile. Or was your downfall the one that gets us all, eventually; the stealth of years quietly tugging at your ankles, until every step rolled into a ball and chain. And one day the ball and chain said no. No more. Not. One. Step."

When I've been on chemotherapy, my world sits in two dimensions; cognitive thought and complete arse-about-face mental mayhem where my brain can't function, and things don't make sense. It took my horse to point this out by politely, but completely, ignoring the miasma of confusion that is 'chemo me', and retreating into a safer world of his own. Luckily, my husband has learnt to manage chemo-brain-on-steroids, although I'm sure his safer world also provides welcome respite.

During a chemo break, my friend, Stacey asked me if I wrote down my coping strategies. When Stacey drops something into the conversation, I've learnt to sit up and take notice, and writing how I got out of various predicaments proved invaluable. When my whereabouts on the mental map were obscure, or finding the way home was difficult, someone just like me had written an exit route in plain English. So yes, I've been in a hole; not like yours because holes are tailor-made, but I know what it's like down there. I know what it's like to focus on how strong you are, and say a little mantra to reinforce superhuman powers, but discover superhuman powers are distant memories, and strength no longer belongs in the present tense.

So, if you don't like where you are, what is there to lose? At least a change of scenery would distract you for a moment, which your current thoughts do not. But how do you do it? Well, we (because you're not alone in this) do it one frigging step at a time and the first step is to recognise where you are. In a hole. Yes, actually *look* at those walls, *feel* that oppression, and breathe in the stale air. Wallow. Stop trying not to think about it because it needs such complete saturation that even with your eyes firmly shut, you know you are down a hole. Miserable, isn't it? You would not even want your dog to live there, would you? (Your cat would have left long ago) and yet you've been dwelling in this hole for so long, you've ceased to notice how inhospitable it's become. It is uncomfortable, cold, the layout no longer works for your needs, and the décor is so eighties it looks positively retro.

Decide today if you want to stay there and if the answer is Yes, that's absolutely fine. You need your hole; you need to hide a little longer and recover in peace. Décor and damp do not bother you right now, you have a snuggly blanket, and your dog will be forever loyal. When you're ready, you'll know. However, if you want a change, then decide it's time to re-decorate; you hate the smell of new paint, so maybe consider moving out for a while? If life on the outside gets too hectic, you can use the space as a holiday hole, so choose the colours carefully and leave the snuggly blanket behind for another day. You never know . . .

Stand up tall on tippy toe, step on the large rock that forms rock bottom and open your eyes; you can just see some light at the top of the hole. They call it 'light at the end of the tunnel' and I promise you it's not the light of another train hurtling down the track. It's real honest clean light, and that's where we're heading. The next step is to take your notebook and write everything you achieve in one day. Even if it's something you wouldn't previously have countenanced as achievement, it deserves noting. Even if you don't consider it worth the pencil lead, *write it down.* You can't be trusted to judge accurately what is and what isn't, so trust me when I say everything you do is an achievement, and you can find plenty to achieve even when you're in a hole; cleaning your fingernails, being nice to spiders and laughing at yourself. Three achievements for free before you've even started.

Your notebook is filling quickly, you didn't realise you achieved so much in one day, did you? You were so busy distracting yourself from your predicament, you didn't notice anything except the predicament. The next step is to focus on now. We're going to consign the past to where it belongs, in the past (the clue is in the name). No more penance because you can't change it. Like everyone else, you're far from perfect and things probably never happened how you remember they did. Nor can you control the future because you are not omnipotent, so stop trying because, like worrying, it's a waste of energy. Instead, use that energy making the present interesting; happiness is not a given, but interesting is something you can create from scraps. Now is probably a good time to mention the voices in your head, the ones that keep shouting at you. Did you know that if you stop listening, they stop talking?

Notice things. Notice your breathing. I am breathing in; I am breathing out. I am doing it all over again. In and out. Nothing fancy schmancy, nothing structured or yogic, just plain old breathing which you've been doing ever since you were born but might not have noticed. Breathing is your new go-to tool. Every time you need a moment to process something, relief from a rising panic attack, fluttering thoughts, just breathe. It's simple, it's free and you already know how to do it. No brainer, huh? Oh, and did I mention you'll climb out of the hole on your breath?

Now you're recognising achievements and breathing, you've stood up and stretched, you've seen the light, you're part of today instead of somewhere else, the voices have stopped chattering so loudly, and you've made a decision that you don't like your current surroundings (don't forget to write down these achievements). You'll leave this day. I don't advocate packing a bag, everything you have down there can stay there. Just like Vegas, what happens in the hole stays in the hole. So, you breathe in. Just in, that's all, and on the out breath you take a step forward, a normal everyday step. Breathe in again, and on the next out breath, you take a step upward. Forward, upward, in and out. It has its own rhythm, doesn't it? You might feel a bit lightheaded with all the breathing, so any time you want to rest you rest, and if you feel a bit emotional and want to cry you cry, and don't forget that anytime you want to laugh and smile, you do that too. Forward, upward, in and out, until gradually the light gets brighter. Forward, upward, in and out until your steps get lighter. Forward, upward, in and out, don't look back. Forward, upward, in and out and you're at the top.

And what you do now is up to you, but remember, today you accepted help to get out of the hole, and accepting help is the biggest achievement of your life so far. Write it down before you forget.

PART THREE

LEARNING TO RIDE A CIRCLE

"He showed me how to let go in the only way he knew. Once I started listening, the lessons came thick and fast. He has changed everything."

20 BRUCE

After my wonderful horse Teddy died and my mum died, and I had a cancer recurrence. I decided after thirty-five years to give up horse-owning, but I still wanted to ride, and a mutual friend put me in touch with Bill Blackwood. Bill's stableyard, situated at the back of an industrial estate, consisted of an open-fronted tractor shed and haybarn facing each other, with broken hard standing between. The twelve looseboxes were roughly built inside with pallets and concrete blocks, mostly held together with baler twine. Bill rarely had time for sweeping or the niceties of appearance, in fact he barely had time for speaking, but his horse knowledge was legendary, his horses at peak fitness, and rumour said he accepted bribes when clients wanted him to take a horse, although if that was true it was difficult to see where he spent the money. Bill wanted help exercising horses and thought I might be capable of doing the tedious hill walking. I liked Bill; he was fair but firm, and I realise now he was taciturn because he was entirely focused on the horse, and horses thrive on a quiet mind and actions. I became expert at riding one horse while leading two, and hours spent in the saddle on the Dorset hills was a profound way to process grief. I rode Bill's horses for two years.

In 2008 the phone rang. "Bill here, you busy?"

"Not especially," I replied, although I was immersed in internet selling.

"Need some help. You on?"

I looked at the boxes of vintage fabrics piled high in the

sitting room, waiting to be photographed and listed on Etsy. I remembered the sold stock upstairs, ready for packing. "Yup, I'll help. See you tomorrow."

To say I fell in love with Bruce the moment I saw his handsome head would be a major understatement. Our eyes met across the stable door, and no other introduction was needed. I lifted a hand to touch his neck. He swayed on his heavily bandaged legs, flapped his lips together and breathed on my cheek.

"No time for gawking," said Bill, standing behind me. "Horses to do."

"Oh, hi Bill," I replied pointedly. "How are you?"

His ironic smile creased the corner of a bottom lip. "Horses ready, I'll come with, see you're still on the job."

As our cavalcade of six clattered out of the yard and along the forest track, I organised my reins and lead-lines and settled in the saddle. "Tell me about the cob," I said to Bill.

"Owner got more money than sense," he spat the words. "Perfect good hunter, ruined. Came last year as vet rehab, this year they stick a novice woman on 'im. Fell off a bridge. Horse, not woman. Not right in the head."

"The woman or the horse?"

"Both."

"Injuries?"

"Skin, maybe bone chip, fire brigade keep pulling him out of accidents, they'll have 'im as a mascot." Bill laughed at his own joke. "Won't settle. Nice horse. Patch him up, he'll go back out." Bill sat back and didn't speak again.

True to his word, Bill patched-up Bruce's wounds and he resumed weekly hunting. I looked forward to seeing him on the days I rode. I can't explain what pulled me towards him because he bore no similarity to Teddy, my 'horse-of-a-lifetime'. I wasn't allowed to ride him and the only time I went into his stable to groom, I felt very intimidated by his incessant movements and sheer size- it was as if, shut-down and physically hurting, all the space around him filled with his machismo presence. Maybe girls just love to love a bad boy.

The Farmer's Meet is a hunting tradition, where local farmers who allow hounds to cross their land are given a horse to hunt for the day. In his ninth hunting season, Bruce was lent to a stout gentleman farmer who had ridden point-to-pointers, and he rode the fifteen-year-old horse in a relaxed and unhurried way. He liked the black cob and simply wanted to enjoy a rare day on horseback. Apart from the relentless rain, the day would have been unremarkable, had the farmer not chosen to jump a gate as an easier option to the high hedge on either side. Unfortunately, the churned gateway was deeply poached, tearing a tendon in the cob's back leg as he took off from the holding mud. Bruce's ninth hunting season was his last.

"Why's the vet out for Bruce?" I asked Bill, nodding towards the stable.

"Done a tendon scan," he replied without lifting his eyes from cleaning tack. "Farmers Meet, last time out this season. Couldn't keep him safe." He threw the soapy sponge in the bucket of scummy water and walked out of the tackroom.

"What did the vet find?" I asked Bill later, nodding towards the bandaged horse's hind leg.

"Deep digital tendon tear. Won't hunt again. Owner's gonna write him off, too old, too crocked. Nice horse."

"Whaddya mean write him off? They don't need the insurance money, do they?"

"Don't need any money as far as I can see, just some horse sense."

"I'll have him." I heard the words and turned around to see who spoke them. What idiot would say they wanted a troubled, lame horse?

Bill was standing looking at me. I saw the corner of his lip quiver. "Yeah, thought you might. I'll tell James."

"You know I didn't want to get another horse," I said to Mark over dinner that night.

"Yes . . ."

"I've got one."

"Yes . . ."

"He's lame."

"And?"

"Needs rescuing."

"And?"

"Big."

"You like big horses. Teddy was big."

"This is different big."

"It'll make a change if he's already lame instead of going lame."

"I think we can get him sound."

"Expensive?"

"Free. It's me or a bullet."

"Ah, he does need rescuing."

"Do you mind?"

"Probably. What's his name?"

"Bruce."

'So often a slip between cup and lip' is one of the truest sayings. Once James agreed to a new home for Bruce instead of euthanasia, he offered the horse to everyone, and a friend of Rosanna's accepted the offer. Bill Blackwood was livid, and I was heartbroken, not so much at not having him myself, but at where he was going. Rosanna's friend had ridden as a child. She had a weekend cottage with a large field and a bucolic vision of Bruce grazing happily for the rest of his days. In order to give Bruce's tendon the best chance of healing, James generously paid for debridement surgery to remove injured and scarred tissue, followed by post-op care with Bill. I was numb when this fine horse was dispatched to be a field ornament, and my belief in Divine Intervention crumbled. I needn't have worried.

Bruce loved all the unaccustomed grass. He loved being able to walk through flimsy fences to the organic veg plot and fruit bushes and he particularly loved the apple orchard until the bucolic dream became spasmodic colic and a neighbour called the vet. Rosanna's friend's husband was livid at her stupidity (and the £200 vet bill) and Bruce arrived back at Bill's six weeks later, a lot fatter than when he left. James wanted rid of him quickly, and Bill phoned me.

"Horse is back. If you still want him, act fast."

Mark and I acted fast. I phoned the livery yard I'd previously arranged for Bruce, but they'd filled the vacancy. I phoned the stables where I'd kept Teddy for twelve years, but they were full, as were five other local DIY yards. There was room for him at a farm within walking distance of home, but the stable was for a small pony, and he wouldn't have got through the doorway with his hips intact! I found two lovely places, but they only accepted horses at full livery; apart from wanting to care for my own horse, I couldn't afford the monthly cost. Anxiety set in followed by frustration. There are lots of private homes near us that keep horses, so I delivered a printed letter to them all asking if they had room for one more, but nobody replied. I put cards in shop windows and a strange man contacted me, saying he had a chicken shed at the end of his garden, and he wouldn't want payment if I stayed as well. I was tempted.

On Friday afternoon I answered my phone to a woman speaking with a cut-glass accent. "Hello, I'm standing outside Furzehill Post Office reading your card regarding stabling. I've just moved from London to Dorset and my new house has two brand new stables and two acres. Might that suit your requirements?"

"It definitely might." I replied and took her address. With indecent haste, Mark and I went to view. And it was perfect. Completely and utterly perfect, and she was happy for me to rent it as a whole and sub-let the other stable so Bruce had a companion. Then she told me the price, and I thought she was joking but she wasn't. Feeling this dream slipping away, I tactfully said prices in Dorset were a lot lower than London, and she must've seen my disappointment because she lowered the price by five pounds a month. I explained that full livery, with everything included, was around £600 per month, so maybe her expectations of a higher amount than that were unrealistic. She thanked me for my time, and we left. The stables remained empty for the following two years. Then she sold the house, and they were converted into a granny annexe.

On Saturday, one of the livery yards I'd visited phoned. "Hi, Louise here. Have you found a stable yet?" I recounted a shortened history of my failures so far, and she commiserated.

"I might be able to help. I've just spoken to my old friend Sheel, and she's thinking about renting her spare stable. D'ya want her number?"

"Yes, *please*, Louise."

"Text her then. She wants someone responsible who knows what they're doing. I said you fitted the bill. Her stables are a bit out the back of beyond, a bit basic, but go see for yourself."

"Thanks, Louise, really appreciated." I texted Sheel immediately and the answer pinged back within five minutes, with a time to visit and directions.

Old Roman Farm was a ten-minute drive from home, along pitted gravel tracks between massive arable fields at the back of Badbury Rings, an ancient Iron Age hill fort. The fields were scattered with unkempt tumuli covered in scrub and trees, rising in eerie mounds from the flat ground, and the expanse of sky was uncannily huge. Sheel walked out to meet me as I got out of the truck, and in a split-second of recognition, we both laughed with joy.

"Elaine, it's YOU!" she gasped, hugging me around my waist.

"Sheila, it's YOU!!" I shouted in disbelief, returning the hug. Sheila was a no-nonsense old-school horsewoman. We shared a birthday, and she was exactly ten years older than me. We'd been friends since the 1970s when she bought my pony, Jimmy for her riding school. We had kept in touch until 2000 when she closed the riding school and moved; I don't know whether she lost my address or me hers. We both started talking at once, then both became tongue-tied, and still shaking our heads in disbelief, she showed me around. Used for storing machinery, the near-derelict farm had a row of four stables housed in an old building, with a wide walkway at the front and a bay at the far end for feed and hay storage. Outside were three turn-out paddocks with a high beech hedge at the bottom forming a solid windbreak, a small well-drained area I could use to ride, and a neatly squared-off muckheap. Sheila owned a broodmare and two younger horses and lived in a caravan behind the barn. The farm was more ramshackle and a lot more remote than I'd envisaged, but I knew we'd be safe and comfortable with Sheila, and a quiet atmosphere was what Bruce needed. The arrangement was DIY Livery, but Sheila was happy to do Bruce for me at any time and gave me a handwritten price-list of services; a business footing makes things simpler even between old friends. We shook hands, we hugged again, and the deal was done. We had found our home.

21 ANGEL FEATHERS

On Wednesday, Midsummers Eve 2009 Bruce came to me. The big old cattle truck grated to a halt, Bill Blackwood jumped out of the cab, opened the rear ramp and Bruce clattered stiffly down the metal slope. The black horse stood, looked at his new surroundings and let out a long sigh. Bill echoed the sigh, turned his shoulders, and without any pressure on the leadrope Bruce followed him into the stable, which Mark had given a fresh coat of white paint. Bill stood the horse to face him and unbuckled the headcollar. I was waiting outside the door and could've sworn I heard Bill whisper, "Safe now. Don't be frightened," but they were such unlikely words for him I must've misheard. Bill handed me the headcollar, walked back to the lorry and pulled out a patched turnout rug and a bridle in one hand, and Bruce's Irish Horse Passport in the other, together with a bundle of vet reports tied with baler twine.

"Useful?" he said.

"Very," I replied, picking up the bottle of wine I had for him and an envelope with a thankyou card and money for diesel. We walked towards each other bearing our gifts like one of those weird East-West spy swaps where neither party wants to act first, and we laughed awkwardly until he put the rug on the ground, I handed him the bottle in his free hand, he gave me the bridle I gave him the card. I wanted to hug him, but I don't think he's a huggy person, so we tried to shake hands which meant juggling the gifts about again until we touched fingertips.

"Thank you, Bill, for everything," I said, feeling a bit over-whelmed.

"Nice horse," he said gruffly. "He'll be fine for you." He looked at me and nodded, and his eyes were twinklier than I'd noticed before. He got back into the lorry, crashed through the gears' and drove off in a cloud of smoke.

"Dear Bill," said the card, which had a cartoon of a sleeping horse dreaming of carrots, and the caption 'I like doing nothing.' "It was really kind of you to deliver Bruce, here's money for diesel. I really appreciate everything you've done for him, and all your help persuading James, which I know caused you a lot of work. Thank you so much. I've loved riding your horses and I've learnt a lot. If I can ever return the favour please ask. Kindest wishes, Elaine" I had toyed with the idea of an *x* but decided not.

The mission was complete. Bruce was here in the stable fate had found for him, and my overwhelming feeling was relief (reality and panic would follow in due course). He was lame on his left hind leg. Both hocks were stiff with arthritic changes (spavins and thoroughpins) and his dodgy hip affected how he bore his weight. Euthanasia was still possible if the tendon didn't heal and he was in pain, but his 'rescue' wasn't a re-run of Black Beauty, and he wasn't emaciated or cowering in a corner. It wasn't until I got a real sense of his distress that I even considered the word rescue, and then hastily un-considered it because labelling him a rescue-case is as bad as calling me a cancer sufferer.

It was eight o'clock when I settled Bruce with lots of hay, and Sheila's broodmare stabled alongside for company. Through the stable window he could see her two young horses grazing in their field. I left him for the night and drove home, lost in thought and the beautiful skyscape.

Mark handed me a glass of wine as I walked through the back door.

"How did it go?" he asked excitedly.

"It went good. He looks bigger than I remember. I can't believe I've got him after everything. Bill found me a rug and a bridle, and here's his vet reports." I put the bundle of papers on the kitchen table and sank down on a chair, suddenly drained of all energy. "Sheila said she'd check him before she went to bed."

"You look exhausted, said Mark. Go have a bath. Egg and chips for tea, I'll make a start."

I love my husband. I love egg and chips.

As I soaked in the bath, I fretted about Bruce. Would he settle, would he come sound. Had I taken on too much, was he worried in his new surroundings? The answer to everything was yes. I was so concerned about getting him, but I had no idea if I'd even be capable of riding him. The only time Bill let me exercise him he'd tanked off across open ground, and we'd spent ages going round in circles until he slowed down. Why had I conveniently forgotten that episode? Mark came in with wine to top-up my glass and a magazine to read. I was going to tell him what had happened but changed my mind.

"Here, read this," he said, handing me a Spirit & Destiny magazine and pouring the wine. "Sara gave me some magazines for you when I saw her this-morning. It's a bit airy-fairy but it'll take your mind off things. Food in twenty minutes"

As I said, I love my husband. I opened the magazine and skimmed the pages until an article about angels caught my interest. Different angels do different jobs, and they like to be asked for help. Archangel Michael is the biblical Angel of Protection, and the writer gave a simple invocation to harness Michael's great protective power. I read the words, thought of Bruce, read the words again, decided I had nothing to lose and spoke the invocation. I closed my eyes and asked, wished and willed with all my heart that angels would look after you. Just to be safe, I said it twice.

Next morning Bruce had his head over the stable door watching Sheila brush her mare. The sound of his flapping lips echoed around the high wooden roof beams, and from the look of his stable he'd spent the night box-walking. Sheila and I exchanged hellos, and she said if I turned him out in the end paddock, we could see how he got on with the others and maybe have a companion later. I remembered she's not a morning person, so I didn't chat. I looked at my horse in his stable. My horse! A wave of excitement ran through my body. Sheila looked up from grooming and caught my eye, and we grinned at each other in companionable silence. As I slipped on Bruce's headcollar he grabbed the noseband and chewed it nervously, then held it in his teeth. I wrestled it out, pulled out the rope which was also in his mouth and led him outside. He walked politely, stood to open the field gate, turned and faced me and as I undid his headcollar he stood up on his hind legs, spun round and galloped off bucking a squealing. It took me completely unawares and as I ducked away from his front leg I stumbled backwards and fell over. Not a good start.

I brushed myself off, retrieved the headcollar from where it had fallen, and went back to the stable. Luckily, Sheila had gone into her caravan for breakfast. I hoped she hadn't seen my first attempt at being responsible and knowing what I'm doing. I wheeled in the barrow and began mucking out. When everything was clean and swept and his bed laid, I lifted the water bucket from the corner to refill. On the floor underneath was two white feathers.

So, Archangel Michael had heard. I carefully put the feathers in my pocket. Maybe things were going to be okay.

22 FAST. VERY FAST.

Bruce was here, and he was truly the most handsome horse I've ever seen. I was going to make everything better, he would become a superstar, and as the storybooks say, 'we would all live happily ever after'.

My initial plan for Bruce (besides making amends for all the horrible things that had happened to him) was spending time walking in hand to help strengthen his injury. A few years before, I'd ruptured the cruciate ligament in my knee and had it reconstructed using hamstring from the back of my thigh. Post-op rehab had been extensive, and it guided me towards what would benefit Bruce. Each day we took a walk along the roads, fields and tracks around the farm, treading different terrains to encourage proprioception and balance. I quickly discovered he behaved perfectly on the road, but as soon as we turned onto open countryside, he became agitated, flinging his head in the air to snatch at the reins, and turning sideways to barge me with his shoulder. I yanked his head down with a sharp "NO!" and carried a stick to try to push his shoulder back, but it didn't help.

I also discovered Bruce hated being touched. Grooming was bearable but not enjoyable and he'd swing from side to side and snap the air until the ordeal ended. He jumped like he'd received an electric shock if you rested a hand on his body, and his muscles went rigid. Hoping to help him relax, I asked Sadie to give him a myofascial release treatment. She dryly remarked she was unsure where to start because he was so tight everywhere, and

Bruce was adamant he was not going to release anything. The physio came to check his pelvis and said there were so many hotspots along his back it felt like he was on fire. I persevered trying to loosen him up with simple massage, but my hands literally bounced off his neck. He got so upset it was counter-productive and I felt frustrated I couldn't help him relax.

Bruce became stressed if you asked him to do the smallest thing and would go through a whole repertoire of movements hoping one of them was what you wanted. The more anxious he became, the more I backed off, until I stopped asking him to do anything because it was easier not to wake his demons. The less structure I provided, the more he took matters into his own hands because his survival depended on somebody being in charge, and non-communication became a rapidly spiraling vortex of confusion. Sheila put one of her horses in his field for company, but he bullied and bit it and wouldn't let it eat so he remained alone and didn't play with the horses over the fence. He was as shut down as he'd been when he was hunting. Physically he might be improving but mentally he was not.

After six fraught months of struggling to lead him along the tracks, I decided I'd be safer riding. Sitting on his back was good, and I felt a swell of pride in my horse as we set off on our first ride together. On the road he was a perfect pro, ignoring passing farm machinery and politely pulling on to the verge so cars could pass. He didn't bat an eyelid when a gaggle of cyclists pedalled past in a gale of swooshing tyres. Riding a horse with a lovely swinging stride and an interest in his surroundings, and with the sun pushing through the mid-November clouds, I was the luckiest person alive. Me and my horse.

We reached the gate that opened into the field, and feeling how relaxed we both were, I couldn't see a problem going home across the grass. Bruce moved to open the gate with the faintest nudge of my leg and stood stock-still while I looped the chain back over the post. I brushed my hand down his neck in appreciation and turned towards the headland, aiming to follow the hedge to the top of the field. Suddenly and without warning, he dropped his bottom to the ground. I thought for a moment a hole had opened up, and then launched himself in the air like he'd been shot from a sling. If you've ever seen pictures of a high-school dressage capriole (airs above the ground) that's how I think it looked, but it felt more like jumping a wide chasm that wasn't there. It wasn't unseating. In fact, his broad back felt like an immovable perch, but it was terrifying and I had no idea what to expect or do next, so I just hung on. And prayed.

When he eventually landed, I thought I might regain control, but as soon as his feet hit the ground his head shot up in the air, nose pointing to the sky and ears flat back, and he fled like his life depended on it. I tried crossing my reins, sawing on his mouth and turning him, but he was galloping in blind panic and dead to feeling, so I sat and waited. And prayed some more. Time seemed to stop, I thought I heard myself shouting, but maybe it was the wind whistling through my ears, and I was more worried about the damage he'd do to his healing tendon than the damage he might do to both of us if he didn't stop.

There was a wire boundary fence at the top of the field, which common sense told me he'd want to jump if he faced it. On the right of the fence was a thick high hedge, planted to break the wind on the exposed hilltop. I decided to try to turn him towards the hedge and run him into it, if I went at an angle we stood a better chance of less injury. Jamming my feet down into my stirrups, I moved both hands to the right of his neck, wrapped the reins around my fist and kicked like mad with my left leg while putting all my weight into my right. Like an oil tanker in an ocean of grass, he started to make the turn, not fast enough to jack-knife but with enough latitude to avoid the fence. The looming hedge whipped us with sharp-as-nails branches as it skimmed his shoulder at speed, and as the sudden scourge of pain brought him back to his senses, he dropped his head and slowed to a trot, and then to a standstill. I slid off, loosened his girth because he was blowing so hard, I thought he'd explode, and I collapsed in a heap.

My body was completely numb and as the adrenaline dropped, I began to shake like a leaf. Then my anger rose up inside and with renewed force, I got to my feet and dragged Bruce back down the field to the road. I dragged him and swore and cursed; he pulled me, barged me and trod all over me. Blood from his scratches was smeared over his neck and my jacket, the branches had shredded my sleeve, and with each step the torn leg of my once-white breeches waved like a forlorn peace flag. As we walked home in the dusk, we must've looked like a pair of leftovers from Halloween trick-or-treating. When we got back, I tied Bruce in his stable, washed him down with warm water, inspected his cuts for thorns and applied Sudocreme to the worst. I was as gentle as possible, but he flinched with every touch. I rugged him, put down two buckets of warm water and a big pile of hay, and stood outside the stable hoping he might take a drink or eat a mouthful, but he just stood and watched me, slowly flapping his lips. The honeymoon was over, and reality didn't match expectation. I'm sure I wasn't the first, or the last, to experience that disappointment.

"I'm sorry, Bruce," I said quietly, filled with remorse and sadness. "I'm so sorry."

Through the winter I persevered as best I knew how. I did everything I'd ever learnt to try controlling my horse, never realising his fear of harsh control was the root of the problem, and what I light-heartedly tried to dismiss as his 'open-country panic attacks' were exactly that. To him, they weren't light-hearted, and I didn't dare drop my false bravado and admit I was shit scared. The day the end nearly came was the catalyst for change. We'd ridden happily along the stony track from the farm for about twenty minutes when we reached a fallen tree blocking the path. With no way round and no way over, the only action was to turn and go back. As we turned, Bruce sprang into action. I had a comforting thought that if I couldn't slow him, he'd stop at the farm entrance, but I hadn't reckoned on the tractor driving down the path towards us.

The tractor took up the width of the track and the trailer he towed behind was only marginally narrower. From his high place in the cab, the driver saw me in plenty of time, but maybe I looked like I was having a fun gallop because it felt like an eternity before he stopped and tried to pull in, except there was nowhere to pull. Bruce's gallop didn't falter, I sat back in the saddle waiting for him to slide to a halt or hit the tractor head-on and neither option was appealing. His third option was to go to the side of the tractor, where the gap twixt wheels and hedge was about the width of a thin horse, but Bruce wasn't thin, and my legs were either side of him. He took the third option. I briefly caught the look of sheer horror on the tractor driver's face as Bruce dived for the gap, and I instinctively pulled my feet from the stirrups and grabbed the pommel for balance, tucking my knees up to my elbows, and stupidly breathing-in as if that would make me thinner. I heard my stirrup and leather drop to the ground as the side of the tractor pulled it off the saddle. At the time it was strangely exhilarating. The horse beneath me was so focused on his task (albeit with no regard for me) that I felt no fear until afterwards. He stopped at the farm entrance like nothing had happened, and Sheila watched us walk down the drive.

"Good ride?" she asked, looking quizzically at my white face and missing stirrup.

"Fast," I replied. "Very fast." And then I burst into tears.

We'd reached crisis point. My horse terrified me and I had no idea what to do. On her next bodywork visit for Bruce, I recounted the story to Sadie. She looked up as I spoke, and when she'd made what adjustments were possible to Bruce's taut muscles, she said matter-of-factly "I can't help you with any of that, but I know someone who might."

23 THE ART OF DOING LESS

I watched as Kirsty Hearne shut her van door and tucked her hair under a leather cowboy hat as she walked towards the stable. For some reason, it struck me that she looked completely self-contained, as if she had everything she wanted and wanted everything she had. I'd explained our problems on the phone, and she was willing to see if she could help.

A woman of few words, she cast her eyes over me and Bruce, ran an open-palmed hand softly down his neck, and nodded towards the schooling paddock, where she'd suggested I have a few poles laid out. As I led Bruce around, she arranged the poles into an L-shape, and asked me to lead him through them. No problem. I walked one side of the poles, he walked through, and I breathed a sigh of relief that we'd done something right. Then she asked me to back him through the poles. I pulled at his mouth, pushed him hard in the chest and loudly commanded "BACK!" and he stood annoyingly still. I shouted the command louder and made the push pushier, but still no movement.

"Do you always have to push to move him backwards?" Asked Kirsty.

"Well, yes," I replied, "I've always done it that way." How else was there to do it?

"And do you always shout?"

"Only if he doesn't obey."

"And does he obey?"

"Ummm . . . no," I said forlornly, looking at the ground. "Not usually, no."

Kirsty walked over to where Bruce stood firm and asked if she could have his reins. I handed them over, feeling an absolute failure. She shook the reins at him, lowered her head slightly, and took a short step forward. He stayed immobile. She lowered her head further, and walked towards him more forcefully, and he took a few hurried steps backwards, put in a buck to show his displeasure, and then stepped neatly around the L to the end of the poles. Kirsty rubbed his forehead and told him he was a good boy. He dropped his nose and rested it by her elbow.

"I think we've solved that problem," she said quietly. "Perhaps you could try asking instead of telling."

Next, she asked me to lead him forward again, this time walking inside the poles with him. We walked down the straight, and when we got to the turn he walked right through me. I jumped to one side and hopped back again to finish.

"Did you think about slowing him to make the turn," she said, and I wasn't sure if it was a question or a statement.

"Ummmmm, no."

"And do you always have him walking ahead of you at the pace he wants?"

"I guess so," I replied, never really having thought about Bruce's position. I'd never really given much thought to leading a horse, I just expected it to do as I said. If it went too fast, I'd pull it back and if too slow I'd pull it forward. When I wanted to stop, I'd apply pressure until it stopped.

Kirsty showed me how to decide where I wanted Bruce to be, and how to keep him an arm's distance from my body so we didn't bump each other. It was the first time anyone had explained how to give a horse clear directions, rather than correct it when it did wrong, and it made perfect sense. I didn't know why I didn't know about it. Then she showed me how to breathe commands instead of shouting them, and we practised going forward on an out breath and halting by slowing my feet, so we stopped in unison without any pressure on the rope. Miraculously, we moved left and right by turning my shoulders.

As we went back and forth through pole alley, walking over the poles, and stopping and starting without pulling or tugging on the reins, I felt an incredible sense of elation at the way Bruce responded. If he noticed my feet slow and my shoulders turn, what else did he notice in my movements? This was all new to me. I'd been taught that being the boss was the key to mastering horses, not breathing.

"I think we'll call it a day there," said Kirsty after forty minutes. "You both look like you've done enough." As she ran her hand down Bruce's neck he dropped his head and snorted. "He's a good horse. You just need to find him his quiet place," she said. I had no idea what she meant or where that search would take us, but I knew it was our only chance to make things work.

It seems obvious now how similar Bruce and I were. Anxiety overruled logic, we both cloaked ourselves in an armour of false bravado and we were both in permanent flight from our demons. Bruce might have four legs, but I was running as fast from cancer as he was from his nemesis. Kirsty's 'quiet place' would prove as mind-quenching for me as it did for him.

How do you find a quiet place? I began by Googling 'meditation Dorset' and found a local MBSR course. Mindfulness Based Stress Release is awareness through paying attention, non-judgementally in the present moment, based on the teachings of John Kabat-Zinn, who 'brought Buddhism to the West'. I'd got frustrated with meditation before and given up, but it's easier to do something for someone else than for yourself, so I joined the weekly group to discover what a quiet place looked like, and how I could give it to Bruce. It was hard going! I abhorred silence and always considered my razor-sharp reactions a blessing, so why would I want to pause first? Mindfully chewing raisins wasn't what I'd expected but I'd paid for the course, so I listened to the reasoning, and gradually learnt how to unhook and release the tangle of what-ifs in my mind; when you stop paying attention to the voices, they stop chattering. Mindfulness gave me the simplest coping tool, breathing, and over the years mindful breathing has changed my life. Pause Breathe Smile. Yay raisins!

Breathing with Bruce was miraculous. While I groomed him, I focused on my breath and spontaneously, great sighs of emotion rose from the pit of my stomach and fell from my mouth like forgotten prisoners fleeing their dungeon. At first, Bruce snorted and cleared his nose, then he yawned. Then he rubbed his nose on his knee, letting out a long out-breath and swishing his tail until it ceased. I thought it was coincidence, but each day I tried to do the same breathing pattern and sometimes he followed suit. Sometimes he just flapped his lips and sometimes he pawed the ground, but he made an action that acknowledged my breathing. (Writing this, I sighed those long out-breaths again without realising!)

With all the vigour of the newly converted, I practised groundwork with Bruce, trying to breathe steadily and stop my mind wandering to a million different locations. Kirsty had me holding the reins as if I was riding, making me aware of how my hands wandered alongside my busy mind. I was also confusing Bruce because I gave no forethought to my directives. Like a garbled phone message, he got snippets of conversation and had to guess the rest. To direct him clearly, I had to set him up not to fail. It sounded straightforward, but it meant unlearning everything I knew. Along with Bruce, I was also starting again.

After several weeks of practise and teaching sessions, Kirsty suggested Bruce might like to move on. I hadn't ridden since the Tractor Dash and was determined to look good, but as the old saying warns us, 'pride goes only as far as one can spit'. I did, however, learn the biggest lesson, the art of doing less. Kirsty stood by the fence as I walked and trotted Bruce around the paddock, changing direction and awaiting instruction. I hoped she'd tell me what to do, but as she just stood and watched, I thought maybe the lesson hadn't started yet. Then she walked into the centre.

"What are you asking for?" she said, as Bruce and I laboured around the arena in a vaguely defined circle.

"A loose trot," I gasped between rising and sitting. "With a good bend," I added, trying to sound like I knew what I was doing.

"And is it working?"

I rode two more laps while I fought the inevitable answer. "No."

"Then why are you doing it?"

"Because I don't know what else to do." The truth in those words stung me to the quick, my ego as flat as Bruce's footfall.

"Have you tried doing nothing?" Said Kirsty, with the merest hint of smile.

Needless to say, I'd never considered doing nothing.

24 CANCER RETURNS

May 2010, Cancer the fourth time.

Cancer returned to its favoured underarm site. There have been so many lumps over the years I can't recall how I found it, probably in the shower. In 1991 I had radiotherapy on that area and it's not possible to re-treat the same site, so after three consecutive operations to get clear margins around the tumour (I did suggest they insert a zip instead of sutures), the consultant recommended I take a daily dose of Arimidex, an aromatose inhibitor that blocks the body from producing any oestrogen. I'll also need regular bone density scans and high-strength calcium and vitamin D tablets as Aromatose inhibitors can cause osteoporosis. I had an overwhelming gut feeling against taking arimidex. It was the best preventative treatment in the circumstances, so I gathered information to help make a more informed decision, but no matter what I read, my instinct still said no.

I saw a new oncologist. He said take the drugs. I talked to my GP who said take the drugs. I asked Mark's opinion, and he bravely replied he completely understood if I went with my gut reaction. I cast rune stones and dowsed, and my gut instinct still said no, and it was causing me unbelievable angst; if I was right then all was okay, but what if I was wrong and having a kneejerk reaction to another tumour and three more drugs? What if the cancer returned with a vengeance? The irony of being the mistress of my own demise was too ridiculous for words. I sat on the floor like a child in a sandpit, drowning in the quicksand of cancer while Mark nursed my needs. I don't remember how long I fought to find a decision, but eventually, my mouth said I'd take the drugs. My body didn't alter its feeling.

I'd always felt the cancers were somehow my fault. If I ate different things or acted differently or hadn't done awful things, I wouldn't have got it, and my efforts to find a reason for my cancers kept leading me to genetics. Wondering why no one had mentioned this before, I requested a referral for genetic counselling. The extensive form-filling needed medical details on familial cancer and while compiling my Cancer Family Tree I learnt that prostate cancer is often hormone-induced (almost the male version of breast cancer), and the lung cancer that killed my maternal grandmother was probably secondary breast tumours. Arriving as immigrants to England in the 1920s with nothing but a verbal past, I couldn't delve further back than great-grandparents, or further sideways than second cousins, but the clarity of seeing a perfect cancer-line spreading down the maternal side of my family shook me to the core. Maybe my cancer wasn't my fault after all? For my own interest, I also made a paternal tree and found a perfect line of heart disease. One certainty was that no one in my family ever died of old age!

When I test positive for BRCA2 gene mutation, the Consultant in Clinical Genetics tells me I'm not alone in the problems I experience carrying this gene. My ancestors were Ashkenazi Jews and along with a self-deprecating sense of humour and curly *jewfro* hair, they have a high incidence of BRCA2 mutation. Thanks ancestors. I'm given copies of my genetic summary so relatives who wish to be screened have all the information. Some accept the information with grace, appreciating the fact-finding that's been researched. Others panic.

Removing my ovaries is a sensible precaution against further cancer, and luckily our local cottage hospital can do the surgery a week later. The hospital is a thirty-minute walk from home, it's a fresh sunny day and I told l Mark I'd prefer to be alone, he can visit in the evening. Along the green country lanes carrying my little overnight bag, feeling like a character from Thomas Hardy. The receptionist greets me with a smile and directs me to the ward where I unexpectedly burst into tears. En-route to the linen cupboard, a nurse pauses and sits down next to me.

"It suddenly gets to you after all the hustle and bustle doesn't it, sweetheart," she says, offering kindness in lieu of a cup of tea.

"It sure does," I reply trying to regain my composure. "I thought I was okay."

"I'm on duty tonight, I'll check you later." She pats my arm before leaving.

The keyhole surgery goes smoothly, I'm wheeled to a recovery ward to join the groggy band of post-opees and offered a much-needed cup of tea and hospital biscuit. Hospital biscuits are always plain, flavourless and immensely comforting. After a day of nil-by-mouth I could've eaten the cardboard packet. Five wan smiles from the other occupants acknowledge my presence, and in sleepy unison we all snuggle under our blankets to doze off the anaesthetic.

When Mark arrives for visiting hour, I'm sitting up in bed in my hospital ward, feeling extremely uncomfortable but smiling my well-practised hospital smile. He isn't fooled by the smile or my pretence that I'm still groggy, but I don't feel like chatting, so he leaves early. I spend an uncomfortable night trying to sleep on plastic barrier sheets and shuffling to and from the toilet unable to distinguish between bleeding and the need to pee. In the quiet, impersonal darkness of the hospital bed I mourned the mother I never became, and the body that let me down.

Over breakfast we all discuss our ops in gleeful detail, knowing these are the last ears to listen without grimace. Mark arrives to collect me and as I'm discharged I say a silent final farewell to my ovaries, unceremoniously dumped in a sluice bin. They did their best, it was the bodywork that failed.

Once back home I experience the intense crippling pain of post-op keyhole surgery which is so awful, I Google the symptoms: "One of the most uncomfortable aspects after having Laparoscopic Surgery is the subsequent organ, diaphragm and shoulder pain. This is caused by the CO_2 gas used to fill the area having surgical repair, becoming trapped against the diaphragm."

I unashamedly (and uncontrollably) fart for England. Nor had I expected removing my ovaries would bring on a second wave of menopause. I unashamedly (and uncontrollably) flushed, cried and grumped my way through the shifting balance of adjusting hormones, stopped brushing my thinning hair and started slapping industrial-strength moisturiser on my parched skin. And I farted just because I felt like it. Deep inside me, cancer quietly chuckled. And a year later the cancer returned with vengeance.

The only way is life.
With cancer, Having cancer, Being cancer.
Terror turns to fear.
Clinging to sleeping pills, I stare blankly as they fail to deliver oblivion.
The grey wraith that I become allows skins to peel away without concern for the bare bones that lie beneath, and I am naked but for my cancer.

Radionic Treatment

Without medicine I would surely be dead.
I've been patched-up and sent on my way more times than I care to recall, and for very many years the plaster stuck valiantly while the wound slowly festered.
Off the Waiting List. Living with Cancer. A winner in the Postcode Lottery.
Healed from the outside in.

Not wishing to make a career from cancer nor be defined by a disease that others found so difficult, my stiff upper lip saw me safely through 20 tough years.

Keep Calm and Carry On. Won my wars or so I thought until the 4th time which, with hindsight should've been called a breakdown, but we called it coping.

The intricate steps towards seeking help are like a dance of desperation for the depressed. Even for one enlightened by otherworldly experiences, playing the card seen as a last resort meant facing reality; I didn't trust my medication, I didn't trust my body. I needed to trust a black box. I've used Radionics in the past always to good effect, but this time the struggle was within myself as if the inner me knew what lay ahead and would prefer to take a Duvet Day.

Surgery, recuperation, decisions, wretchedness and grief. . .moving steadily through the healing process the Treatment worked its wonder and when I reached acceptance, I felt strong enough to go it alone. One more notch on the post, one more episode to be lived and re-lived in the fear of a midnight mind and one more smile to greet the day.

May 2011

And so, to the 5th time. . .

If cancer doesn't get me then I shall die of boredom from hearing the same diagnosis over and over and over and over and over again.

Because Arimidex was unable to stop my cancer the oncologist suggests Chemotherapy followed by a different hormone blocker pill. I nod agreement, I just want this to be over. I feel relieved to have chemo and the relief breeds false hope that it'll cure me. Make me better, stop the cancer coming back.

How it Feels

Inspired by the Olympics I want to try extended trot with Bruce. So, I ask Kirsty in our lesson if we can work towards it. . .little do I know.

Collection and power. Collection of your hugely powerful body, how can I gain that?

Trot-halt-trot we get the hang of it eventually....to strike off as your last back leg comes in ready to stop. We motor but with lightness. I sit up with such immense pride that your chest comes up your neck lowers and you're like a steam train harnessed by the lightest touch. I'm totally amazed and you're so happy that for once you're allowed to be you, to show what you do, to go forward unrestrained, but contained within my framework. We turn the corner to the long side, and I allow. You perform- one two three four and then I lose it. Exhausted. Laughing- Kirsty smiling and laughing. I want to applaud. I can't believe we did it. Fours strides of extended trot. US! In our silly little slanting school. If I'd won the Olympics I couldn't have been happier. Thank you, dear Bruce. You glow. I glow. Phew!

HA! I'm stronger than Chemotherapy.

"I have different ways." -Cancer.

These next months of chemotherapy are going to come at a very high price. Living will be suspended and replaced by enduring. This is the price I pay for life.

25 A PROPER COB

On our next lesson, Kirsty asked me to rise one beat and sit two while trotting. I understood the action, but my body was clumsy. Sauntering round, Bruce seemed happy not doing anything strenuous, but his mood suddenly switched, as if he decided he was being ignored and might just as well go home. He sprang into a gazelle leap and galloped towards the gate. I couldn't see enough space to stop and prepared myself for a fall, but with cadence that would've impressed a dressage horse, he halted square from a gallop and stood quietly with his chest against the gate. I wriggled back into the saddle, open-mouthed and speechless.

Kirsty walked unhurriedly across the field. "Nice halt," she said.

"Do you think I could get a stronger bit?" I asked her. "He can't keep tanking-off with me."

"Doesn't matter what you put in his mouth you won't stop him if he wants to go." She replied.

I felt crestfallen, more at her seeming lack of concern than my predicament.

"But of course," she continued, "you can always learn to turn him and that'll stop anything."

"Turn him?" I replied, puzzled. "He doesn't turn."

"Oh, I think he will if you ask in a way he understands. Tom Dorrance, who was the master of enlightened cowboy training had a phrase called double-your-colt. Basically, if you disengage a horse's hindquarters and ask them to move laterally, they can't go forward. It's a way of directing when things start to go shit-shape. Instead of waiting for Bruce to gallop off and try to stop, be ready to turn as he lands from his leap, keep his quarters moving across, and you'll slow on a circle and stop. Eventually, you'll be able to bring his head round as soon as you feel the danger signs."

I looked at Kirsty, she looked at me, and we both grinned. "What are we waiting for?" I said. "Let's get learning!"

Bruce didn't stop running away, but with Kirsty's help I began to see things from a different perspective. His running wasn't an act of disobedience, and it wasn't directed at me personally. He was running because that's what flight animals do when they're terrified, and he was terrified; just because I couldn't see the danger didn't make it any less frightening. (Years later I discovered that when he was hunting, James galloped him up and down the field, beating him at every turn as a punishment for not standing still. The turn was the trigger, especially in open countryside, and for him, it was as real as the days it happened).

I stopped calling Bruce's escapades bad behaviour and re-named them 'expressing his opinion,' and they became a lot less scary. I didn't know if I could actually alter a situation by approaching it differently, or if I was sidestepping the obvious to avoid misery, but I felt I had a choice. I couldn't change the situation, but I could change the way I looked at it and labelled it, and that was something to being going on with.

Mindfulness helped me clear my head and make room for response, instead of disciplinary reactions towards Bruce. To help him relax I had to know what I wanted to do, and I began visualising my request, so he received clear instruction. When he got anxious and needed to move his feet it was more sensible to direct him somewhere than try to stop him and working with my breath meant my hands didn't grab his sensitive mouth. I also tried to take emotion out of the equation, but that's still a work in progress. It wasn't a one-size-fits-all panacea, but it helped, and our confidence grew. Kirsty lent me Mark Rashid's book Life Lessons from a Ranch Horse, and as I read about Mark's experiences with his horse Buck, thoughts I'd had back in the nineties with Teddy began to re-surface. At the time I'd wanted to make my horse feel better about his life, but I didn't know how. Monty Roberts burst on to the scene in a blaze of join-up glory, along with Parelli instructors in cowboy hats, and I'd watched clinics, read the books and bought the halter, but that new environment was alien. I lacked the courage to travel unfamiliar paths back then, but the seed was sown and now those thoughts were ripening. They might even bear fruit.

Kirsty always began lessons by asking me what I'd like to do or aim for. Initially, it surprised me because she was the teacher, and I thought she should know what to teach me, but it gave me focus on what I wanted from myself and Bruce. On our next lesson I asked if we could jump.

"What would you like to jump?" She asked.

"I've put some branches by the hedge, and there are some buckets for stands."

"One jump or a course?"

"Just one will be enough."

"Okay, you shorten your stirrups and ask for a nice forward trot on a circle, and I'll set it up." She quickly arranged a row of poles along one side of our working space, with a small brush jump in the centre. "Trot over the poles a few times from both directions, and remember, not any old trot, but the trot you want!"

Bruce pricked his ears as we trotted over the poles, raising his back and lowering his neck. I tried to make my breath slow and steady because I was horribly nervous.

Once she was satisfied we were ready, Kirsty gave instructions. "Next time, come round to the brush after the row of poles, still trotting," she said. "What's your plan after you land?"

"Err, I don't have one."

"You'd better think of one before you try. We haven't done this before, and we don't know what he'll do."

"I'll be ready to turn him," I said smugly. "And then we'll stop."

Kirsty looked up and smiled. "Good plan."

I never thought we'd do it, but we did, and Bruce carried me like I was precious cargo. It was only a little jump but to me it was like jumping the moon. As we landed, Bruce shot into the air with ears flat back and I sat still and brought him onto a circle because that's how confident I felt after jumping the moon. The second time was in canter, and he didn't panic afterwards. Kirsty's word rang in my ears, "know what you want, set it up and let it happen." Jumping branches balanced on buckets, in the corner of a sloping field, on a horse who had been written-off meant everything I had wished for this horse came true.

Emboldened by new-found confidence, I entered a local in-hand show. On the morning of the show, I got to Sheila's at the crack of dawn, bathed and polished Bruce until he shone, and plaited his tail to show off his wonderful backside. He was an Adonis, and I was a nervous wreck. Sheila drove us to the show in her battered old trailer and regaled me with showing stories from her youth. She'd lent me her 'lucky' tweed jacket with assurances it had never let her down. It wasn't the jacket that worried me.

The other entrants in the cob class were all gypsy cobs with flowing manes. Their naturally hairy legs feathered-out at the hoof, like seventies bell-bottoms, and Bruce was the only maxi-cob, with a traditional hogged mane and clean-shaven legs. His paces were faultless, but he obviously wasn't the type of cob the judge favoured. As we came out of the ring proudly clutching our 5th place rosette, an elderly countryman stopped us. "Excuse me," he said with a broad Irish accent, putting a hand out to my arm "I hope you know you were the real winner there."

"I'm sorry," I replied, slightly confused.

"Yours was the only horse who moved like a cob should

move. The horses above him only shuffled. Judge didn't know what she was doing. She should see more proper cobs. Don't get many like yours these days, he's made like they should be. Like they used to be."

"Oh, thank you, how very lovely of you to say that!" I was truly overwhelmed.

"I wasn't the only one stood here who thought it."

"Thank you, you've made our day. But the judge was fair, she said he had hock spavins. Mind you after nine years hunting he's entitled to have arthritis in his joints."

As the stranger studied the offending pair of hocks, Bruce stood as still and square as he had for the judge, flicking his ears backwards as the man spoke. "They don't look too bad to me, and they're far enough from his heart not to cause any trouble. As I said, judge knows nothing about cobs." He ran his hand softly down Bruce's neck and looked him in the eye. Bruce held his head by the man's arm and smelt something familiar that he couldn't place. Then he flapped his lips.

Bruce and I were on a high. After a fearful first year, we were finding our way of working together. I couldn't say I trusted him, and he certainly didn't trust me, but we had compromised to find a way to keep moving forward and still breathe.

My next goal was riding a walk-and-trot dressage test. But once again, cancer got in the way of plans.

26 CHEMOTHERAPY.

Poison. It does what it says on the tin.

Suspended from the drip, the bag of Docetaxel wears a black plastic hood to protect it from the light and reminds me of an executioner anonymously administering his blow.

"I can't do this" were words I hadn't expected to hear let alone say, but they screamed from my mouth like the last plea of a condemned soul. As short but terrifyingly intense panic attacks turned into days filled with overwhelming anxiety, I began my journey to the centre of hell, flailing and kicking against the crushing vortex, but propelled ever downward by the all-consuming instincts of a body under attack.

With each repeated dose of this treatment designed to save my life, the adrenalin-fuelled fight-or-flight mechanism fought to save me from the imminent danger it knew would kill me. A body torn in two by itself. The indescribable spiral into meltdown was swift. I stopped eating, I stopped sleeping and I stopped being rational. I screamed, and rocked, and paced, and followed little rituals only I could understand.

"Strong? In control? Managing with cancer? What were you thinking, Elaine? I'm the one who's strong and in control. I'm Cancer."

7 a.m. in the morning, Mark has just left for work.

Alone, I sit at the kitchen table. In a split second an insurmountable rage wells up inside me

I CAN'T DO THIS!!! I CAN'T FUCKING DO THIS!!! I CAN'T I CAN'T I CAN'T

The newspaper is hurled across the room, the table thumped with such venom the legs almost buckle and the cat jumps up with all four feet in the air and lands running for the catflap.

My face is contorted, my body pumped.

And then it goes. Gone. Completely gone. Like it never happened. I sit and sniff, I say to myself "blimey, what was that all about?" but myself is too shocked to answer.

Welcome to the Weird World of Steroids.

My anxiety was there for all to see, except I didn't see it I just felt it, and Mark didn't want to see it. When he had left for work, I screamed and flung myself to the ground, writhing in a terror of isolation. I could only function if I switched on all the lights and left the back door wide open. When he returned from work, the outbursts shocked him. I couldn't pull the curtains in the evening; I couldn't cope with quiet time. I slept so fitfully I stayed downstairs on the sofa, bolstered by pillows and warmed by firelight. I paced the room at intervals throughout the long nights. I silently dusted every nook and cranny. I emptied drawers. I counted.

I'm well and truly Down the Rabbit Hole and there ain't no tea party.

The hospital prescribed sedatives. They were lovely. Little blue pills that semi paralysed muscles and put me in a little blue in-between-land.

I slept deeply and awoke in a stupor of sickness and sweat, which wasn't so lovely. I was unable to talk properly, and the little blue pills DEMANDED to be taken at increasingly higher doses and increasingly frequent intervals otherwise they threw an extremely violent tantrum. That wasn't lovely at all.

Because of the blue pill sickness, I took more and more of my chemo anti-sickness pills. Many years later I read the contra-indications in the accompanying leaflet "

The hospital suggests I see a counsellor. The Breast Care Nurse says she'll write a referral.

Tim

Tim the District Nurse came to the house the day after chemo to inject Neulasta, which stimulates the growth of new healthy white blood cells in bone marrow. The injection was simple, the after-effects less so. Pain that felt like your hips had separated to the point of no return. I couldn't climb the stairs; at times I couldn't stand.

You could talk to Tim. He saved me. I told him about the panic attacks, the anxiety and sleeplessness and he took it very seriously.

He asked, "Who is your Macmillan Nurse?"

"Macmillan Nurse? I thought you only got one of those if you were dying." Awkward pause which needed no explanation.

"No, you can have a Macmillan Nurse to help you and your family through cancer. They're attached to the doctor's surgery. I'll fix it up for you."

It was a turning point.

Frances

Frances quickly phoned and arranged an appointment. Was she so quick because I was dying and no one was telling me?

On the day I was very anxious. I made tea, and I re-made tea, and I re-washed the cups and made the tea again. Then I had a blue pill and re-washed the teapot and re-made the tea, and then Frances arrived in a wave of efficiency and calm. She didn't drink tea, so I made coffee.

She took all my details and gave me a little test to see if I was depressed. It said I was. Then she gave me a little test to see if I was anxious and it said I was that too.

I explained it was all from the chemo and the steroids and once it was over, I'd be back to my normal sunny self. Even through the little blue pills I could see she didn't look convinced.

On her next visit, she suggested (very firmly) that I start a course of ant-depressant/anti-anxiety drugs.

She contacted the doctor's surgery and made a telephone appointment with my GP. She also gave me the phone number for the Cancer Counseling Service at Forest Holme and asked me to call them for an appointment. She said it would help.

Cetalopram

My GP prescribed Cetalopram which he said would be excellent in this situation. He reassured me I would sleep. I would eat and my anxiety would reduce. I thanked him and put the phone down.

Then I phoned straight back and asked him if it was okay to take with chemo and he said yes, it was.

I put the phone down. Then I phoned straight back and asked him if it was okay to take with the blue pills. He said yes, it was.

Anxious? Moi?

I began on a 10mg dose. If you survive the first month then Cetalopram can be an excellent drug of choice, but in the early stages it has a habit of exacerbating and exaggerating every single anxious thought, even ones you haven't yet had, but the moment it was prescribed, before I'd even collected the prescription, I felt cured. Of course, that was simply relief.

The first day I popped the Cetalopram, I stopped my blue pill, stopped my sleeping pill and waited. The anxiety came like a tidal wave. I could've torn my brain out.

The panic continued to escalate.

I phoned helplines but they didn't have an answer that I could hear.

I tried acupuncture but cried so much he felt it best "not to treat today."

I read web pages full of anecdotes from similarly anxious people who also couldn't find sense in the grip of their anxiety.

I phoned Stacey, "I'm having the most awful panic attack."

"Take one of the blue pills."

"I can't, they make me feel awful."

"And how are you feeling now?"

The doctor doubled my dose to 20mg, and the strength of panic surged higher.

The kitchen drawer was open, and I was looking at the array of kitchen knives. Big black handles, wide razor-sharp blades.

How cold it would be to hold a flat blade against my wrist. How comforting to turn the blade to its sharp steel edge and draw a thin line of blood. To FEEL something real. But the blood would spurt. I'd have to explain. There would be more panic and fuss and they'd lock me away. But how cold it would be just to hold that flat blade against my wrist.

In the morning I concocted a story of wretched nightmares and asked Mark to hide all the big sharp kitchen knives. I think he believed me because they disappeared immediately.

Laying in the bath, scented to the stinking point with relaxing lavender.

A special CD of 'Sleep Inducing Piano Music' playing gently in the background.

Eyes shut, trying to breathe pleasurable thoughts.

A vision of someone standing in our garden. I creep up behind them and smash them over the back of the head with a rusty horseshoe (?!). The blood pours and I carry on smashing. I pulverise their head. The someone is Mark.

I'm physically sick at what I've just thought.

In the early hours of another sleepless night, I wanted to phone The Samaritans but some deep-seated fear stopped me dialling. I'm sure I'm not suicidal.

I phoned a medical helpline. I told the man my symptoms, but I didn't mention the knives or the head smashing. He was calm and spoke with the voice of an angel.

"This is all medically induced. This is Cetalopram speaking, not you. This will subside and it'll stop but it frequently happens in the first month of treatment as the drug makes changes to brain function. I can't help you, but I can stay on the phone for as long as you want and hold your hand through the night."

I thanked him. He had helped me more than he knew.

Eric

Eric is a hessian sack and we've stuffed him with straw. The top of the sack is twisted and tied so he looks like a sack with a man-bun. I don't know why his name is Eric and quite frankly I don't care. Today is Eric's day and I feel trepidatious, but strangely excited about our upcoming encounter.

He was my idea, encouraged by Mark.

Eric lays on the lawn at the top of the garden. We approach him with stealth, armed with kitchen knives, garden spades and a length of metal chain. Mark and I look at each other and Mark nods to go-ahead.

I take a deep, deep breath and exhale a guttural, primal scream which echoes around the trees and startles us both into a split second of inaction. But it's just a split second, and then I strike, screaming, shouting cursing words I didn't even know I knew. The carving knife plunged into Eric's heart, his stomach and throat, wrenched back out and ground into his eyes. I kick him and stomp on him. Murderous words and names scrabble through my mouth and scream into his face. Cancer cunt cancer cunt cancer cunt you can't kill me. You can't you won't you can't. I beat him with the garden spade (expecting blood to fly) and stomp some more and scream some more. . .and then I collapse in a sobbing, exhausted heap on the damp grass, gasping for air that won't come. Mark's face is white as a sheet, he picks up the chain and whips Eric until the sack splits and his stuffing is spilling out. He stabs him over and over and over, and his words make mine sound like a nursery rhyme. I cover my ears, hide my face as Eric is totally pulverized, whisps of straw floating to the ground and pieces of hessian littering the lawn. Mark collapses next to me, shaking like a leaf. We've killed Eric. Killed cancer.

We're blessed to have no neighbours.

I suggest a nice cup of tea.

"You might have killed Eric but you have not killed me."
-Cancer

27 UNDERSTANDING BRUCE

So, I thought I'd do my first Reiki on you, Bruce, seeing as you are the instigator of the journey. You knew something was afoot and approached it with enthusiasm.

I'd just started. . .the crowscarer ripped through the sound waves like a crackerjack and you jumped in fright. Head up, I felt the pulse in your neck beat. I put my hands on you and you settled so quickly.

It was lovely for me, treating you, my dear boy. With my hand cupping (what I hoped was) your solar plexus chakra you lifted your tail and let out a huge fart- rivalling the crowscarer. That was to be my message!

Afterward you followed me into the field and wouldn't let me go, following me up and down, "If there's more of that about, I want it!"

Sometimes Bruce, you leave me speechless.

In order for you to relax and respond, I have to be in charge.

In order to be in charge, I have to know what I want to do, and what I want you to do.

If I'm not in charge, you will take over.

I have to give to instruction with intent. Not any old trot, but *this* trot.

If I tell you, you're so keen to do that you respond. . .the fault is that I don't tell you…that I don't know.

Hands come from elbows not wrists...elbows come from back.

Open pelvis slightly to walk on. Lift up not forward, lead with sternum...energy going forward.

Turn your head when you toss *consistently.*

Tread down a step to turn...from the hip.

Your back leg has to be under my weight.

Set it up, know what you want, then it will happen.

Front and back two huge circles. Sit on the part where they cross.

Softness before the movement, the movement itself will not make softness.

Without the front relaxing, the back cannot push.

Make yourself big, flick energy.

Rattle the rope to remind that I'm here.

Think of feet going backwards when I ask for back up.

Breathe in, breathe out through seat, head lower, back anywhere there's tension.

Listen to you.

I was grooming Bruce last night and he kept walking away, round his stable and coming back to face me full on. I itched all of his itchy spots, rubbed ears, muzzle, eyes, scratched neck and withers, but nothing was what he wanted. He put up with my attempts for a few seconds then walked back round to face me again.

When I got home I told Mark that he must think me so dim because he was plainly asking for something somewhere and I was darned if I knew what.

I just want to spend time with you and listen to what you have to teach, Bruce.

After our ride this glorious morning I realise you've taught me to be in the present- that you need me to be in the present, and then you'll yield your head. I have to earn that reward.

Fifties and sixties: I stop thinking and begin feeling.

Bruce facilitates the change.

I meet a horse who says it's his job to carry me, but his remit does not extend to filling-in my gaps. He makes his feelings quite clear; clarity, consistency and boundaries are non-negotiable, and self-preservation is his priority.

I stand firmly by what I know for the first year, then it occurs to me I know very little.

My leather-bound stick is the first thing to go, followed rapidly by conceit, ego and expectation. Over the years, pretty much everything else follows suit.

This mass exodus makes space for new ideas. Who knew breathing was the antidote to most problems? Why are win and fail the only options? I quickly learn to change my vocabulary; label something a problem and that's what you get. Behaviour I consider 'bad' becomes 'expressing an opinion', and by listening to that opinion, I discover what panics my horse. The day he pauses before bolting is a day of celebration.

Your grace and generosity, your immense ability to forgive, your heartfulness and honesty and the pleasure you bring to the eye, to simply see you brings a smile to my soul.

28 UTTERLY COOKED

One day a single word filtered through the fug. "Knitting."

I bought wool, and a pattern, and I tried to knit myself out of anxiety.

When I finished the back of my cardigan, I un-picked it and knitted it all again, just because it felt nice to do.

When I sew up the finished garment, I find one side is four inches longer than the other.

Christine the Counselor

I phoned Forest Holme Counselling Service, and they made me an appointment.

I looked on their website for directions and realised it was a hospice. I couldn't look at the website anymore and I didn't want to go. I wanted to be sick.

It was a h o s p i c e.

Mark put me in the car, it's difficult to physically pace in a car so I did it in my mind.

He held my hand as we sat in the waiting room and smiled encouragingly when Christine came to collect me.

Christine was small and slim, wearing black clothes and straight grey hair cut into a sharpish bob. The room was small with some chairs, a table holding boxes of tissues, and a large window overlooking a pretty courtyard. A courtyard where dying people could sit.

She sat neatly in a chair opposite me and indicated I make

myself comfortable. I wanted to pace but I didn't want to appear totally bonkers. She passed me some papers and asked me to answer the questions, but I'd started crying and didn't have my glasses so between sobs we did the job together.

It didn't seem I was going to stop crying anytime soon.

She asked me if I was willing to try something new.

"Anything" I gulped.

"I'm going to ask you to fix your attention on something in the courtyard for five minutes. Then I'll tap the box of tissues on the table to say time is up"

So, this is counselling? Looking in the garden for five minutes is going to cure me? Great. Great fucking rubbish.

But I do as I'm bidden and after the five-minute tap I turn and face Christine with a deep exhale and look suitably bored.

"Did you notice that?"

"Notice what?"

"You just let out the greatest breath and your shoulders dropped right away from your ears. And you've stopped crying."

The last bit was easily remedied as the tears returned on cue, but I have to admit they may have been tears of relief.

"That's it for today. I want you to practice that exercise all week whenever you feel anxious."

We made an appointment for the following week. I wanted to come back earlier, get it done quicker but Christine said no, a week's time would be fine. As we parted at the door I mumbled "I've just started on Cetalopram. With the counselling am I going to feel better?"

"I don't know" she replied, "I really don't know."

Back in the car I knew Mark wanted to know what happened but didn't know if he should ask so I saved him the trouble.

"We filled in some forms, and I looked in the garden for five minutes." He looked suitably crestfallen.

"Fucking counselling. Waste of time."

I practised my breathing technique all week. I still practice it to this day.

Fucking counselling was one of the greatest turning points in my life.

We explored so much, Christine and I, sat opposite in that small room overlooking the courtyard. Initially each week, stretching to fortnights and then monthly, we slowly but very surely unpicked each layer, laid it bare and forensically examined its whys wherefores and what-nows and decided whether to keep or discard. Christine was very clever- she didn't let me evade the difficult things nor charm her into slipping through the tragedy unseen. It was utterly exhausting.

One morning she suggested drawing something. I can't remember the exact sequence of events, only the outcome, which was that I drew an armoured jacket and we recoiled simultaneously when we realised what it was. We discussed it. She asked me if I wanted to put it back on? I stood silently, screwed the paper into the tiniest ball imaginable, and put it firmly in the bin.

My fledge had begun.

Mark is driving around Fleetsbridge roundabout. I'm sitting in the passenger seat pacing, when it occurs to me that I can't cope anymore and it would be polite to tell him.

"I can't cope anymore."

He carried on driving without his eyes ever leaving the road, and in that single moment, I began to cope again.

November 2011

After the fourth cycle of chemotherapy, I declare defeat. Or retreat, whichever spin you prefer.

If I have any more I'm going to end up in a psychiatric ward because I'm totally and utterly cooked. Surprisingly to me, everyone nods in agreement.

The oncologist prescribes Exemestane, an aromatose inhibitor that does the same thing as Arimidex via different pathways.

I'm anxious about taking it and postpone the start until after Christmas.

Frances the Macmillan nurse goes on holiday, and I don't die through lack of handholding.

My hair starts to grow, grey pallor lessens, and I try to piece my life back together once again.

In January I obey orders and begin the Exemestane.

Post Traumatic Growth

Although the chemotherapy meltdown was a nightmare I never wish to repeat, the aftermath re-building was *so* necessary and the day I discarded the armour was momentous.

I remember quite clearly taking it off and how it felt to be free.

I'm able to receive now that everything doesn't bounce off. Asking for what I need to be given. . .well that's coming with practise.

I feel less concerned with the future and able to live the present.

In those quiet early morning moments thoughts are still sombre, but worries appear to be carried in a stream or in grey clouds which are always behind me, so I'm thinking they are past residues draining/floating away.

Crumbs...what I went through to get here. I'm very grateful to have arrived. It was like I opened the windows wide but instead of fresh air coming in all that happened was the dust blew around like a tornado. I screwed up my eyes and put my fingers in my ears, but the sound was mind-blowing. Literally.

I spent a year picking at a scab until I was raw with pain, unable to find what I had to know, yet powerless to stop and heal.

I shed weight, I shed tears, I shed friends. Those who could hack it kept arms open in readiness and ducked when tantrums flew. Those that couldn't made a hasty exit. Rats and ships.

I became a bulimic feasting on grief and vomiting bile until my stomach churned in anguish and I could see myself from the insides out.

I berated my insides. I called them all the horrible disgusting names I knew, and then some. I wanted to kill my insides; murder them slowly and horribly until their mutilated remains were unidentifiable, and then some.

After the tornado, the voices came. They mocked and they clamoured and they demanded to be heard. They ALL demanded to be heard. ALL the voices. ALL the time.

I shouted at them to stop, and they laughed. They knew I wanted to murder my insides and said they'd dance on the grave. Said they'd tell everyone I'd done it. Said they'd tell the cancer. Said it would seek revenge. Said I'd die.

But I didn't.

My soul became a desert, and like my ancestors, I became a wandering Jew.

Moses had his tablets, I had mine. I fought the cancerous plague. I fought the thunder and hail in my head, and I fought the plague of darkness. I fought the death of the unborn and glimpsed the barren wilderness left by locusts and flies.

My mind burned in the relentless heat as I journeyed aimlessly towards my Promised Land. Somewhere, under the carefully visualised star-strewn sky the sands slowly shifted. Manna fell and I tasted hope.

As the dunes receded I found firmer footing in three steps:

I asked for help.

I gave myself space.

And openly, I waited.

And it came because I let it. I deserved it and I let myself deserve it.

Hairshirt, sackcloth and ashes. My body had atoned for a crime it never intended to commit. GBH upon itself; a life sentence reduced to 20 years for good behaviour. Enough bullying, enough punishment.

No welcoming party, no fanfare, just quiet satisfaction as I was reconciled with an old friend.

I fell in love with that friend and at last I forgave that friend.

Buddies. Me and myself. And cancer.

Like the stoical Capricorn mountain goat, I had hauled myself up every steep, stony, craggy, death-infested inch of that forsaken rockface, each faltering foothold forever etched in a memory overflowing with pain, avoiding the unthinkable abyss below.

Reaching the summit was never an option; the climb itself was my reward, my claim of triumph over adversity, my distance between now and then, and climbing both focused and numbed the mind.

Unexpectedly seeing sunlight, breathing the heady intoxication of summer blooms warmed by love, being bathed by a nurturing breeze and finding a supportive, grounding, caring earth on which to place my blistering burden was like finding the lost haven of Shangri-La, and this I did not expect.

This was new and not only took away my breath but showed me breath. Showed me deep, meaningful, life-giving life-prolonging life-enhancing- life-LOVING gulps of pure fresh untainted energising cancer-free breath.

And I trusted. I took baby steps amid fields of shoulder-high happiness. A toddler in paradise chasing damsel flies, giggling with glee at the pure pleasure of simply being in a Well World. A world of optimism and understanding. A world I didn't think could be mine.

This panorama of peace stays behind my eyes, eclipsing sorrow like an indelible stain of salvation as I go onwards and upwards, climbing once more. A touch of the Well World endeavouring to keep the distance twixt what is, what was. . .and what could be.

29 BRUCE BOLTS.

New Year's Day January 2012

It's a bright winter's day and I decide to take Bruce for a walk, leading him across the fields. He's not as eager as I am to enjoy a sociable ramble. The connection we lost during my raging anxiety still discolours the edges of our relationship.

We turn left off the gravel track onto the bridleway, and with ears pricked and muscles trembling at the sight of wide-open space he begins to bounce along beside me, turning sideways to evade the contact I have on his bridle. I move off the central track to the headland by the fence but the long grass tickling his belly aggravates his excitement, and with his head high in the air I'm having difficulty keeping my footing in the deep earth. By the time we reach the wire fence at the bottom of the field we're both breathless, hot, sweaty and thoroughly wound up. I have a choice of turning and walking back up field or returning on the gravel track. I decide to make my point and regain some control in the field. Little weak bod me versus big hulking him.

As we go to turn, he tries to walk right through me. I reprimand him and ask him to step backwards. He plants all four feet firmly on the ground and shoves his nose hard against my chest, knocking away my breath. I tell him to step backwards and get two reluctant shuffles which, in view of the situation, I tactfully decide is more than sufficient. As we walk forward once more he stands straight up on his hind legs and spins around to face home. The force knocks me sideways, but I hang on to the reins for grim death. THIS IS STUPID I'M GOING TO GET DRAGGED, JUST LET GO!!!

As he starts to gallop, I let go, and in the gleeful spirit of freedom, he puts in an almighty buck. I've always trusted it wasn't aimed at me, but maybe I flatter myself. Wedged between half a ton of fleeing horse and a barbed wire fence there's nowhere for me to go. The surreal vision of his back feet coming towards me freezes me with fear. The earth is soft, and somewhere a bird sings quietly. A tractor hums in the distance. I reckon from the intense pain in my chest I'm still alive, and if I'm alive, I'd better get up as quick as possible and catch my loose horse. I test my body parts. Legs are mobile. Moving anything above the waist causes great racking waves of pain across my chest. My neck, head and hip throb from being the point of impact.

I call Sheila from my mobile; she doesn't pick up. By rolling and screaming and making a hundred little shuffles, I drag myself up from the ground and, bending double and lurching slightly sideways, I move like Quasimodo up the hill where Bruce is watching me from the gateway. He drops his head for me to take hold of his bridle, and very, very slowly we return to the track for the mile-long walk home. Holding his bridle is too painful to bear so I hold nothing, and he steadies his pace to walk alongside me, unattached. I keep having to stop and take deeply painful gulps of breath, then go back to my bent-double stoop. He stops quietly when I stop and moves carefully when I start up once again. Behind us, a farm tractor rumbles over the gravel. I pull to one side to let them pass but they stop, and the girl in the passenger seat jumps out asking if we're okay? As I explain briefly in short breathless bursts, she suggests I climb into the tractor cab while she leads Bruce back but there's absolutely NO chance I'll ever climb up to the height of the tractor door, so she joins us walking, with the tractor bringing up the rear guard.

Once back at the yard she puts Bruce into his stable, removes his bridle, wraps him in a warm rug and wraps me up in a warm coat. She leaves her phone number and returns to her tractor driver just as Sheila arrives. Sheila listens to my breathless story, checks Bruce, then bundles me into her car. I can't speak anymore, it's too painful to cry, and I'm grateful for the silence as she drives me home. Mark is just about to get in the bath for a relaxing early evening soak. "I think I need to go to A&E" "What now?"

The A&E phone handler says (in exasperated exhaustion) that the waiting time to see a doctor is four hours, but I can book an appointment to see a doctor in the emergency out-of-hours clinic at 7.15 pm that evening. Gratefully I book. I sit down. I gasp, and I wait. Happy New Year one and all.

Mark is ashen-faced. I haven't the energy to look at mine. The doctor listens, aghast as the story unfolds. She checks breathing and bones, sight and cognitivity. The conclusion is minor concussion, whiplash to my neck, severe bruising to my hip, probable broken ribs (we don't x-ray for broken ribs) and my mastectomy implant appears to be completely ruptured. I make a weak joke about being fitted with airbags.

"See your GP if you get further pain, dizziness or shortness of breath (can it get any shorter?) If you rest, everything should heal in the next six weeks."

30 BIRTHDAY BLUES

January 7 2012

To say it's not been the best of weeks is a major understatement, but I've survived. I've coped with a level of pain I didn't know existed and I've learned (extremely quickly) how to stifle a sneeze. I had an ultrasound scan to confirm my right breast is completely mashed, most of the silicone is lodged in my armpit, but nothing can be cleaned out until the ribs heal.

The radiologist tells me years later that he has many ladies coming to appointments panicking that they've ruptured their implants by walking into a door or some such minor impact. "I've only ever seen one implant completely ruptured," he tells them, "And that was caused by a direct kick from a half-ton horse."

It's my birthday, and my birthday treat is lunch at Hugh F-W's Riverside Café in Bridport. Except that I awake in the morning with a cough, and despite trying to hide it Mark notices I'm coughing every few minutes and my breath is exceptionally short. I say I'm fine, I'm sure I am.

I phone the out-of-hours doctor who tells me to go to A&E immediately. No lunch in Bridport then.

I report to reception and am whisked straight through to a small waiting room where three doctors examine me, ask pertinent questions and send me straight to x-ray.

I have two broken ribs in the upper part of my chest and a punctured lung which has started to collapse. I'm to be admitted, oxygenated and fitted with a drain directly into my lung to remove the fluid. I say I want to go home; I don't want to be in hospital. I don't want them to stab my poor broken post-chemo veins in an attempt to take blood and I certainly don't want a tube fitted through my ribs directly into my lung. It's my birthday and this can't be happening. Except it is, and my poor husband is at the end of his tether, and I'm trapped into a hospital stay.

He leaves for home with a list of necessities as I'm wheeled, feeling like a condemned prisoner into critical care for observation.

Through painful sobs, I beg the nurse for the empty bed by the window. She wheels me over and leaves me to cry it out.

I'm fitted with an oxygen mask, blood is taken, and I'm handed a menu card.

Opposite, a nurse is hastily feeding a frail elderly wraith a cheese and pickle sandwich. "What dear? Can't eat anymore? Okay, we'll take it away." She hasn't taken a bite; I don't even expect she can bite.

Any sympathy is short-lived as she proceeds to pee and poo in her bed for the next twenty-four hours. At one point in the night, I think she's so still she's died, and then comes the noise. How can such a frail person fart so incredibly loudly? The Care Home must be enjoying their respite.

My friend, Julie, comes marching down through the ward, every inch of her a nurse in recognisable surroundings. "I'm sure if you didn't want to have sex, you only had to tell him."

"Don't make me laugh" I snuffle through oxygen masked words.

We both have a fit of giggles which turn into a bout of tears, and she takes my hand and holds it tight in hers.

Julie leaves, Mark arrives, doctors visit and prod and poke, nurses check charts, and I continue breathing. In. Out. It's all I can do besides cry.

Tears slowly subside. I sit watching the fading light through my saviour-window and try to grapple with reality. Accompanied by the slow rhythm of the oxygen pump, I fall into fitful sleep.

At unearthly o'clock I'm sharply awakened by an energetic young doctor and his cohort, explaining that I'm using the wrong oxygen mask. Or trying to explain, but my brain can't comprehend. "I've recently read a P A P E R" he loudly whispers for the third time "This is NOT the BEST-CHOICE mask for a collapsed lung, it can cause MORE DAMAGE!"

His cohort looks suitably impressed by both his knowledge and his ability to whisper so loudly, and with much fumbling and total lack of any bedside manner, they swap my mask for a different style, re-hook the oxygen supply and chatting to each other about a tea and toast break leave me without neither a backward glance nor word.

A woman is brought into the bed next to me. She has severe stomach pain from suspected gall stones. She screams into her pillow until the morphine kicks in, and then she snores like a banshee and vomits at equal decibel levels.

Disturbed from their sleep, the obese diabetic lady in the next bed asks the nurse for a mug of hot chocolate to accompany her KitKat, and opposite her, an obviously dying soul re-counts her bed sores.

A stroke victim is the next nighttime arrival, her head swathed in towels as her eyes try to avoid the glare of hospital light and crying with frustration as her withered arm and leg are declared immovable despite her most heroic effort. She can't comprehend why or where or even whom. "Do you know where you are, dear?"

"In my chair"

Awake again at 6 a.m. The HCA tidies my bed and delivers a cuppa. She tells me about her uncle who got kicked in the spleen by a horse and died a very painful death. I thank her for that information, but the words stay in my mouth. Maybe the oxygen mask serves a higher purpose?

At 9 o'clock sharp, The Consultant arrives in his expensive suit, exquisite Italian leather loafers, open white coat and casually slung stethoscope (the devil is in the detail). Surrounded by a gaggle of junior doctors, the eldest of whom appears to be twelve. He demands silence from the group, introduces himself, places half-moon glasses on his nose and reads my chart. Questions are directed to the group first and I assume my place as a supporting extra. The Lead Diva role is clearly his.

"Lung drain," he declares.

"No, thank you," I reply.

He slowly removes his glasses, curiosity definitely ignited by having a patient disagree with his expert diagnosis. "??" the expression says words are not needed.

"Well, from seeing the x-rays, the puncture is at the top of the lung. It's lasted this last week without deflating so it must be healing up and wearing the correct oxygen mask has done its re-inflation task. Surely, fitting a drain would introduce a site of possible infection into my already weakened immune system (play the Cancer Card, play the Cancer Card) besides being incredibly painful?"

The gaggle stand open mouthed. I sense one of them wants to take a photo for posterity.

The consultant shakes his head, then nods it, then looks at me quizzically. "Right you are then."

Discharged. Come back day after tomorrow for another x-ray." He turns on his expensive heels, summons the dumbstruck flock and strides from the ward.

I stare out of the window to the sky, silently mouthing eternally grateful thanks for my salvation. At three o'clock in the afternoon my discharge papers are completed, I vacate my bed and head for home.

31 SCANS, BIOPSIES AND ONCOLOGY APPOINTMENTS

January 2013

From the Radionics Practitioner:

"Hi Elaine, Now that comment about Spring cleaning opened a flood gate on the treatment front!

Here is a list of things to think about or look up if you wish:

Detoxify the spleen chakra, crown chakra, and mental body.

Bach flower remedies Crab Apple and Gorse.

The colour pale green.

A crystal Rutilated Quartz onto the thymus.

The symbol for Aries, like a pair of horns with a downward v between, representing the Fire element and indicating a lack of fire.

To help bring in and balance the Fire element, a Bailey Flower Essence 'Heath Bedstraw.'"

Yesterday afternoon I had a definite shift of mood. I felt a smile start deep in my body and radiate through, and while my lot is far from ideal, I don't feel unhappy.

I feel I'm out of the mire, still on soggy ground but way

ahead I can see firm terrain and even though there's still a bit of a plod to be done, I know I can head towards firmer footing and get my bearings. With the snow thaw has come my thaw which got me thinking that we count the snow as disruption to life whereas snow is life, and we should learn to fit the minutiae around it. Perhaps in the same vein I could think my wobble is life, not a disruption.

Think with a simple mind and try not to hold on to anything from the past that you don't need anymore. Is that the message?

February 7, 2013
Cetalopram Working

Things continue steadily; the Cetalopram's taken effect and it's rather like looking at life from behind glass doors—I feel like perhaps I didn't need it after all, but then that's probably because it's working.

The doctor has said I need to go on to statins because of the high cholesterol. He explained that "it won't make any difference if I spend the rest of my life eating rabbit food," it's so high because of the anti-cancer meds destroying protective oestrogen and the only way to lower it is with more medication. Other people take all these pills so why should I be so reticent?

June 13, 2013

Feel very well and happy with lots of nice things happening.

We had a trip to USA at the beginning of May which was both interesting and tiring but I don't feel quite over it yet.

I've booked a new larger venue to hold my Vintage Fair in October which is exciting, and I have my vision of how it will be, so working towards that.

Bruce and I are getting along great guns and working with visualising energies which he loves.

Since I took off my armoured coating, I feel so well supported by people and nature.

Penny, who runs the mindfulness meditation course, asked me to help at her sessions as a meet & greet and extra pair of eyes/hands which I feel very honoured to do. I've been doing a little healing on the horses (and Mark) and am overwhelmed by the response. Not really proper Reiki, just my way.

November 4, 2013
Off Cetalopram

We had a tree come down bringing our electricity and phone cables with it and were without both for 60 hours. . .it was rather pleasant lighting with oil lamps and the Rayburn kept us snug and well fed. It's amazing how much you get done in a day with limited daylight hours and no internet!

I've stopped the Citalopram. It's there again if I need it. Right now, I'd like to see if this veil lifts and I feel a little more me/a bit less the result of a medication. I've been having a little anxiety in the night, feeling trepidatious about the quiet times. I do my breathing and don't try to deny that there are quiet times, there just are. It's interesting this recurring bugbear, I'm working on getting to the bottom of it.

Otherwise, I feel fabulous. Still tired a lot, but tired, not exhausted. My knees are rather stiff after riding last week, which is new. I'm having a lesson with Kirsty tomorrow and we're going to explore doing less, being softer. Dear Bruce receives it all with interest!

Gifts are given but unless they are recognised and acknowledged, karma is not cleared. Look out for the colours lavender and purple, these are the colours of the spirit. Often, though not necessarily, spirit guides are seen to wear these colours when they first appear to you.

February 28, 2014

You know what it's like when you drop a pack of playing cards and they scattered randomly all over the floor. . .well, each morning when I wake up I feel a bit better and a bit better, like I'm being gathered up and put back into place in a neat stack, like I'm supposed to be.

June 15, 2014
Come Off Anti Cancer Meds

I'm feeling a little overwhelmed by all I have to do, which is ridiculous seeing as I'm the person in charge of allocating the doing.

I'm struggling a bit because I think I've made the decision to come off my anti-cancer medications. I just can't get away from the feeling that taking it is wrong for me. I don't know whether it's the Aromasin that feels wrong, or the hi-dose vitamin D/calcium that supports it. I've talked to the oncologist who recommends taking it for at least another 2 years, so we've agreed that I'll come off it for one month and see how I feel.

It's a hefty decision.

July 28, 2014
Radionic Treatment

From the Radionics Practitioner:

"Working with you just now, I feel that you have lost a little of your direction or purpose in life which will make you feel anxious and a bit confused. It is possible that you have reached some sort of crossroads and are undecided which path to take."

"If you feel this is so, my treatments to you today will be helping, but I also ask you to go into your meditation and ask to be guided. Don't expect the answer to come very quickly. Try to go with the flow on this and prepare the soil to receive the message by being flexible. Be quiet and observe because I think there is a new goal for you to work towards which is part of your life plan."

It's the anxiety that's really surprised me like someone has switched the Anxious ON switch and here it is back again gaining momentum. I've started thinking I should go back on the dreaded Cetalopram? What is it with me?!

A lovely thing happened on Saturday afternoon. In broad sunny daylight, a barn owl landed on the garden fence post and stayed around for nearly an hour, hunting and sitting on the tree while Mark photographed him. Sitting on the fence by the road, he nearly caused a pile-up as cars slowed to look at him. So lovely to see.

I've been getting too affected by other people's stresses and problems, can't seem to brush them off.

I've been getting angry. I see that it's flight translated into words because they're always angry-and-rushing-off phrases. I've been making tons of stupid mistakes which is down to poor focus.

So, I think the counsellor will help clear some of the undergrowth; I have a lot to work on, and I see it all. It's very good to be so supported.

Try to remember that we are a soul with a body, not the other way round a body with a soul. The body is a bunch of chemicals, some of which we can control, and some have minds of their own as far as I can tell. So, when in a state of anxiety, think okay, I don't much like this, but it will pass.

I just wish I could find the enthusiastic me and have her come back again.

September 16, 2014
Hiatus Hernia Scan
Chiropractor Appointment

The gastroscopy yesterday showed I have a hiatus hernia. I'm not sure how it got there but now it's been found out it can jolly well go away.

It's been a bit of a week here, lack of sleep, no appetite, feeling pretty worn out. I made a lovely pot of chicken and barley broth so have been having as much of that as possible.

I wanted to move Bruce to a new yard, made my decision, but then Sheel's other livery had to be put down, so don't feel I can add to her burden at present. . .perhaps it's just not meant to be at the moment.

Off to the chiropractor in a moment, really hoping he can loosen all this tension but a little concerned lest lots of emotion might come out with it. . .still, better out though!

Chewing almonds is said to be good for acid reflux.

Yesterday, I felt like I had blossomed. Just that. That I'd come out of being that tight bud, afraid to open.

Towards the End

It's been an eventful journey and I feel I've arrived at the outskirts of where I was heading.

November 2014

There's a tiny, grisly lump on my neck just above my collarbone, which I wiggle back and forth in a vain hope that it will simply disappear. I'm still wiggling a week later. A week after that I make an appointment to see The Consultant.

She also wiggles, checks my other hotspots and declares "it's very, very small, and I don't think it's anything to worry about. Keep an eye on it and come back if it gets bigger."

Because I so very much want to believe her, I do. And that is my downfall.

I show the lump to my GP. He says it doesn't look/feel ominous, but to monitor it.

Monday July 27, 2015

It grew bigger. The Consultant organises scans biopsies and oncology appointments in a flurry of hindsight haste. The person who has used so much skill over the past years to save my life has now been the tool of my downfall. The irony is inescapable.

Tuesday July 28, 2015

I'm lying on a bed in the ultrasound room peering at the radiologist standing by my shoulder. Guided by the images on the screen he's taken biopsies from my neck via a long needle within a sealed box, which clacked as it bit the sample.

This is a very odd time; I feel split in two beings.

Person one is me as I feel I really am: kind, hopeful, happy, enthusiastic, practical.

Since the start of December, this other person flits in who's anxious and jagged. She feels isolated and weary; physically depressed rather than mentally so. We both work on being mindful and accepting all things will pass but while I'm doing most of the work, the other one is overstaying her welcome!

I have a doc appointment tomorrow re liver function tests, the results may shed light on this imbalance but I'm thinking maybe I need to go back on Cetalopram, maybe I'm just an anxious person who's having trouble coping- with what I don't know.

Physically I feel good but have this whirl of isolation and flutteriness going around my mind; it's as if I want to receive a lot of "there-there-ing," if you know what I mean!

"You're right to be uncertain Elaine, you probably can't do this again." -Cancer

Monday 10 August 2015

The desk is not the only obstacle between The Consultant and me.

I cannot understand how she did not act immediately seeing a lump in one of the most common places for breast cancer to spread on a woman who has had the disease five times previously. But she did, and now it's all down to Damage Limitation.

"Localised Spread. . .the cancer has spread but remains close to the original site."

I ask that she completely clears my axilla with surgery and tries to reach and remove the neck tumour from within. If it ain't there anymore it can't cause any more trouble.

She falters, "The aim of surgery is to alleviate pain or cure disease. . .it's not causing pain and we cannot now cure this disease (panic: is she just thinking aloud??) With such a radical axilla clearance there's an extremely high chance of causing severe lymphodeama and reducing your quality of life through impaired movement."

"I want as much removed as possible and your skill lies in doing that to the very best effect. My skill lies in making the very best I can out of life with what you leave me. It's impossible for you to put me back to how I was before, so I make the most of what remains. I've not had lymphoedema yet so I can't see why it should suddenly start now."

Surgery is booked for Wednesday with a stay overnight in hospital. Radiotherapy marking-out is scheduled for the following week.

32 RIDING THROUGH

We all arrive at fear with real and imaginary experiences that are as unique to us as our DNA.

Unlike any other marathon, fear has no common starting place, no midway point of motivation, and no perceivable end, but if we can gain succour from refreshments offered along the way, we can survive. If we can hear the shouts of encouragement through the deafening cacophony of self-doubt, we have hope. Moreover, if we can accept that our personal best is simply putting one foot in front of the other, we'll stay the distance, and the absence of a finishing line will become irrelevant.

What are your greatest fears? Mine are incapacitating illness, living without Mark, and I'm fearful when riding my horse. I have not listed them in order of greatness. Life without Mark is self-explanatory. Being incapacitated means I don't want to helplessly linger on the edge of death; I want to say a quick "Goodbye," grab my coat, and leave while you still have something bad to say about me.

My most closely guarded secret is that I'm a fearful rider; I could never say riding frightens me, so is there a difference between feeling fearful and frightened, and where do these feelings originate?

I love my horse with all my heart, I love riding, and the joy it brings is like nothing else in the world. Yet every time I climb into the saddle, all pleasure is obliterated by the voice of fear screaming relentlessly in my head. It tells me I have just signed my own death warrant. Like a spit roast over an open fire, my fear rotates continually, basted by terror and dread. The juices are so intensely flavoured I can taste them dripping down the back of my throat.

So, what do we do with fear? I can't predict what fate has in store for Mark, any more than I can arrange my demise as a speedy episode between breakfast and lunch. However, there's surely a way to restore the equilibrium of riding my horse.

The fear has been with me for many years; I just chose to ignore it. Ignorance was bliss, but it wasn't constructive. Mind and muscle memories have replayed past events so many times in a vain effort to warn me of the peril that what started as a faint speck of anxiety has become an overwhelming stain of panic.

When I mount my horse, I breathe deeply, and focus mindfully on my actions. I smile as my body lightly greets the saddle, and sigh like a granny settling into her favourite chair. I thank my horse, check my girth, wriggle my toes, shrug my shoulders and thank my horse again. All is good.

Lightly and politely, I ask my horse to move off. Bruce responds (as always) with a quick snatch of the reins and a wobbly hind step as his dodgy hip adjusts to my weight. We both breathe through his momentary anxiety, and I thank him again for his compliance, and for being him. We walk down the track to the arena, his steps are guarded as unshod hooves tread on stones, and he re-sets his balance to negotiate downhill with a slanting camber. We've done this hundreds of times, and don't deviate from his favoured route, arriving at the arena in the correct place to neatly open the gate, enter and shut it behind us with well-executed sidesteps and turns.

We begin our swinging, relaxed walk up the long side of the school towards the top, and as Bruce raises his head and pricks his ears to better see the horse grazing beyond, I feel my hands tighten, my face reddens, and I'm like a stuck pig in a slaughterhouse, with the blood of fear oozing from every orifice. I have a lucid moment of trying to regain composure before the panic in my gut rises to meet the panic descending from my eyeballs.

I start to sing aloud, and Bruce's ears flick back to me, as the familiar words of 'Ten Green Bottles' follow him around the school perimeter. He walks mechanically forward as if I wasn't there (which I'm not), and I try to let his solid body soothe me. My panic swirls around before joining forces with a heartbeat that's faster than speeding time. It's a gamble whether I'll implode or explode, and I grit my teeth, awaiting the outcome.

"Breathe…breathe…green bottles…" I gasp "hanging on the wall…" Gasp. "Breathe…breathe…green bottles…" gasp "should accidentally fall…" two gasps and an out breath "and there'll be nine green bottles" out-breath "hanging on the frigging wall."

Throughout all this, I smile and pretend. My stoic horse rubs his nose on his knee and pretends; the critical fault-pickers who watch surreptitiously would never know how much each ride costs. When I've put myself through enough penury to prove we're both 'ticking over nicely', we halt squarely to dismount, and as my leaden legs reach terra firma, the frustration of my feeble fear kills me slowly once again. I can't even manage a walk around the arena. It's been a year since we ventured out of the farm on horseback, and two years since we trotted. Once I'm standing on the ground, Bruce shakes himself from head to toe, ridding his body of my burden, and rests his nose on my shoulder; he knows a placatory peppermint will follow the litany of apologies.

Where did this fear begin? In the beginning is the only answer. Countless horses over countless years have done things that scared me, but I always coped with whatever they did. Bruce added his substantial weight to the fear load; from the start, he had an unpredictable streak that belied his steadfast appearance, and when he accelerated from fright to flight quicker than I could anticipate, it took a chunk of courage to sit still. When I recall the events without emotion, I clearly see I coped competently, if not entirely effectively, but fearful feelings cloud logic. I'm not frightened of the horse; I've managed the worst he might do. What frightens me is the feeling of fear.

My confidence waxes and wanes with the stages of my treatments, but I recognise the real Me differs from the chemotherapy-induced wraith, who wouldn't dare put foot in a stirrup. I no longer have anything to prove, least of all to myself and in a skewed way, fear reminds me I'm still alive. Perhaps it's time to accept that fear is as much a part of riding as limbs aching the next day?

My fear is mine, and I'm grateful for the reminder not to do something dangerous, but like an auto-immune condition, fear doesn't know how to stop. So, is the answer to work on its responsiveness and not its potency? A stronger bit is never the answer for a horse, but perhaps walk-halt-walk transitions would work, direction not correction? Partnering Bruce began when I learnt to sit still, breathe and trust, instead of trying to control with dominance as simple as it was difficult. Could fear be diluted by guiding it to a place of acceptance, rather than obliteration?

Today I've shared my secret, aired my fear, and I feel lighter. Life is a work in progress, and perhaps by keeping our enemies closer than our friends, we can choose when we visit them, instead of having them hammer on our door demanding entry. My horse, my ride, my fear. My choice.

PART FOUR

SEE ME

The layered scars,
bestowed along years of treatment
would tell their own story
if only I could let them.
But the cutting removing
re-arranging and healing
are neither sights nor tales
for the faint of heart,
and my cancer is not yet public property.
I don't want your sorrow.
Don't wear pink for me
and run marathons in my name
because my life, (what's left of it)
is not yours to pity.
I'm the same bitch I've always been,
I still laugh at misfortune and
swear freely without shame.
Cynicism sharpened by poison.
See me
before you see the cancer.
See the curly hair even when I'm bald
and the smile flying at half mast.
See the mismatched-on-purpose clothes
and the defiance
lingering behind my eyes.
See the terror, the pain and the loneliness

separating terminal
from curable.
Rest with me in my silences.
See me pleading for time that you take for granted
but see me first.
I am not your drama
you cannot steal me.
I am not a crutch enabling your betterment
and I have no silver lining.
I'm the bad news you wish you hadn't met,
sent to spoil your healthy day
but in my way, I'm happy.
I see joy where you cannot.
Love, birdsong, friendships, kindness
are spread so thickly on my slice of life
that I grow fatter each day
in the moment of every mouthful.
And the best? I save that for dessert.
I am not yet dead

33 SCANS AND MORE SCANS

2016-2018

For the past two years, I've had a CT scan every twelve weeks to monitor the cancer's progress. I joke that I'll die of radiation poisoning before I die of cancer, and one year when the tumours were in retreat, the radiographer took the threat seriously. Then the tumour cavalry appeared on the horizon and the cancer advanced again, so we stayed at twelve weeks and watched the skirmish unfold.

The scan itself is no longer arduous and I don't feel 'invaded' like I once did. I trust the radiography team. I've made friends with the machines and drinking a lot of water thirty minutes before the scan is uncomfortable, but easily remedied afterwards. Having dye injected that makes you feel like you've peed yourself is sadly something I've gotten used to; I've even stopped worrying if I really have.

The scan report goes to the oncologist, and then to the cancer team for discussion. The radiographer's expression is always professionally deadpan. The only time his mask slipped was when two huge embolisms showed in my lung, and he called a nurse to escort me to the hospital ward for emergency clot-busting drugs. I had no idea they were there, no symptoms, and they frightened me more than the cancer. Those things can kill you.

Waiting a week for scan results is difficult and something I have given up trying to master. Cancer causes worry no matter how many 'positive' quotes tell you otherwise. I know I can't change the course of events but that doesn't stop me hoping I won't be more incurable than I was before. The only balm brought by familiarity is not needing to face the music until it starts to play; I'm well until they tell me otherwise, and this might be my last week of being well. If you think that's a crazy thing to hang on to, then welcome to my world.

Results Morning dawns with a feeling of impending doom. The oncologist will phone at noon. Keep busy keep busy! Drinking too many cups of tea too quickly gives the equivalent of a coffee buzz, and in a blitz of activity, the house gets dusted and swept, the toilets bleached, cutlery drawer tidied, and ten things listed on eBay. Applying lipstick makes me feel more in control (why?) but then I chew my lip and it all comes off. I look at the clock, check the phone to make sure it is working and do the newspaper crossword, then the Sudoku puzzle, then abandon Sudoku and start on the word search. Check the clock again, check the phone again, and start prepping dinner. In the middle of trying to stop cheese sauce sticking to the bottom of the pan, the phone rings. With arms outstretched, twixt pan and landline, I answer with my best, nonchalant telephone voice.

"Hello."

"Hello Elaine" says the oncologist "how are you?

"Umm, you have my scan results, so you tell me?" I reply, and then, thinking that sounded a bit rude I add, "How are you?"

The oncologist knows me well enough not to waste precious seconds on small talk (that'll come afterwards) and he quickly translates the scan results.

"All is well."

I imagine him leaning slightly forward in his chair to see the laptop screen better, one manicured hand resting on his chino trouser leg while the other steadies against the edge of the desk. And I breathe out.

"There are no new tumours, the lesion on your liver hasn't changed, and the only remarkable note is the stomach lymph nodes are continuing to get larger."

"How much larger" I ask anxiously.

He gives me millimetre sizes, and sensing my lack of com-prehension, compares millimetres to vegetables so I have a better idea of my stomach node sizes. They were peas and now they are radishes. We discuss many things in foodie terms and the pea-to-radish ratio makes sense to me; the oncologist and I bonded over a shared interest in what we eat. We agree to con-tinue with my current tablet treatment rather than returning to the higher infection risk of chemotherapy, continue to monitor the nodes, which are impossible to biopsy, and speak again in a few weeks.

The scan showed things are no better and not a lot worse, which these days we call 'good'. So, if all is good, why am I not happy? I should be waving flags, phoning everyone and pop-ping champagne corks! But I'm not doing that because where my health is concerned, good means precarious, and it also means bad is simply postponed. I'm not being pessimistic, I'm being realistic, if a tad gloomy. For some stupid reason I expect the scan to show improvement, as if someone has worked out a way to cure incurable. It won't sink into my thick head that no progress is as good as it will ever get, that not being any worse is the best-case scenario. I am not grateful enough, and I probably never will be. I am angry. I am angry I have cancer.

Full of anger, I get in the car and make the short drive up to Bruce. The frothy white swathes of cow parsley swaying in the grass verges, the hawthorn blossom, the deep pink wild cam-pion flowers don't soothe me like they did yesterday. I drive past the swans on the river, viewing it all without actually noticing any of it, hands gripping the steering wheel until my knuckles turn white.

At the stables, I get out of the car, pick up Bruce's halter from the tackroom and stomp down to the field where he's nibbling the remains of today's strip-grazed grass ration. He looks at me sideways, lowers his head and walks over, fat belly swaying like a galleon in full sail. I offer the halter and he drops his nose, not into the noseband but on to my cheek. He breathes, sighs, and as I lean into his sweet grass breath, he caresses my skin with his whiskers. I close my eyes and we stand, nose to cheek in the afternoon sunshine, not knowing which is horse breath and which is human. Then, without warning, a huge slippery wet tongue comes out from between his soft pink lips and in one long sweep, he licks from my neck to my hairline. I open my eyes and see him looking down at me, his deep, honest eyes slightly cloudy with senior cataracts but still twinkling with incorrigible Irish humour. And I love him. And I love life. Again.

[Elaine discontinued Chemotherapy and began Targeted Therapy under Professor Tutt in London in 2019. -Ed.]

34 COLIC.

Mark and I were getting on each other's nerves. Not a lot, but enough to make snappy, slightly-too-sharp replies. Neither of us are confrontational and we don't argue much, but he thought I was having a go at him, and I thought he was being stubborn. Neither of us wanted to talk about the real issue.

Over the years and through the troubles, we've drifted into a comfortable friend/lover/partner-in-crime combo, built on mutual respect and a huge dose of humour. We've become an Old Married Couple. How that happened I have no idea; two rebels aren't supposed to mellow into Mr & Mrs Boring, but boring we are, and it turns out that eating dinner on a tray in front of the TV (me wearing my pyjamas) isn't such a bad thing after all.

It was time to do something a bit special, so I decided to make a proper roast beef dinner with Yorkshire puddings, onion gravy, and all the delicious trimmings. On Saturday night our oil-fired Rayburn range was due to be turned out for its summer holiday. The continuous heat is necessary in the cold, but too stifling for warmer weather. It would be the last opportunity before we swap to hob and microwave cooking, and Mark's eyes lit up at the plan. We decided to dress for dinner. There might even be a glass of champagne. Time to re-claim a bit of 'us'.

Spring grass is Bruce's nemesis. He eats too much too quickly without a pause. Spring grass is unforgiving, and he gets colic. If I strip graze him, he will limbo-dance under the electric fence to reach the grass, and if I graze him in a bare paddock, he jumps out. Over the years I've tried pretty much all the preventives . . . but he still gets colic, especially if it rains. I've become attuned to his behaviour, spot warning signs early, and he responds well to a couple of homeopathic treatments and a sachet of painkiller. We do our deep breathing together, a little Reiki (from a distance if he wants to be alone) and if he's still bad, the vet comes with IV pain relief and cramp-relieving Buscopan. It's comforting to have a plan.

On Saturday evening, the colic arrived. After a long dry spell, we'd had light rain mid-week, I didn't think it was enough to make a difference, but it must've given the grass a growth spurt. Having done dinner prep and put the pot-roast in the oven, I drove to the stables to bring Bruce in, give him a quick groom, and be back home in time for a fragrant shower. I'd even painted my nails! Bruce was listless and kept resting his forehead against my chest, a sure sign he needed me to know something. He had a lot of gassy wind, but ate his bucket feed with customary greed, so I gave him the homeopathic pills as a safeguard, and phoned Mark to say I was going to stay for an hour. Mark was in the bath and memorised the veg instructions. If he felt disappointed or annoyed, he hid it well. When I gave Bruce his hay, he pricked his ears and leaned forward for a sniff, then uttered a deep guttural groan and dropped to the ground in front of me. I thought he'd died. He laid, heaving and moaning with his legs stretched rigid as the colic spasmed through his body. It was a fearful sight. I've seen him do it before, but familiarity isn't a shield; his pain looked horrific. I tried to distance my emotion, deal with the practicalities and phone the vet. The receptionist knows his name and my voice, respects my diagnosis that it's an emergency and says Maria will be with us ASAP. Now we just have to wait. I pray to the horse gods to help the colic pass; I don't dare think maybe this one won't. I update Mark; he sounds disappointed and offers to come over. Bless that man.

Bruce is standing again now, breathing hard but not sweating. The cacophony of gut sound is drowned-out by his farts, and I tell him what a good boy he is to expel all that gas. He walks towards me and rests his forehead on my chest, and we stand in silence before I feel him tense with the next wave, and as his legs fold underneath him, he goes down. He doesn't roll, he just braces himself against the cramp, so I see no reason not to let him lay down. I've tried walking him to ease the pain, but it doesn't help. I empty a water bucket, turn it upside down and sit in the corner of his stable. His eye flicks towards me, saying my presence is okay.

This horse. I've had some good horses over the years, but Bruce held the key that unlocked my future. He led me to the changes that unleashed a real, better me and accept what that entailed. And I thought I was saving him. Thinking back to his predecessor, the big, wise Teddy, it seems horses take us on a path and it's our choice whether to listen. Bruce is up again and standing in front of me, nose on my knee. I silently say the words *good boy*.

A few weeks ago, when I was grooming Bruce, I found a cluster of raised lumps around his bottom. They weren't scabby or infected, and my first panicked thought was MELANOMA. I went hot-and-cold; please don't let my boy have anything cancerous. I sent some photos to Kirsty, and her quiet opinion reassured me that they probably weren't melanoma, but even if they were, they would be slow-growing. Has this colic got anything to do with the lumps?

I recall how the seasons affect Bruce more than any horse I've had, or maybe nowadays I just notice these things better. The summer is too hot for his bulky body, and he has a paranoid hatred of flies, so he spends daytime dozing in the shade of his stable and grazes the paddock at night. In winter he detests the rain and despite being insulated with waterproof rugs, shows his grumpiness with impatience and tantrums. He's at his best in the autumn; as the sun cools, his hoofbeats sound less like a plod and more like a happy dance, and vigour refreshes his body. His countenance dips at 'blackberry time' when the fruits ripen and his coat gains a bloom of fuzzy growth, but once he's adjusted to the change, he's back behaving like a youngster and generally forgetting his manners. I'm pleased to see him jolly and know manners will only momentarily have slipped his mind. I'm in awe of this horse with his gleaming coat, and ready aptitude to have a go at whatever task I suggest, be it my madcap idea of walking into his stable backwards to improve his core stability or being solid enough to nanny a nervous horse through traffic in the village.

And now he lays like a beached whale. I owe him such a debt, but I can't help him through this pain. I watch his breath rise and fall and wonder how he got old? How we both got old. Whispers of grey hair have gathered around his eyes and muzzle, and his unshod hooves have spread to counteract the uneven placement of his back legs. We've stopped and restarted so many times over the years. His life must be like Groundhog Day, but he always shows the same enthusiasm for work, the same stoicism. He wears his Elder Statesman countenance like a medal.

Twenty minutes later, Maria arrives and sets the routine into action. She checks his heart rate, gut noises and temperature before administering the drugs. He flinches to register discomfort. I tell him what a good boy he is, and Maria strokes his neck before performing a rectal exam. The drugs start to kick-in, and he stands quietly while she reaches inside. No tumours, no impacted blockage. We both allow ourselves a small smile. He once needed hydration fluids pumped through a tube in his nose, it was touch-and-go, and I don't want that again. We chat about something; I have no idea what, until Maria is happy the drugs have worked. When he relaxes sufficiently to doze, she packs her equipment and leaves. I stay awhile, watching him carefully and then go home for dinner.

Mark has 'rescued' the beef too early, and it is tough. The potatoes are bullets and the Yorkshire puddings doughy, but he saved the veg and the gravy is tasty. We eat on trays in front of the TV and the champagne stays in the fridge. I grab a chocolate bar and eat it on the way back to the stable. Bruce is waiting at the door asking for his hay and his heavily lidded eyes are brighter. I'm relieved, but that night I don't sleep very well. Next morning he's still drowsy, the stable is full of poop and his gut is quiet. We both agree the best medicine is turnout in his paddock. Later that day he's as bright as a button, and when I tie him outside his stable, a steady stream of stableyard visitors arrive to ask after his health. News travels fast.

He greets them gregariously, with all the grace of an old pro. "Oh, I'm much better, thank you for asking. It was very painful, but nothing for an old hand like me. Now, have you brought me any get-well gifts? Fruit? No? Oh well, move along then please, the next in line may have food . . ."

Everyone loves Bruce. Most of all, me. That night we have cold beef, new potatoes and pickled red cabbage. We open the champagne. I sleep better. And we've stopped annoying each other. Just like the colic, whatever caused the blockage has cleared.

35 FUCK THE RAINBOW BRIDGE

"The horses at Rainbow Bridge play together in the sunshine until each of their owners comes to claim them, as the owners themselves pass away. The souls of horses and their owners finally reunite and cling together in joyous reunion, never to be parted again."

To take responsibility for ending your own life is tough, but if it's the wrong decision, you only have yourself to blame. To end someone else's life with or without their agreement is illegal, although Death Row and warfare continue. But to snuff out the soft breath of one so dear that the mere thought of it leaves you feeling like you've been eviscerated with a blunt fingernail, is the task we horse carers accept each time four hooves and a velvety nose nuzzle their way into our hearts.

It is our job to order destruction of the life that lives above those hooves, and forever close the eyes of the soul we have worked so hard to keep safe. There will be no more silken coat to groom, no more smell in which to bury our face, and we will never again see the blink of trust that passes between two opposing species. When we nod our head to signal the felling of the body beside us, the world instantly changes. Is becomes was, and wisps of memory are the bittersweet legacy of love.

"I'm…So…Sorry" are the three words you never want your vet to say, because "There's Nothing Else We Can Do" completes the sentence. It's not a life sentence, it's a death sentence. You nod, and as you mime an answer, trying to swallow rising bile, find a spare breath, and fight against the urge to run away, three huge tears plop out of your eyes and your horse turns to look at you. The vet stands back until you win your fight for air, and when you can agree coherently, she brings you the death warrant to sign and you can't write your own name. We have the idea that living creatures deserve a good death, but many didn't even get a good life. You can only do the best you can do and there's a whole future ahead to beat yourself up with what-ifs. Doing the best by your horse is a commitment to love even when sparing him pain means sacrificing his life.

Death and sex (which ironically started the dying process the moment it gave life) are very similar. In reality neither actually resemble the misty-hued scenes depicted in the movies, but they do both leave you feeling totally exhausted, or disconsolate because the end came too soon. From Here to Eternity has the right title, but in death the waves only ebb and the tide never returns to the shore.

Euthanising a horse is not a pretty sight. Don't let the Rainbow Bridge fool you for a minute, because horses don't really metamorphose into a unicorn and trot across the coloured arch to heaven. I've stood with enough horses as they received anaesthetic overdose or bolt gun to know they all die as individually as they lived. Some struggle with surprise or fight to stay alive, some are thankful to go and some hardly notice. The sight that is unreal, and the one that I can never un-see is half a ton of horseflesh laid dead with its tongue lolling to one side. If you need to sob into a still-warm neck before your own heart breaks, brace yourself against the sight of a corpse because this is your last opportunity. You've held it together this long, and the vet will busy herself checking his pulse and heart even though you all know he's dead. Touch his body, smooth his coat and stroke his ears. Whisper the prayer or the thankyou or tell him he's a good boy because part of him might still be watching you, just like he always watched from the gate until you were out of sight.

He's free at last. This magical creature had such a strong will to survive evolution. He paid for domesticity with his freedom, his ability to roam in a herd, and his fundamental right to just be a horse. He buried his wants, forgave constantly and learned to work through pain. He served people as best he could, if he was lucky, he got his own girl and when she heaped the worries of her world on him; he carried them as stoically as he carried her. Mankind wanted a horse that suited their needs, not his, and the horse has made all the compromises. It's not wrong to want something back from our horses, but don't assume because you pay the bills and make the decisions, you own them.

We want a partnership but how many people communicate with their horse in his language? If you scratched his withers in a one-sided attempt at mutual grooming it's a start, but then you put him back in his solitary paddock. Horses acquiesce and dominate and find safety in the herd pecking order, but we humanise their reactions and 'protect' them with fences. We leave a flight animal to watch 24/7 for imaginary predators instead of having a herd leader to do it for them, and then wonder why they get anxiety, or fat because they aren't moving with interaction.

Connect with your horse in his language while he's still alive. Lower your eyes, lower your expectations, empty your mind and take the opportunity to just be with him, breathe with him and be quiet. Give him a holiday from your constant chatter, verbal and mental. Knowing that you've tried to meet him halfway will mean more to him than all the treats and titbits, and when the end comes, he'll know you know that the weakest has to leave the herd and he'll trust you to be the swiftest predator.

"The horses at Rainbow Bridge play together in the sunshine until each of their owners comes to claim them, as the owners themselves pass away. The souls of horses and their owners finally reunite and cling together in joyous reunion, never to be parted again."

Don't make Bruce wait for me, he's done his time with people clinging to him and claiming him. His soul is his, not mine.

Just as he lived, he died with a force that shouted, "That's it, I'm off," but this time I bailed out and let him run because there was no reason for him to stop. I might have paid the bills and taken responsibility, but I never owned one single hair on his body. How can anyone own magnificence?

36 TRUST

Do you ever wonder if penguins stand around laughing while one of them pretends to walk like a person? The thought hadn't crossed my mind either until I tried (in vain) to distract myself this week from real life, and real feelings.

Meditation has been too scary because I don't want to be alone in my head. Going for a walk seems pointless without a destination, and although people irritate me like never before, I've leant on shoulders from four corners of the world and sighed as friends caressed me with words, hugs, cups of tea and compassionate silence. And goats. Mark has shown a depth of love I'm incapable of reciprocating, and as each shard of my grief bought another ticket and re-joined the queue, I felt it say to Mark: "When she goes, you'll feel like this too." Just as money goes to money, death highlights death.

Kirsty's goats deserve more than a passing mention because goat solidarity is very solid. Lupin, whose mother was the sagacious Libby, has inherited her mother's serenity and happily shared what she could spare. Kokomo the kid bounced about demonstrating life with a carefree heart, and Honeybee the movie star, who views the world as only a diva can, stood quietly offering no opinion, just support. The other herd members cudded thoughtfully, radiating constancy. Thank you, goats.

It seems I'm the only person surprised at how shaken I am. Astra, Barley, Paddy, Barney, Will-Be and Teddy lamely answer "Gone" when their names appear on my own euthanised roll-call, and I thought their numbers would numb the blow when it came to Bruce. I've stood with others as they died, some I knew, and some I only met just before the ceremony like an ironic arranged marriage, and while no death is easy I stood firm. This time, I can feel my bedrock crumbling.

For the past few years, it's been a toss-up whether Bruce died first or I did, and statistically it should've been me. In the eleven years we were together I had three cancer recurrences in the first seven years and have been 'incurable' for the past four. Bruce preferred me to stay in the present moment, so morbid thoughts became black jokes, and the future wasn't a place we explored. With his death, a significant part of my world closed (I'm the mistress of re-invention so don't start muttering about one door closes blah blah) which deserves some grieving of its own. My life keeps shrinking. I feel like I'm being funnelled into a concentration to discover my essence, and I'm a tad concerned what happens when the distillation is complete. Physically I'm incapable of doing what I did, but mentally I'm still a horse person. I don't want the sheer hard work of keeping another horse, nor the responsibility, but I want the connection and I want to put stuff Bruce taught me back into the world.

Meanwhile, Bruce is gone. His bridle, which I spent too much money having made-to-measure, hangs on its hook but he'll never wear it again. All my horses have worn hand-me-downs and hand-me-ups and I never throw anything away that's repairable. Having a traditional bridle made from best English leather that fitted Bruce's head perfectly was my gift to him. The plain cavesson noseband took three fittings to ascertain the perfect width, and cut-outs on the headpiece meant the base of his broad ears would never pinch. It was a bridle that signified we were working together in a way neither of us had done with another partner, it was a bridle worthy of the horse that wore it.

My health is having a bit of a wobble. I'm desperate to come off my steroid meds, but the low dose hasn't controlled inflammation levels and instead of respite, the rheumatologist has increased the dose. I sought out the best medical practitioners for treatment so I can't complain when pharmaceuticals are their weapon of choice, but by stopping my over-active immune system from behaving like a drama queen, what does that leave me with to fight everything else? For the first time since I began writing, I'm actually feeling sorry for myself.

Not fitting my daily life around Bruce has created a new routine of having time, and maybe time is what I need right now. Time to do nothing, time to just be because there's nowhere left to run. Time to write. Doing nothing, trying less and noticing what happens was my first big Bruce lesson. The concept is as scary as it is compelling, but it was Bruce's parting gift and if there's one single thing he taught me, it was to listen. And to trust what I heard. And to stop feeling sorry for myself because an answer will come.

37 TIN HAT

My life as a lab rat / the guinea pig strikes back.

It occurs to me that I'll never die, that my legacy will live on forever in the form of other people living because of what I've been through.

I'm thinking that to survive nigh on 30 years of cancer is something not necessarily to be proud of in the way you would choose a vocation to dedicate your life to, but certainly to own, and be proud you've made the best of the situation you were given. Now, I have to take care of myself very well because in my new capacity as a research resource, with b-tests better able to determine why I'm still alive, I have to be available to take more drugs and see how the cancer reacts, in order for other people to benefit from my misfortune.

There is so much that I can contribute towards without doing anything more than having cancer and living with it, which of course isn't as simple as it sounds.

There are times when I've felt guilty about the advantages, I have over other cancer patients. In the 1980s my dad urged me to take out 'health insurance' which was a new concept here in National Health Service England. Why would anyone want to pay extra for a service provided for free? Well, because I was a dutiful daughter, and my dad was an insurance agent for the health insurance company, I did as he said. When I left my husband, he cancelled the payments (fair) and the premiums were a chunk of money for me to earn by cleaning other people's houses, but by then I'd had cancer once and I knew I wouldn't get cover cheaper anywhere else. So, I stuck with it. Today the yearly premiums are £4,500 which is still a chunk of money for me to earn.

But, I've had access to treatment the NHS could not fund. And yes, I feel guilty about that but in order to pay the premiums I go without things some other people have. I've also tried to be pro-active in my cancer treatment, and understanding it, have spent hours researching not only treatments but also mental ways to combat my situation, and have made quite dramatic changes to my way of thinking in order be able to live with the disease. Some of the changes weren't easy, and they don't make patches to slap on when you get cravings for your old personality like they do for nicotine withdrawal.

When I found Professor Tutt, I knew he was my man, and he is saving my life. He agreed to take me as a patient because of my history- all those cancer years already under my belt have provided a way of giving me more years of life.

In those same years, Cancer has been battle-damaged and now wears a Tin Hat. He doesn't like this research because it undermines his status. I might have given my consent, but he didn't give his, and his legacy becomes weaker as mine grows stronger. He may well be afraid he'll have no legacy. Tin Hat sat at a table in his underground bunker, pulling out the straggling remains of his hair. From time to time, he leaned forward and banged his forehead hard against the table edge, knocking the WW2 tin helmet further back from his forehead and exposing a mass of matted scabs and dried blood. His eyes were bloodshot, blue and red, his face ingrained with lines of misery.

Tin Hat had grown old alongside me. When we first met, his enthusiasm knew no bounds, and he'd taken on my challenge with the glee of a fast won victory. He thought I would be a walkover, but he had met his doppelganger, he had met one as tenacious as himself.

Tin Hat surveyed the list of drugs in front of him but felt no joy in having overcome, circumvented and schemed his way

through and around them. fluorouracil epirubicin and cyclophosphamide anastrazole carboplatin taxotare Exemestane
tamoxifen letrazole capecitibine Eribulin olaparib. Until Olaparib they were known drugs. Some of them had taken a while,
but the key to unlocking their potency was there if you looked
long enough, and he had all the time in the world to look. Then
a spread occurred which was like wining the jackpot. It wasn't
entirely due to his skills, but it was fortuitous and he thought
it would be plain sailing towards the end. All he had to do was
coast to the finish line and collect his prize. What his prize
actually was, he wasn't certain.

But the young bloods, the upstarts, had taken advantage of
his advancing years and tried to take control after all his years of
diligent work. They wrestled to unbalance him, shouting scare
stories about DNA therapy and targeted medicines that acted in
ways previously unheard. Not only did Tin Hat have to regain
his stature amongst the riffraff, he also had to learn a whole new
way of managing his way.

Tin Hat had to go on-line. He called on colleagues of old, and
they brought their own dripping greyness to his already grey
world. He sought the counsel of epidemics and virus spreaders,
dust-bowl pioneers and poisoners. They plotted and planned
and together; they found the solution to olaparib was to repair
the DNA fault that it targeted. It was a pyrrhic victory because it
weakened Tin Hat's strength and resolve and pulled in so many
favours that he was now at the beck and call of others, while
still fighting his own war. However clever, however tricksy and
however powerful Tin Hat was, the one thing that he had never
stopped to consider was that when he succeeded in killing his
host, he also killed himself. Neither of us would be the winner
and neither of us would collect anything except oblivion.

38 THE ONCOLOGY PROFESSOR

Today I spoke to the oncology Prof on the phone to discuss my latest scan results. The past couple of months have not been good ones. When I started on Olaparib I had an inflammatory flare-up

I love a free offer. But when it's another life-limiting disease I should have read the label before I put it in my shopping basket. Greed will be my downfall.

The new recruit goes under the name Polyarteritis Nordosa. Polyarteritis Nordosa is a rare inflammation of the arteries, caused by a malfunctioning immune system. My immune system was sheltering between a rock and a hard place, killing off stray cancer cells with accurate sniper fire. Now it's come out all guns blazing, shooting at the cancer, the drug that keeps the cancer stable, or anything else in its sights. Imagine *Tombstone* meets *Reservoir Dogs*; apart from Val Kilmer, it ain't a pretty sight.

Polyarteritis Nordosa showed up for duty about a year ago, bringing with it mysterious bruises that wouldn't fade, and fingertip-size red lesions on my legs. It quickly added a random purple pattern to my thighs which looked like crazy-paving, and, just for good measure, a strong dose of swollen aching joints and hit-the-brick-wall-fatigue. If this was cancer's new buddy I hoped the courtship would be brief, but alas, they've become besties.

The London oncology professor diagnosed the problem at first sight, but it took months of different opinions, investigations and skin biopsies to confirm his suspicion. Now he and a wonderful London rheumatology professor are working (gloved) hand-in-hand to stabilise my condition. I was a multi-disciplinary medical case, now I'm a multi-professor medical case.

The inflammatory levels in my blood are ridiculously high. I'm an over-achiever but this is silly even for me. Large doses of steroids reduced the inflammation but caused a major flare-up when I came off them, and now I'm on longer-term low dose steroids. I have a love-hate relationship with steroids, which varies from trying to conquer the world with manic activity, to sleeplessness and mood swings that drive me crazy. Or crazier.

Playing host to two serious diseases isn't a barrel of laughs but it does have its lighter moments. I wonder how/if they consider each other; do they fight to invade my body space or do they divvy-up areas that aren't already diminished and toss a coin? If my waistline is the border, will cancer cells attempt risky crossings in a migrant dinghy to reach my pelvis, and will Polyarteritis Nordosa send an army to my upper torso, like the Romans marching north to crazy-pave Hadrian's Wall?

Last week I had a phone consultation with the rheumatology professor. We both agreed there wasn't much to do at the moment except watch the situation, which I've learnt over the years means they're working on best-guess scenario. I don't have a problem with that. When you go past your expiry date you can't expect instant answers because there aren't any. I never set out to be pioneer woman, in fact I've always thought this heap of shit is pretty much wasted on me because I've got more important things to do, but hey, next person in line gets the benefit of my experiences, and that's the most positive spin I can muster for this situation.

Before we finished the consultation I asked the professor if he was happy to continue overseeing my treatment.

"Yes of course," he replied. "I'm more than happy. I specialize in rare and esoteric diseases, which you have, and I'm very interested in your case."

"I seem to specialize in them too," I replied flippantly, and he laughed out loud; the rheumatologist has a similarly dry sense of humour.

For some reason, between thanking him and scheduling our next appointment, the word esoteric escaped me and I thought he said erotic. Rare and erotic disease.

"What did he say?" asked Mark as I put the phone down.

"I have a rare and erotic disease." I replied, shrugging my shoulders nonchalantly. I quite liked being rare and erotic. For a moment I had visions of turning into a burlesque dancer until I remembered my crazy-paved thighs.

"What did he say?" Texted my friend.

"I have a rare and erotic disease." I texted back.

She replied with **???!!

I feel a tad disloyal towards the cancer. We've been together for so long, how do I explain I'm having a fling with a younger disease? I'm no cougar but Polyarteritis Nordosa sounds more outlandish than stage 4 cancer, and definitely more erotic!

My plan for terminal cancer was neater than this. I'd have some good times, then things would get worse, then worse would become the good times. Eventually, my organs would pack-up and I'd die, and I hadn't calculated on something else elbowing its way in. After all this time, cancer should at least get the credit because having an understudy steal the limelight as the curtain falls would be ironic. I hadn't expected to die of something randomly erotic, but maybe I'd prefer multi-orgasm failure to multi-organ failure? Just sayin'.

In the past month, I've had to increase my steroid meds to a dose I find unacceptable, I feel I'm insulting my body, but I understand keeping the inflammation down is the priority. I develop acute gastritis which PPI inhibitors seem unable to cope with, stop eating because it's easier than the pain of food, and the indigestion brace that locks right around my ribcage stops me sleeping for the few meagre hours that the steroids allow. I want to fart, but it's all trapped inside and when it does erupt, it sure ain't parma violets. Constipation seemed so easy in comparison, where is it all coming from if I'm not eating? Welcome to the nitty-gritty of illness. Many times I consider calling an ambulance because I'm at my wits end, and the only thing that stops me is Mark's stricken face as I mutter through gritted teeth that "I'm okay really, just uncomfortable." I wonder if I'm going to die, and as I pace the kitchen floor at three in the morning, it seems a reasonable option. Bruce went and left me holding his colic.

Today I spoke to the London oncology Prof on the phone to discuss my latest scan results. I'm pretty certain there has been some progression so I'm upset but not surprised when he says the lymph nodes in my aorta have grown in size and multiplied, and the Olapraib targeted treatment has failed and is no longer effective. Mark's sitting next to me, but I don't put the phone on speaker because I want to digest this momentarily before I tell him, I need to grab a grain of control. The steroids have only reduced the inflammation slightly and I'm angry enough to let rip at the Prof.

"I've gotta come off these fucking steroids," I say slowly and forcefully. "They've brought me to my knees. I'm not eating, sleeping or resting. I can't tolerate anything beyond a dry bagel. I've lost too much weight. How in heaven's name am I supposed to keep my immune system working enough to fight cancer when I can't manage the basics? Not only have the steroids not worked, I'm now beyond negative, they've worked against me."

The Prof doesn't point out that without the steroids I may have had kidney failure, nor does he flinch at my tirade. He speaks kindly and explains matter-of-factly about the next line of treatment and gives me time to cry my tears of frustration and release while I listen. Carboplatin Platinum Therapy. It sounds grand but it's chemotherapy by any other name and I last had in combination with Taxotere chemotherapy back in 2011. That was a very pokey combo, and he assures me the platinum therapy alone will be more tolerable. More tolerable than what?

Glumness descends and Mark and I spend the day looking at each other and muttering "You okay?" No, we are not okay. During the night it dawns on me that something had to give. Olaparib had probably helped cause the inflammatory disease and was continually stoking the fires. In order to treat the inflammatory disease, steroids had exacerbated the situation into negative equity. A vicious circle of three powerful drugs fighting each other for supremacy is not a good situation to be hosting, and if I continued, the thing that gave would probably be me. Now the chain was broken. I'd turned a corner and was trying another route. It was still a forward step. My cancer has responded well to chemotherapy even if I haven't, and it would also dampen my immune system enough to stop the inflammation. Yes, it would be difficult in the midst of Covid to stay healthy and virus-free, but when the choice is between a rock and a hard place, you just keep going until the rock gets less rocky and the hard place softens. I start to feel mighty relieved and that's the feeling that I wake up to next morning. Oh, I woke up, that means I slept!

39 SECRETS IN MY FREEZER

Is your deepfreeze a depository for experimental batch-bakes that taste awful but you can't justify wasting? Do you have packs of Supermarket Ready Meals reduced in price, but so reduced in size they barely constitute a snack? While the tasteless foods stay on the top shelf pleading for a purpose, the homemade pizzas hide out of sight, impossible to find without satnav, and the unlabeled frost-fugged bags become an unlucky lucky dip; frozen pasta bake can be such a disappointment when you thought it was apple crumble.

Well, my heart has got just like that. Overcrowded with dour-tasting stuff that is well past its use-by-date, and by the time I've found something nice to feel, I've gone off-the-boil fumbling through the detritus. So, in the spirit of tackling long overdue jobs, I donned my metaphoric apron and rubber gloves and set to work de-cluttering and defrosting.

First out are family arguments, they don't improve with age and won't mend now. A rickety relationship with my father needs releasing. He's been dead for so many years he's probably forgotten about it and that's just what I should do. I decide to dump the lot, but its roots are so deep they're tied to the gates of hell. As I chisel and scrape, the mess begins to thaw but no matter how hard I scrub, the stain spreads further. It's more stubborn than my father. With a massive heave-ho I finally wrench it out. It overflows onto the floor, so I mop with strong disinfectant until no trace remains, not even a whiff of remorse. Gone. Probably never forgiven, but it's gone, and the jettisoned weight makes my heart flutter. I was being as stubborn as dad by hanging on to it for so long.

Broken friendships go straight in the bin; they taught me the disappointment of expectation. Would I go back for a second helping? Once I could have been tempted, but none of those people fought to keep me and I don't want to re-live the pain of losing someone I've shared myself with. Friendships are never truer than the adage "A reason, a season, or a lifetime." Wrapping the love of my lifetime friends around my shoulders stops the chill of sadness.

Envy for my ex-sister-in-law's Biba coat; black velvet maxi with dagger collar and leg o'mutton sleeves, it was deservedly covetous back in the 1970s, but why has jealousy sat there so long? She and I had known each other since we were seven years old, we shared all the people we became, and nowadays I miss the reference points nobody else knows. Was jealousy on both sides the reason we no longer speak? Whatever the reason, neither of us would fit into each other's lives these days any more than we'd fit into the coat. No need to wear regret, the coat goes.

My first wedding day wrapped in the lingering scent of bouquet freesias. As I tenderly lift it out, unexpected emotion weaves through the floral perfume. I hear the voice of the cantor echoing around the synagogue and catch my mother's face filled with pride. It was a poignant day in many ways because we married to make everyone else happy. My second wedding day smelt of hope and love and fear, spoilt when cancer gate-crashed the party. Mark and I tried to ignore the unwanted guest and battle through the day together as best we could. It's what we still do, and will always do. Till death do us part is for quitters. You cannot deny your own history, nor can you discard it, so I tuck the wedding days together, side-by-side, and blow them a kiss.

Old cars: doesn't everyone hoard a little bit of love for them? Oh, you don't? My cars all had names and when I recall certain events, I remember who I drove at that time. My first car was a 1955 MG, collectible now but just an 'old banger' back then. I saw her as characterful, grand old lady, but others only saw the rust. Some sensible hatchbacks and a fabulous (but juice-guzzling) Range Rover followed, before I settled into my stride with pickup trucks. I think I'll leave my cars parked where they are.

Trying to save other people, smart answers, rigidity and control. They're past their sell-by date and I can chuck them all. Impatience is at the back and tramples everything to get out first. Impatience dives headfirst into the bin.

Animals: I usher Horses I Have Loved into a large field. They graze happily together, safe in the knowledge they will never be discarded. Cats and Kittens snuggle back down with a contented sigh, as do the special chicken souls of Henny and Martina. The rest of the flock fly upstairs to be stored in Memory. I killed my pet rabbit when I was eight years old, his name was Thumper and I loved him. I forgot to close the hutch door, he got out and a dog ate him. Now I'm a stickler for double-fastening doors. Lesson learned, time for Thumper-guilt to go. Teenage angst still there? Oh, for goodness sake, I won't need that again!

Dead family, other people's dead families. Dead friends. All gone but somehow staying. Broken promises on both sides. They were promises made and meant at the time, but broken things always have a story and maybe the story was more important than the promise?

I'm midway down now, touching the bit where the therapist would ask if there was anything else and I'd smile my brightest smile and make small talk, and we'd both know what was going on. Secrets, dark stuff, middle-of-the-night-nightmares. Peek and poke or tiptoe away? I breathe deeply and decide to poke. There's a lot of heartache, a lot of grief. Do I carry grief with me to prove my love, if I let the grief go does love fill the void? Maybe it's time I tried.

I let people down. I was rude and said the C-word at a dinner party. I sulked, I was jealous and unjust. I was unkind unfair unbending and downright cruel. I lied. And my punishment has been holding on to it this long. Grant absolution, in the bin.

I shouted at my mum when she was ill. I shouted at her for being ill. How can anyone do that? I know she instantly forgave me so why can't I?

Challenge. Why does my life have to be such a challenge? I know I thrive when I've got my back to the wall, but these days I'm scared to venture out into the middle of the room. To let that fear go I need a steady supply of resilience, but nothing is steady anymore. Illness. The sickening glimpse through the portal that shows how ill I actually am. I consider myself a well person suffering the indignities of endless treatment, when in real life I'm an ill person who needs treatment. Just like challenge, I can't change the situation I can only change my perspective, and today's the day for action not pondering.

This stuff is getting too much so I make tea and move on down, and there, stowed right at the back of the bottom drawer, where you only ever look for old boyfriends and boots you once loved is a very *secret* secret which makes me smile.

I love challenge. If life is steady I create a project. I didn't want a challenging illness (or two) but I accepted the challenge and said fuck off I'm too busy living to spend time on this. Sometimes I hustle my inner Jewish Princess to the surface and pull rank, sometimes I plot my next move and sometimes I let change take place organically, re-inventing myself to take advantage of the situation and the openings its limitations have created. Start a new business, learn to milk a goat, bend the rules, fall in love with a troubled horse, use a spreadsheet. I wouldn't know how to live a life that wasn't challenging and when I whine, it's not the challenge that gets me, it's overwhelm. Time to take a step back, admit I'm pooped and get a good night's sleep. That admission isn't something I've quite grasped yet, but I'll work on it, it's my next big challenge.

The best thing I found in the freezer came last. Maybe I had to make room for it to find it. I'm a secret challenge diva, and

I ain't chucking that one out. The bin is full. My heart is light. Time for ice cream.

40 LAST CHANCE CHEMO

Well of course you probably guessed something was afoot here, so it's time to update you with cancer and treatment news which is surprisingly good. I thought if I set out to explain it in an email, you can ponder bits and not get worried.

I spoke to Prof Tutt on Monday for my scan results. Interesting. No organs are affected. The para-aortic lymph nodes are more enlarged and multiplied and they are certain now this is not inflammatory disease but cancer progression. The Olaparib is no longer effective. I've stopped taking it, I have a two-week break to clear my system. Then he planned to start me on a weekly Carboplatin (platinum therapy) chemotherapy dose, which I would have at the local hospital.

My inflammatory response is down from 120 to 100, which they also put down to the cancer not the vasculitis so I can reduce steroids to 10mg but have to stay on them for the time being.

I've felt for the past month that something had to give. I'm sure Olaparib was causing the vasculitis, the vasculitis was needing steroids, steroids were/are causing yet more grief and pulling me down below where I need to be. I think this new path is NOT a backwards step but a different way to go forward. I'll be relieved to have the local hospital security lest I feel ill- I've been concerned about not having a familiar port-of-call in an emergency. All in all, I feel I'm where I should be at this time, although of course, change is always a tad scary as is disease progression. I need time to get my book finished.

Yesterday I spoke to Prof Tutt, which had an uplifting and surprising outcome!

When I spoke with him on Monday, I was under the impression that as the Olaparib was no longer working, I was being 'handed back' to local care, with him in a supervisory capacity. I accepted that. To be honest, I was quite relieved to have my local hospital involved again as it feels secure. I've been going there since 1995 so it's almost my second home.

Prof Tutt wanted me to go to London for a consultation on Monday 19th to have a full DNA blood test- a Guarda 360 which was revolutionising cancer treatment by providing in-depth info. Whether or not there are treatments yet available to back up that info is debatable. My health insurance declined it, and at £3000 it was beyond self-funding. Mark and I felt quite fragile after the news about progression (face to face with everything once again) so I emailed him and cancelled the appointment, explaining why.

He phoned at 9 a.m. yesterday morning, saying I had the wrong end of the stick. He had persuaded the drug company to give me the blood test free, as I was an important member of his research!! He also felt now the lymph nodes had grown, a biopsy might be possible if I was agreeable. And having discussed my case with his multi-discipline team, he thinks instead of chemo I may be suitable for Fulvestrant injections plus Ibrace tablets. I'll leave you to google those if you need to know more details. These are monthly buttock injections, and he wants me to have them at Guys which will be trips up to town again. I turned down these injections four years ago because at the time the liver biopsy showed a mixture of oestrogen positive and negative tumours, and Fulvestrant only blocks oestrogen. Now the liver tumours have cleared, if we can biopsy the lymph tumours we know exactly what we're treating rather than best guess.

On Monday morning we're going to Guys where I'll have the DNA blood test and then a PET scan to better see if any lymph nodes are in a biopsy-able place. If they are, I go back up again and have the biopsy under guided ultrasound at Guys. I can see his point about preferring to trust his own team, although I do find the travel arduous.

So, I feel like the bullet has gone overhead once again and now I need to regain my strength, mental attitude and magic powers and step lightly into this new adventure. Something more to write about!

I'm just about to make another switch, from Olaparib targeted therapy back to Carboplatin platinum therapy which I last had in 2011. Luckily, I don't feel it's a backward step, just turned a corner and trying another route. At present, I have one more line of available treatment to try after that, which is endocrine therapy. It hasn't got us yet babe, however hard it's trying. I do believe us stubborn ones get a cancer that matches our personality! It's a way of life, it's our way of life and we're living, not dying. Go girl.

I'm aware that platinum therapy might be my last line of treatment. It's a sobering thought. I don't want to go back on chemotherapy, I don't want to have stage-4 breast cancer anymore, and I'm beginning to realise this might not be the beginning of the end, but it's definitely the end of the beginning. I could just get it over with and die, that would save having to think about dying all the time, watch Mark's face as he tries to stop it crumpling, but then I'd be leaving him alone and that's the thing he dreads. Who can blame him? My life will have ended and as far as he's concerned, his has too. And I'm going to inflict that on the person I love the most. Endless pain grief and heartache, my gift to you. Nice eh? Just what a loving wife should wrap up for Christmas.

Best case scenario? The chemo knocks it all back and after six months I get a break and start back again a few months later. That would give me a year. A whole fucking year. We know how quickly they fly by, don't we? I don't want a year. I want a lifetime, the one they promised me.

41 THERE SHE COMES

In six months' time, Mark and I will have been living with my cancer for thirty years. Princess Di was lucky she only had Camilla as the third person in her marriage. We deal with it in our own ways, and together. When our boat gets blown into the rocks we go into survival mode and when it's washed-up, we sit and wait for deeper calmer waters and then we venture out again. Although it's a vast ocean we sail, we both know we edge nearer and nearer the horizon where one of us will inevitably slip over the edge.

I am standing on the seashore.
A ship sails to the morning breeze and starts for the ocean.
She is an object and I stand watching her
Till at last she fades from the horizon,
And someone at my side says, "She is gone!" Gone where?
Gone from my sight, that is all;
She is just as large in the masts, hull and spars as she was when I
saw her,
And just as able to bear her load of living freight to its destination.
The diminished size and total loss of sight is in me, not in her;
And just at the moment when someone at my side says, "She is gone"
There are others who are watching her coming,
And other voices take up a glad shout,
"There she comes" – and that is dying.

Luther F. Beecher (1813 – 1903)

Whether the other one chooses to stay out in the ocean or head back to shore and find dry land again remains to be seen. That's another lifetime, another story, and it won't be mine to tell.

PART 5

MARK CONTINUES ON

"Till death do us part… is for quitters."

42 INTO THE ABYSS

As you will know by now Elaine has gone, but the end of her story has not yet been told. I'm Elaine's husband Mark, and as I am now the 'last man standing' from the book title, I guess it's down to me to complete the journey with you that she began just a short time ago.

There are two reasons for my doing this:

1. Elaine herself. To leave things just hanging and unfinished was not her style. She loved writing and the interaction with her readers, and I believe telling of her struggle to stay one step ahead of cancer, intermingled with observations on life and her surroundings really did help to make sense of what fate was casting her way. I know she would want to see the final full stop in place.

She asked me on several occasions to contribute to horse husband cancer, "They've heard from the horse, the cancer and from me. I want them to hear something from your side, but I can't say it for you."

I simply never got round to it, and neither of us would have envisaged these circumstances for me to begin.

2. Myself. You would think after thirty years to practise, I would be fully prepared for Elaine to die. But let me tell you that no amount of prep' can ready you for the total and utter finality that is death. The fact is she isn't coming home again, but it's a fact that I just cannot at present grasp or believe in.

Elaine was simply my world, and I'm left feeling like some future space traveller, able to stand on the event horizon of a massive 'Black Hole' , I'm staring down into the abyss to where my life, love, hopes and dreams once existed, but there's fuck-all left, empty, gone stolen away, and I've not a clue as to where to begin looking for any of it.

Maybe writing this will bring me some ideas.

Please understand that I am not the eloquent wordsmith that my wife had become. The only way I can do this is to tell it using my own words and language. I won't praise it by calling it a style! I have help with the more technical side of this but words, expressions and emotion are 100% me. The events are true.

Elaine was quite candid and open about her illness and treatment, so I'll carry on in the same vein. Her last post was December 10th, so we'll pick up the reins from there; Elaine had not eaten properly for some time, nor was she drinking a great deal. She had awful acid reflux and recurring hiccups that was getting on her nerves as much as it was getting her down. Her abdomen had become very swollen and painful. There was also pain in her lower and middle back.

She had a high pain threshold so if she said something was hurting, I knew it had to be pretty bad. We assumed the bloated tummy, (Looks like I'm full term with twins!) was due to IBS caused by all the steroids she was on, to counter internal inflammation in turn caused by the Targeted Therapy, but this proved not to be the case.

It was one of the Macmillan nurses who first mentioned a condition called Ascites. This is a build-up of fluid in the lining of the abdomen. The cancer stimulates an over-production of this fluid and as Elaine's lymph system was badly compromised by tumour growth it could not rid her body of the excess. It simply stores the fluid where it can, hence the bloating and the pain. An ultrasound scan confirmed all of this. The fluid would have to be drained.

She had an overnight stay in hospital where they drained off 5 litres of fluid. A week later it was all back.

Always before it had been the treatments to halt the spread of cancer which had caused Elaine most of her health problems. What was happening now meant we could no longer keep our heads in the sand, it was apparent the cancer had upped the game and was cruising in overdrive around her body.

An arrangement was made for Elaine to have a semi-permanent drain fitted. She was quite pleased with the idea of this solution saying to me, "Isn't it strange how things become appealing when the choices are so limited."

And so, the date and time was set, and then un-set, as corona virus put staff out of action her op' was canceled and re-scheduled for Tuesday 22nd of December.

Lack of sleep was now the norm for both of us. Elaine would go to bed around 10pm, and then be back downstairs about an hour later. She then would try to get comfortable on the sofa or maybe sat at the kitchen table. The painkillers she had seemed to be fighting too much of a rear-guard action. She was becoming desperate now as the fluid building up was causing the pain and discomfort to increase rapidly.

I came downstairs one night around 1.30 to find her sat at the kitchen table. In front of her was a small jigsaw puzzle of a plate of Brussel sprouts. Trying to get her mind focused on this was her way of distracting herself from the discomfort and reality of the situation that was now unfolding.

I sat beside her, and we tried a few pieces of the puzzle together. She spoke first, "It's not looking good is it?"

"Sprouts never do, even in a picture."

"I don't mean the fucking sprouts, you know what I mean."

"Yes, I know, I just don't want to believe all this is true. I want to wake up from this shitty dream."

"So do I babe, so do I."

I went back to bed around 3.30. We'd got half of the 'sprouts' done by then. Elaine completed the rest on her own.

By Friday 18th the pain had reached new levels as the pressure from the Ascites fluid increased. Elaine was on stronger pain medication, but the results were limited so the hospital brought forward her appointment to that afternoon and she was in there by 4 pm.

Not allowed to visit, I didn't see her until I picked her up 24 hours later. When Elaine came out I was full of hope, but this was dashed when I saw her. She walked very slowly and looked so tired and weak. The drain and a small bag with a tap came with her. Nearly 4 litres of fluid had gone already.

"Don't expect too much Mark, I'm not so good."

Her words were flat and toneless, and I helped her into the car without comment. She wanted to go home via the Christmas street lights in town, she always loved to see them.

A voice inside me was screaming," She knows it's the last time." Somehow, I managed to silence this liar.

Despite more painkilling relief, Elaine suffered another bad night being unable to sleep for no more than about 45 minutes at a time. Sunday morning saw some relief, as an early call to Macmillan at the Hospice resulted in permission to increase the morphine dose, she even managed a couple of hours sleep.

Elaine kept herself busy for much of the day, at least as much as the fatigue allowed, even now she refused to give in to a situation which would honestly have floored most mortals. The fluid kept draining.

I wasn't to know it then, but that Sunday night would be our last ever at home together.

It was an utter bastard…!"

43 A NIGHT TO REMEMBER (?)

I can't believe that she's gone.

I was there when she died. I've seen her dead in her coffin. We've had her funeral, but I still can't believe that she is not going to burst through the door any moment now saying "YEA! fooled you all. Now, which miserable sods didn't cry or send a card."

Sunday 20th December. Elaine goes up to bed about 9.30. She's been on the go all day, as much as depleted energy levels will allow. It looks to me as though she is tying-up loose ends, getting things in order. She is back downstairs inside an hour.

I say the stupidest thing possible, "You okay?"

"No, I just can't get comfortable Mark. I feel bloated and my tummy and back have started to hurt like hell. I'm up to date with the pain-killers. Just wish they would bloody well start working."

She is on slow-release morphine-based meds' plus morphine sulfate liquid as a back up. Elaine feels thirsty so I make ginger and lemon in hot water, a favourite, but it is hardly touched. Any attempt to eat or drink and she gets awful acid reflux and violent hiccups.

We sit and watch TV for a while. Christ knows what was on, I don't remember. Elaine becomes more and more restless. She tries sitting on the stairs, in the kitchen, lying on the floor and back to the sofa. Nothing seems to help her as the pain level creeps upwards.

"You go to bed Mark I'll shout if I need something."

So, I go upstairs but sleep and rest elude me entirely. I hear her moving about and after half an hour or so I go back down. One look tells me this is getting bad. Elaine has never been a complainer but if ever desperation had a face I'm looking at it now. I suggest more meds, but Elaine tells me none is scheduled for another two hours.

"Bollocks to that you can't put up with this lot, take another 2.5ml now at least."

She doesn't take much persuading, so I prepare the syringe and she swallows the sickly-sweet liquid and rinses her mouth with the offered water.

We wait.

We try bed together for a while, but the result is the same. Elaine has to keep moving to try and stop the pain from catching up with her. We're back downstairs by 1.30.

Time comes round for the slow-release meds' but over an hour passes with little relief to show for it. Elaine calls the emergency helpline direct to the Hospice and speaks to a nurse who advises another 2.5ml of the liquid. There is concern that Elaine's medication is not working correctly.

(We find out why later in the week).

It's difficult for me to express here how utterly helpless I felt. Here was the person who I love more than life itself, yet I could do so little to help her at this wretched hour.

Why do these things always happen in the middle of the fucking night?

When I was in my early teens my mother started to suffer severe asthma attacks. I well remember the look of hopeless desolation on my father's face as we watched mum fight for breath on so many occasions. We could do little to help and it always seemed to be worse in the early hours.

I knew if I looked in the mirror now I would see my dad.

At 4.30 I ring the Hospice.

"Hello, yes Mark, my colleague spoke to your wife earlier.

She should be having a better response to the pain relief by now. If she were my patient here, I would give her another 5ml of the liquid now. It may take up to an hour to kick-in, the only other option is to call an ambulance and get her to hospital."

"Hospital?"

"I'm afraid so. We can't take her in tonight. I'll put her down as an emergency case for the Macmillan nurses, they'll contact you after nine o'clock in the morning."

I hang-up. Hospital, A&E no bloody way! We've been too many times before. If Elaine ends up in A&E with all the covid 19 restrictions I can't stay with her, she'll think she's been abandoned, this next dose just has to work. She's sat on the edge of the bed when I go up.

"What did they say?"

"Take another 5ml now, another 2.5 in two hours."

"Are you sure?"

"If you don't take it I fucking will, it's that or A&E."

This is all the coaxing she needs, and the sickly liquid is quickly dispatched. We sit together on the bed, Elaine takes my hand.

"I can't continue like this darling, I need to be somewhere where this pain can be controlled."

"That means Hospital or the Hospice."

"It's got to be the Hospice. If I go to Hospital I might catch Corona Virus and die. Then the cancer would be so pissed-off."

We both giggle, then sit in silence. Later she goes onto the landing and curls into a ball on her side. I feel so helpless.

Elaine has the other 2.5ml around 6 am and settles sitting upright in bed. She now seems sleepy, also slightly confused. I put it down to the medication and am just grateful we seem to have dodged A&E.

Downstairs I make coffee and leaning on the rail of our Rayburn cooker I look into the mirror above it. My hair is now so grey (when did that happen?) and my skin appears to have a misty morning tone to it, but it's my eyes that hold the attention.

They are completely without any light whatsoever, none from within and none reflected back. Just soulless hollows looking back at a lost soul.

I turn away leaving the glass to its own reflections and pour the coffee. I don't eat, breakfast is the mouthful of fear I've been trying to swallow all night.

I'm back upstairs at 8 am. Elaine has been quiet for some time, and I find her propped up in bed eyes closed. I'm not sure if she is sleeping but deciding not to disturb her, I sneak back downstairs. The phone rings just after 9 am.

"Hello, Mark? My name's Hazel, I'm one of the Macmillan nurses. Sounds like you've had a rough night?"

"Bloody awful Hazel, we can't do another like it. Elaine needs help."

"You both do Mark. Do you think she would be happy to come into the Hospice?"

"Yes, she'll be okay with that."

Right, I'll try and make the arrangements this morning, will call you back after 10."

Upstairs Elaine is awake. "Who was it?"

"Hazel, the Macmillan nurse, she's trying to get you into Forest Holme. She'll call back after 10."

"Thank you, darling."

Julie, Elaine's best friend, is coming round at 10.30 for the traditional Christmas present swap. I ask Elaine if I should cancel, but as always she wants to see Julie very much, so the arrangement stands.

At 10.15 Hazel calls to say a final decision on Elaine is yet to be made and she will call back after 11.

Julie arrives a bit late due to a fallen tree blocking the local road. Her smiles disappear as I tell her the situation. She fixes them back when she goes upstairs to see Elaine.

I make tea and Elaine tries some, but two sips and the acidy hiccups start again, and she leaves the rest. She seems very weak. Julie and I communicate with silent looks.

Hazel calls back shortly after 11. "Hi Mark, all fixed, Elaine can come in today. They want her here by 1.30 at the latest to start some blood tests. She's only being admitted for assessment at the moment, not palliative care. Shall I arrange an ambulance?"

"No don't worry about an ambulance Hazel, I can bring her in myself." (An idea is forming in my mind).

"Okay, Mark if you're happy to do that fine, but please be here by 1.30."

"We'll be there, thank you, Hazel."

"It's why I'm here, good luck."

My idea is a slight deviation off the direct route between home and Forest Holme.

I go back upstairs to where Elaine and Julie are now opening presents. They look up as I come in.

"Pack a bag, we're off to the Hospice."

44 A DRIVE IN THE COUNTRY

Elaine always did say that the saddest thing when doing a house clearance was coming across the Christmas decorations. "These people never knew when they put them away that it was for the last time ever."

We had to keep many of them so that they would 'live- on" somehow, or so she thought. Consequently, our own trees used to groan under the combined weight of so many other people's Christmas pasts.

Eventually, she was forced to purchase a seven-foot artificial tree with a metal frame and limbs that could handle the annual load. Testament to it's being one tough son of a bitch, is the fact that when we got Sammy and Rita as kits'-four years back- they lived in it for two weeks, only coming out for food or a crap or when captured at bedtime. It's well over twelve years old now and still going strong.

Monday 21st December

"Do you want to open Christmas presents now in case you're still in the hospice on Friday?" I ask Elaine.

"Do you think I will be?" Her voice is steady but quiet.

"To be honest, yes," I reply.

"Okay, just a couple maybe."

I am looking at my wonderful wife of almost twenty-five

years. She is pale and fragile and obviously physically weak. We've just been through possibly the worst night of our lives together. Her painkilling meds aren't working right, and she has suffered so much because of it.

The pain has eased somewhat, but the vacancy is being filled by fatigue and mild confusion. Cancer is on the move now, regardless of us believing it or not.

There's not much time as we've got to be at the hospice in less than two hours. But I don't want to rush these oh so precious moments that are left to us. Elaine has always been like a big kid at Christmas. She loves everything about it especially the presents and always has to have a present on Christmas Eve to placate her until the big day.

Her 'big' present this year is a Samsung Tablet which I bought with the help of our good friend and IT-expert Bob. He's got it all set-up ready to go, we switch it on and she runs her fingers lovingly across the screen.

"I've always wanted a tablet. Thank you, darling."

There's also a couple of items I bought from the other Vintage Barn sellers and a metal watering can shaped like an Elephant that she saw in the Summer and just had to have.

I can never be certain about presents for Elaine. She loves the offbeat and quirkiness in things most of all, (don't quite know what that says about me!!).

I change clothes and leaving Elaine to get ready, go downstairs. My insides are in complete turmoil. That voice inside me is talking again.

"You're taking your wife to a hospice. That's the Last Chance Saloon, isn't it? People go there to die, don't they?"

This can't be real can it, CAN IT! Twenty minutes pass and I go in search of Elaine.

She's sat on the floor of our spare room, her work room, packing material into a large 'boot bag'.

"What are you doing love?"

"I want to get this ready for Liz, to go with the rest."

Liz and husband Jack are fellow Vintage sellers and Fair organisers. Elaine has asked them to come and collect all her material and costume stock as she knows I won't know what to do with it if she is not here.

"We've got to get going, Elaine."

"It won't take long."

"Leave it, darling, I can sort it out with Liz when the….if the time comes."

"It's just…"

"Now sweetheart."

"Okay, help me up."

I collect her bags and other items, including the tablet, and go downstairs. Elaine follows slowly and stops halfway down the stairs to catch her breath. Watching her, I feel fear nibbling at the shrinking hope inside me. She walks straight through the kitchen to the far door and goes outside. I follow and lock up behind us.

I notice she hasn't said goodbye to the cats. Nor does she look about her outside. She just looks ahead of her and keeps walking. This is totally out of character. Normally she would make some comment about the trees, the garden or the sky. She'd look for birds or gaze across the park. She was always observing life, looking for fuel for her writing and the inspiration of new ideas.

I open the gate and then the car door for her, and help her in.

It's time to leave, and I'm sure now Elaine knew well enough that for her it was going to be for the last time.

Now there are two routes open for us to get to the hospice. The most direct is through the park then turn left out of the security gate and drive up to meet the main road. To turn right is to follow the route taken by Elaine every morning and evening to get to Bruce. It's a journey she had been doing for several years, until recently. It follows through a narrow country lane leading to a winding country road for just over two miles.

Not long ago Elaine said she wanted to take the car one morning and drive this way again just to remember Bruce and for the love of the trip itself. His death hit her extremely hard, I don't think I realized quite how hard at the time.

She has her eyes closed as we pass out of the gate and turning right head downhill. We finish the narrowest part and turn onto the slightly wider section. At any time, it is a captivating drive. In Spring Summer or Autumn, the colours, smells, and sounds vie with each other to dominate the senses. But Winter bleakness gifts it a beauty born of desolation and quiet solitude.

The green of the damp fields shows bright against the grey and muted browns that make up everything else. The air is fresh, but not cold, and the sky white rather than blue, shows a vibrant life of its own to the world below. A bump in the road, and Elaine opens her eyes and looks around.

"Do you know where we are?" I venture.

"Yes…yes I do."

She's looking all around now, like a child seeing Wonderland for the first time.

That fabulous sunshine smile dawns over her face. It can't mask the truth of her condition, but it brings its own light to force reality briefly away into the shadows. I feel the lump in my throat as if it were real.

We pass hedgerows and fields so familiar. There's a particular meadow beloved of swans and many other birds and Elaine cranes her neck to see into it as we slowly drive by.

Her blue eyes, wide open now I notice, have a gentle milkiness to them but no sign of tears. The smile shines on. If she is feeling any pain it's been diluted in a sea of unexpected happiness lapping on the shore of memories. I thank God or whoever for our coming this way.

We cross the narrow stone bridge over the river and head into the village beyond. Elaine closes her eyes, but the smile remains, and I know she is ahead of us now and turning into the yard to see Bruce waiting at the stable door.

The voice inside me is saying that she knows this is the last time she'll pass this way. Deep inside you know it, too, that's why you chose this route.

But I don't want to believe in voices or intuition or any such bloody thing, they can all go to hell for all I care. We're a team Elaine and I, and you can't have a team of one. Who's Bonnie without Clyde? Butch without Sundance?

I will not believe in her dying, I just can't. But the voice is persistent and getting louder.

We re-join reality at the main road and turning left head towards Poole, and the hospice.

45 FOREST HOLME HOSPICE

hospice (noun): "A home providing care for the sick or terminally ill."

I first set foot here about eight or nine years ago. Elaine had had a terrible reaction to the chemotherapy drugs and steroids she was then taking. They de-stabilized her mind, causing massive anxiety and horrific panic attacks.

As she gradually got over all this she wanted to have counselling and having seen what her illness had put me through insisted that I go too, though separately from her. I really didn't feel that it was necessary for me, but Elaine pulled the "Please do it for my sake" card so my fate was sealed, and an appointment was duly made with Linda.

I clearly remember sitting alone in the waiting room thinking "What the fuck am I going to talk with a complete stranger about for the best part of an hour."

Linda appeared on time. Middle-aged, slim, neatly dressed with short well-cut grey hair and kindly inquisitive eyes. We went through to the counselling room where I had to fill out a questionnaire about myself. I well remember the one asking, "Have you had suicidal thoughts?" Might answer that differently today!

When this was all done we sat facing each other and Linda said, "Well Mark tell me why you've come here today."

I almost replied "Because Elaine told me to" but it was too early in our relationship to be flippant, so I began with Elaine's history of cancer and it was honestly like spitting petrol on a candle flame.

I didn't stop talking, it just poured forth. Poor Linda hardly got a word in, but she was very patient, and we went on to see each other over several years.

It was so easy to give up despair and fear to someone who is at first a stranger and later, not quite a friend, but who you know understands with impartially. I never regret going to this day…. reckon I'll be back again soon.

Monday 21st December pm.

Elaine and I complete our journey to the hospice arriving there about 1:15. Since we turned onto the main road Elaine has seemed asleep most of the time and we have not spoken. I don't think she was asleep that much, more pretending so as to avoid conversation which really could have had only one subject matter: our destination.

I've parked opposite the hospice as the little car park is already full. As I help her out Elaine's weakness and fatigue is evident, and I gather up her bags quickly as she slowly makes her way to the front door.

My phone rings.

"Hello Mark? It's Doctor Chakrabarti here." (Elaine's oncologist in Poole). "I've been informed that Elaine is being admitted to Forest Holme Hospice sometime today."

"Yes, that's right we're here now – just about to go in."

"I see, I think this is the right course for her now, it's the best place for her to be."

Oh God, he'd just as well have been stood in front of me and kicked me straight in the balls. His saying that this is the right place now for Elaine to be is like an official confirmation of her fate. A rubber stamp if you like, signed, sealed and delivered to death.

I'm reminded of Pilate, washing his hands as they led Christ away to the cross. It's unfair I know. If it weren't for this man, his team, and their dedication, Elaine and I would never have gotten this far, it's just the timing that's at fault.

"Okay, Doc, thanks," I manage to say and hang up.

"Who was that?" asks Elaine.

"Doctor Chakrabarti" I reply.

"What did he want?"

"Just to wish you well."

"That was nice of him."

"Yeah, it was."

We're at the door now and I press the buzzer for admission. Inside we are greeted by Sister Gill and one of the nurses. After passing our temperature checks for Covid 19 they lead us through a short corridor to what is going to be Elaine's room -number 9.

We pass through odd sized double doors, one containing a small, curtained window, into what is quite a large room. There's an easily washable fake wooden floor throughout, and a large window taking up most of the wall opposite the doors. The window blinds are up. A wet room with shower and loo is to the immediate left, and a basin and bin next to the door leading to it. The room is dominated by the large hospital bed at its centre. A chest with drawers is off the end of the bed with a flat screen t v on the wall above.

Between the bed and the window is a huge electric reclining chair. Its bizarre colour scheme of bright blue and baby shit brown can only have been decided upon late on a Friday afternoon, when all other options had been dismissed. I do not realise at the time just how familiar this chair and I are going to become. Directly in front of the chair there is an outside door, leading to a path which I later discover goes around the building and to the car park.

Outside and opposite this door there is a tiny patio area with an even tinier metal table and a single metal chair. I assume this set-up was for the smokers, so they could suck cancer into their lungs whilst their loved one in the bed was trying to cough it out of theirs. I note there is no ashtray now. I put her bags down on the bed as Elaine sits down in the chair.

"Would you like a few private moments before you go, Mark?" asks Gill.

"Please," I reply.

So, Gill and her companion retreat and close the door behind them. I sit down on the bed and take Elaine's hand, she speaks first. "Thank you, darling."

"What for?"

"Getting me in here. I feel safe here, they'll know how to get this pain under control, we couldn't manage it at home anymore."

We are sitting looking directly at each other. Elaine continues, "I'll be okay, Mark, this is the best place for me to be right now, I know it is."

(The words of Doctor Chakrabarti from a few minutes ago come back to me, "It's the best place for her to be.") There wasn't a hint of self-pity in Elaine's words, no fear either. But it was a bloody hard job for me, fighting to keep back the tears, I just didn't want to leave her there.

Sensing this she continues, "You'd better go now Mark. Have you got something for your tea?"

"Eh…yes, no. I'll stop in Wimborne on the way back and get something."

"Make sure you do, don't just go home and drink a load of Stella's."

"I'll drink the Stella's anyway, but I will get something to eat."

"Okay, babe, then I'll call you later."

"You know I won't be able to come and see you for a while?" (No visitors are allowed due to the pandemic situation. There may be some leeway on this for Christmas day only, but that's four days away.)

"I know Mark, but I've got my phone so we can still talk to each other. I'll be alright. You'd better get going now."

"I love you, darling."

"And I love you, too, and drive careful."

We kiss, and then again, and I kiss her hands. Then I walk

round the end of the bed to the door. Pushing it open I turn back to Elaine and mouth the words I LOVE YOU. She smiles and waves as I close the door.

Gill and the nurse are waiting there. I don't know which of them reached me first as my knees just went and I slumped against the wall crying like a child whose toys have all been broken on Christmas day.

The voice was there again, deep inside. "You know she'll never leave that room alive."

And the bastard was right.

46 NEVER GIVE UP

Kempton Park Racecourse hold their antique fairs on the second and last Tuesdays of the month. Out of all the ones Elaine and I did in the 90's and early 2000's, they consistently proved to be the most lucrative.

They start at 6 am so we had to sort and load-up on the Monday beforehand, then travel overnight- a ninety-mile trip- to get a good pitch, then try to catch a few hours' sleep in the truck before kick-off.

The buyers who turned-up were serious spenders. They didn't just look and poke and make comments like "Oh we found one of those in grannies loft, but we chucked it out. Ha-ha."

(If I only had a pound for every time!) We always did well, but being outside had to be wary of the weather.

One Tuesday small, fluttery flakes of snow started to fall out of a slate grey sky at about 5.30 am. It got harder and harder. Some sellers didn't even bother to unload. A few die-hard buyers came out early, but soon retreated against the white onslaught.

We unloaded everything, but after some early sales to regulars it all just died off. The blanket of snow made our gear look as good as everyone else's, but Elaine's face just shouted of disappointment. She always put such effort into it all, as indeed she did with everything she turned her hand or mind to. Elaine would simply never admit defeat so even though many around us packed-up and left, we remained, determined to stick it out.

By 11 am though it seemed hopeless. The weather had eased off but there was hardly anyone left around so we started brushing off the snowy foe in preparation to packing up ourselves.

We were always near the top end, close to a separate parking area where large vehicles could drive in, via an alternative gate, for loading purposes.

The sound of heavy diesel motors made us look up, as into this area drove three huge coaches followed by a large panel van and then a 7.5-ton truck. The coaches proceeded to disgorge hordes of foreign passengers on an antiques buying tour-the van was for any items too large for the coaches. The truck was with film prop buyers, who were regulars, but all had been stuck the other side of London due to the snow.

They descended on the few of us left like a plague of starving locusts. The snow didn't seem to bother them at all. Pleased to be out of the confines of the coaches, they laughed, took photos, and bought and bought and bought.

It turned out they all feared everything would be over by the time they reached Kempton, so they were overjoyed to find some of us still there. Elaine, of course, was in her element.

We were on our way home before 1 pm. There were only a few odd bits to load back up. It proved to be one of our best days anywhere ever.

Elaine's beaming smile all the way home, could have melted what was left of the snow.

Monday 21st December, evening

I'm at home when the phone rings just after 6 pm.

"Hello, is that Mark?"

"Yes."

"It's Doctor Kevin here, I'm Elaine's doctor at Forest Holme."

"Hi Doctor Kevin, everything alright?"

"Yes fine, no cause to worry, just a courtesy call really, to introduce myself."

"Okay, thank you."

"Elaine has settled-in, we've taken blood for testing, should have some results in the morning. Our main concern is getting her pain under control."

"It's been pretty bad, doc, for her to complain it has to be."

"Yes, so I understand, she told me about last night. We can't allow a repeat of that." He continues, "Mark, please understand Elaine is with us for assessment purposes only, at present. She is not a palliative care patient at the moment. Is there anything you wish to ask me?"

"I can't think of anything."

"OK fine. If I call at the same time tomorrow, I may have more news for you, would that be alright?"

"I'll be here."

"Till tomorrow then, goodnight."

He sounds like a nice guy, but there was no real news there. I always suspect that they know far more than they wish to tell.

Elaine calls about 9 pm to say she's been asleep, that they've taken blood, and is on her oral pain medication, so fingers crossed for a better night. She sounds pretty sleepy as we say our goodnights.

It's a strange night for me home alone. There have been so many others in the past when Elaine has been in hospital. But this one has the element of a countdown beginning about it and I am feeling very uneasy. Could this now be the bullet we can't dodge, we've got away with it so many times before, but what if?

Neither Elaine nor I are quitters, we simply could not afford to be. We've never given up to the cancer, just once would be all it needed. Our life together depends on our refusal to change our position or compromise.

We've both been born with an obstinate streak. With Elaine, it's pure determination, whatever.

In me it's unwavering stubbornness, and most likely a refusal to see what others take as common sense. The two of us together make a formidable crew and I'm damned now if I'm going to let the creeping doubts get the better of me.

I stay up as late as possible, hopefully to gain sleep quickly, and not have to lie there trying to best guess scenario the future. I hate going to bed alone. There is a coldness about it that always feels slightly too familiar.

Elaine calls just after 7 am on Tuesday morning. She sounds groggy and says she did not have too good a night. "Couldn't get comfortable, pain kept me awake."

She's 'tried' some toast and porridge for breakfast. But I know 'tried' means she ate very little. We agree to speak later that night.

For the life of me I can't remember how I passed the day but the phone rings again dead on 6 pm.

"Hello, Mark." It's Doctor Kevin as promised.

"Hi, doc."

"How are you, Mark?"

"That depends on what you have to say."

"Well, we've run quite a few tests, some of the results are a bit bizarre."

"That figures."

"One thing we have learned, Elaine's sodium level is low. In fact, it's very low, which would account for the confusion that she's experiencing. It's a known symptom."

"Any idea of the cause, doc?"

"Not at present, we're running more tests."

I think back to my conversation with Elaine this morning and mention that she said about not having too good a night.

"Yes, I know Mark. We've now changed tack on the pain medication and have put her on a syringe driver to by-pass the digestive process. This should work a lot better for her from now on." He continues very quickly, "Mark, would you like to come and see Elaine tomorrow?"

"Yes, of course, I would but what about the Covid restrictions? I thought Christmas Day was the only chance to visit."

"Well, I don't see why we can't make an exception in this case. Perhaps I could come and meet you then to?"

All of a sudden alarm bells are ringing inside me. I may have been born in the morning but it wasn't yesterday morning.

"Doctor Kevin."

"Yes?"

"I've got the feeling you're trying awfully bloody hard not to tell me something."

There are a few seconds of silence before he takes up again. "Okay, Mark, she said you both always wanted the truth, however hard." I remain silent so he continues.

"I gave Elaine a complete examination this morning, and afterwards we had a long talk together. You want me to be honest Mark, the fact is Elaine is now far too weak for any more anti-cancer treatments. Chemotherapy now would just result in killing her outright. The cancer has spread quickly, and she hasn't got anything left to fight it."

No more chemo' means there's absolutely no chance of halting the cancer. It means my wife is going to die.

As Doctor Kevin continues he seems to confirm my voiceless thoughts. "Mark, in light of this our view on treating Elaine has changed, she is now under palliative care."

I don't speak. Diplomatically he carries on "What time do you think you'll be here tomorrow?"

I gulp down the fear, "How about midday?"

"That's fine Mark, I'll come and find you after then, goodnight."

"Okay, doc – and thank you."

My mind was struggling to grasp the enormity of what he had just said. How the hell had it got to this stage so quickly?

Just a few months ago, Elaine was still on Targeted Therapy and all was going okay. But was it? That treatment was causing the internal inflammation she was experiencing. Were they so concerned with that, that they took their eye off the cancer, long enough for it to gain a stronger hold?

All these treatments are wonderful in so much that they prolong and save lives. But there is a price to pay, the side effects. The other conditions they can, and do cause, can be as dangerous as the cancer itself. These latest developments for Elaine are the only real time that the cancer has made her ill, all the others have been caused by the treatments. But without those treatments she would have been dead long ago.

I realise I'm sat staring at the phone as it makes a funny noise to tell me the call has ended.

I can't help but feel that it's calling time on my wife and marriage too.

47 DOWN TO EARTH...
AGAIN

Elaine had always wanted to fly in a hot air balloon. One year as a surprise I booked us a flight that hopefully would take us over our home and locality, which is what she particularly wanted to do.

These flights are very weather sensitive and after many cancellations, we reluctantly took a trip from Fordingbridge (some miles from home) which took us over Salisbury, one beautiful summers morning.

It was all very pleasant, I can recommend floating 1200 feet over Salisbury Cathedral in a wicker basket as a grand cure for constipation and any desire on my part to do it again. But Elaine really wanted to fly over home so she 'blagged' a reduced cost flight to try again.

After the usual false starts, we walked from home one evening, the mile or so to the local school playing fields for our next adventure. It was a lovely summer evening, but take-off was considerably delayed due, I believe, to concerns over the wind. However, we were eventually up and away and heading for home when the wind started to gust and took us over meadows and towards the river.

I gather the pilots sometimes like to show off a bit by skimming down to the water then shooting upwards, just in the nick of time. This duly happened, and as she could no more swim than fly, Elaine's face was a picture.

So must mine have been, when with a large oath ending in 'er', the pilot hit the gas as another huge gust took us towards a big sod of an oak tree on the opposite bank. He wasn't quick enough.

The basket crashed into the treetop then we shot upwards taking plenty of 'oaky' camouflage with us. We then levelled out across meadows and road but were heading straight for the only house on the hillside in front of us.

People were having a barbeque when we all but dropped-in, our pilot was struggling a bit. They weren't best pleased, and much swearing followed us as we only just made it over their roofline.

We floated around a while longer, but it had all gone a bit quiet in the basket by now and we were pleased to hear we would be landing soon. This took place in a field the other side of town. But as we touched down another big gust caught us. The balloon went sideways, tipping the basket on its side, and dragging it along the ground.

We were stacked and helpless like wine bottles in a wicker rack.

When we eventually stopped Elaine crawled out from under me, looked around then gasped and pointed. Running across the field towards us was a small figure all in pink, with wings, and a wand in one hand. Turned out to be a little girl just a few years old. She'd been to a party and had just got home when she saw the balloon and unable to contain herself had rushed out to see it, hotly pursued by her mum.

"Christ," said Elaine, "I thought she was an angel and we were all dead."

"Hope I feel better than this when I'm dead." Said a guy behind us, and we all managed a laugh or two.

On the way home I asked Elaine if she wanted to try for, 'Third Time Lucky', and fly over home. Her reply of "Bugger That" sealed the end of our ballooning days.

Wednesday 23rd December

I arrive at Forest Holme just before midday. Though it is less than 48 hours since I left Elaine here, it seems like half a lifetime has elapsed. After last night's conversation with Doctor Kevin and then a later short chat with Elaine, I'm left in little doubt as to the misery of our situation.

My hollow prayers all the way here have been said knowing there is now no chance of my darling ever leaving this place, alive that is.

The staff who greet me as I am let in all act with the obvious knowledge that they are expecting me and why. After temperature checks for Covid 19, and a fresh face mask, I'm led around the outside of the hospice, through a side gate and along the path that leads to the outside entrance of Elaine's room. As I pass the window she sees me, and I'm rewarded with a big smile and a little wave. She is sitting in the gaudy recliner alongside the bed and speaks first as I shut the door.

"Hello darling, how are you?"

"Fine sweetheart, now I'm with you again. You okay?"

"Yeah, I'm alright."

We as humans always do this, don't we? "How are you?" "Great, and yourself?" "Fine thank you."

Why can't we just be honest; "How are you?"

"Like a flat turd actually, and yourself?"

 "Still fucking dying, far as I know."

I know this is how she would have preferred the conversation to go but perhaps the gravity of the situation got the better of us just then. She is smiling still as we kiss our hellos and I perch on the bed beside her. Elaine continues; "Well, this is all a bit strange, everything seems to be happening so quickly."

"Too damn quickly, love, but you had a better night I gather."

"Yes, thanks to this," she replies proudly, and pats an object tucked down by her leg in the chair. It's a syringe driver. A battery powered machine about the size of a large packet of biscuits, it supplies a constant amount of medication, via a tube and needle.

"It's even got its own designer bag," she continues, pointing out the cover that surrounds it. I reason this must be a staff/patient in-house joke, as it looks to me more like a large beige sock that doesn't fit too well, but I keep quiet.

Elaine is surprisingly bright, but she does close her eyes quite frequently and is still prone to sudden bouts of violent hiccups, especially if she sips a drink. I've hardly time to settle in when a gentle knock on the door announces the arrival of Doctor Kevin.

He comes in, wearing the blue attire that doctors seem to favour plus mask and protective apron. He brings a small chair with him. He introduces himself and I like him straight away. An average height, stocky, with short cut light-blond hair and the pale complexion that goes with it. There is a benevolent smile in his eyes and his whole manner brings to mind a country curate from a Victorian novel.

Doctor Kevin places his chair opposite Elaine and sits down with his back to the outside door. I sit back on the bed by my wife.

"Well, have you had a chance to talk yet?"

"Not yet, Doctor Kevin, Marks only just got here." Elaine replies.

"Okay, will it be easier for me to go through everything we've found out and decided?" says Kevin.

I reply that I think I need him to do just that. Elaine and I are holding hands and she has a gentle contented smile on her face that I find strangely puzzling.

Doctor Kevin continues; "As I mentioned last night Mark, I have been able to give Elaine a thorough examination now that the fluid in her abdomen has gone down somewhat, and I can feel the cancer mass here, around the stomach and also in the middle back area."

He points this out on himself, Elaine is still smiling. "It's not in her stomach, Doc', is it?" I ask.

"No, but it is all around and is pushing her stomach to such an extent that it is restricting its capabilities. This is why the oral pain medication was not working. It has to pass through the stomach lining to be effective and was not able to do so. Now that we've got Elaine on the syringe driver we can by-pass that particular problem."

"Has the cancer spread anywhere else, Doc? (Me again).

"It's travelled extensively throughout the lymph system, which is now severely compromised, and I see from her last scan that the liver is effected also. As I said Mark, she is now far too weak for any more anti-cancer treatments, it is only a matter of time, I am so very sorry to say."

I look at my love. She has her eyes shut and still the smile is present. There is an expression of gracious acceptance in that smile. It is the look of someone who understands that they are exactly where they are meant to be at this moment in time and have made their peace with it.

It's as though this conversation was nothing to do with her whatsoever. I just feel a deep-rooted sadness. Even though I know this is real there's a part of me that still can't, or won't, believe it. I suppose I didn't want to believe it. The idea of living without Elaine was, I think, just too big a thing to grasp…it still is!

"How much time, Doc'?" It's me that's spoken, but it wasn't a conscious effort.

"That's difficult to say, Mark." He replies. "Everybody is different but my opinion is that it'll be more than a week, but not much more than two, if that."

How many times has this man been asked that question, I think to myself. It's a stupid one really. He hasn't got a crystal ball, for God's sake. There's nothing definite about any of this now, except the end result. He can only guess, but then he must have had a lot of practise, mustn't he? By now I'm inclined to think that Doctor Kevin would have made a bloody good diplomat.

He continues; "Elaine and I have had a long talk about all of this, haven't we Elaine?"

Elaine opens her eyes. Even though they've been closed, it's obvious that she has not missed any of the conversation.

"Yes, Doctor Kevin, we have. I understand it all okay." "Doctor Kevin" she continues. "What'll happen at the end, will I just explode inside?"

There is a ripple of the giggles between the three of us.

"No Elaine, you aren't going to explode, I assure you." Says Doctor Kevin. Then he continues; "As the pain and discomfort get worse we will up the dose of pain killing medicine and introduce another syringe driver. The medicine works with a sedative to relax the body into accepting it. This will make you sleepy, and with your low sodium levels you will begin to lose concentration. As you become more uncomfortable, we will increase the doses of everything. This will in turn, make you sleep more, then at some point you will start to get quite agitated in your sleep. We will then introduce more drugs to settle you down and you will fall into an even deeper sleep, then deeper still, until you are at the point where we will no longer be able to wake you up, and then…"

There is a momentary silence before Elaine pipe's up quite cheerfully. "Oh, that all sounds pretty good."

She looks at me "Doesn't it darling? So, I'll be asleep most of the time, better than I'd thought."

I can hardly believe her. Here we are discussing the imminent end of her life, her death. Yet her only question is an almost comical one as to how it will take place. There is no concern, absolutely no fear at all, and I know it's not the drugs, she's been like this all along.

My sadness is now bolstered up by the immense pride I feel in this incredible woman who is still, for the moment at least, my wife.

48 TEARDROPS

At the top of our garden is a stone patio area in the shape of an inverted teardrop. I built it in '96 when Elaine was undergoing her first ever course of chemotherapy. I was given the stone after building some mini dry-stone walls for a friend's mum and Elaine and I decided it would be nice to have an area to put a bench on and maybe sit outside of an evening.

We were married in late '95, being told the previous day that the cancer had returned and after our honeymoon Elaine would have to have quite radical surgery and then a course of chemo' afterwards to hopefully save her life.

Chemo' day was once every three weeks, with a total of five gruelling sessions in all. After each session, Elaine was completely wiped out for about a week, and I would stay at home to look after her.

She was always feeling sick with no appetite whatsoever (she couldn't taste anything anyway). Her energy levels crashed, her hair thinned out, and she just felt diabolically ill all the time. Naturally, she spent most of her time in bed, and while she was resting of an afternoon I would mix-up some cement and then go and lay some of the stones. It was a slow process, but I had plenty of time.

While I was doing this, I would occasionally glance up and notice my wife carefully watching me from the bathroom window. I didn't let on that I'd seen her, but she was often there, though when I went indoors, she would always be back in bed. Both the chemo' and the patio were duly finished, and though a bench, now long gone, was placed on the stonework, we rarely sat there.

One afternoon when I came home from work, Elaine made tea and suggested sitting outside to drink it.

"Let's sit up the top." She said, so we went to the teardrop and sat down.

After chatting for a while, we were quiet until Elaine broke the silence. "I used to watch you. When you were building this, I used to crawl out of bed and watch you from the bathroom window. Did you know?"

"Yes, yes, I did know. I used to catch glimpses of you peeping over the windowsill."

Then as an afterthought. "What were you thinking then?"

"I used to wonder if we would ever get to sit here together. Whether we would ever have a first wedding anniversary, or would you be sat here alone of an evening, tearful and miserable, and me, sat beside you unseen, unheard, unknown and unable to comfort you."

"What did you think when you saw me?"

"I was thinking, she had better not go and die, or I'll have built this fucker for nothing. I don't want to sit here alone, sod that, I'll go and watch the telly."

"Mark Edsall, you are incorrigible!"

"Maybe, but if you go, wherever I sit I'll be miserable without you. I think I'll just imagine you're there and talk to you anyway."

"Don't worry- I'll be there to listen."

Wednesday 23rd December. Late pm.

I leave Forest Holme about 5.30 just before Elaine's supper arrives. I've always found it difficult visiting in a hospital situation when the patient is trying to eat their food. You tend to 'hover' somehow, and whatever you do it just feels awkward being there. So, we say our goodbyes, and I head for home.

Two anxious cats are waiting when I get back. Cats love

routine. But lately that routine has all changed. They know that something is not just different, but wrong, they can sense the tension in me I'm certain.

They've started to get very 'clingy' and hang around me more. The aloofness, especially in Sammy, Elaine's boy, has mostly gone, they are unsure and want to stay close. So, I light the wood burning stove in the lounge, then feed them thinking they'll head for the fire after food. But they pick at the meal, then lurk around the hallway and stairs, sitting and staring, sometimes at me, sometimes seemingly at nothing.

Sitting down at the kitchen table I pour a beer as the quickest form of sustenance and start to think. Something is playing on my mind, and I just have to sort it through. It's to do with Elaine's attitude. Something has altered over the last few days, but what is it?

I sit and rack my brains (not a long journey) and slowly a dawn breaks over the valley.

Elaine is not afraid of death, I know that much. We've lived with its probability for years now. It's more likely the manner of death that she would worry about, but of the actual event, she is more curious than fearful.

That's not to say she's been looking forward to it in any way. She has fought and fought to stay alive and stay with me but there is a definite change now. As I've stated before, we ain't quitters. But I can't ignore the acceptance in her attitude that was not there previously.

Where did it come from? Has Elaine now chosen to give up? I can't believe that. It's the dawning in my mind that brings the answer. She has been given official permission to call it a day. There is little point in trying to fight on when all the ammunition is spent, all reserves are exhausted and there's nothing left to fight with.

They've told her this now is the end, and I believe she has known it for some time but hasn't wanted to hurt me with that knowledge.

For Elaine the worrying is over, she can fully relax for the first time in decades. She is safe in the hospice, they'll look after her, do the worrying for her. There'll be no more operations, scans, ultrasounds or x-rays. No more radiotherapy, biopsies or blood tests. No more endless hospital visits to arrange or keep or fearfully awaiting of results and having to plan life around cancer. No more drugs, blood thinners, steroids and tablets by the dozen every day. No more utterly vile endless side effects and no more hated chemo' to endure.

Plus, no more having to see the disappointment on my face as some news comes to confirm what is always feared.

Free of it all she has passed the baton. The overwhelming odds now mean that Elaine can stop running. She can turn, at last, to the cancer. It is the dark child of her existence. Born into her from the moment of conception it has lived within her like a stunted twin, a broken embryo that never knew life of its own and has always tried to steal that to which it has no right. That which nature has denied it.

Elaine is now staring into it without fear. Its threat lay in its hiding. While it remained a shadow, a whisper, almost unseen and unheard, its power was mighty. But now exposed in the open that faceless shadow, that unrelenting darkness, which has haunted her days and her dreams, now at last she can fully embrace it. She can stare into the eyeless face that has been trying to push her over the edge for years and hold on to it tightly.

It is in her death grip now and she will dictate the terms, taking it with her to the end. If only that face had eyes. I would love to have looked into them as the realisation dawned that Elaine's dying would mean the end of its trying to live, all hope gone. That soulless bastard would cease to be, but Elaine somehow, somewhere would carry on, free of it at last and forever.

As this all comes to mind I smile and raise my glass to the picture of us tucked in the frame of the mirror before me. It is a bit of a hollow toast as I don't feel joyous, just numb, everything is now feeling too adult for me, too coldly real.

Tomorrow is Christmas Eve, always a favourite day of the year. Not quite the event itself, but with that anticipation of good things to come which is almost as enjoyable-but not this time.

I'm at the hospice by 1 o'clock and am a bit dismayed to find that Elaine is still in bed. She is sitting upright but apart from the occasional hiccup, she seems very peaceful. She is very pleased to see me, and we hug and kiss hello.

I notice her lunch is on the bedside table, virtually untouched. Elaine is sleepy, but she has had a pain-free night, thanks to the syringe driver, which is under the bed cover beside her. She has talked with friends on her phone, sent and received texts also. It doesn't take much to tire her, so she dozes for a couple of hours, while I sit beside her, reading and watching.

The nurses offer me a cup of tea mid-afternoon, and Elaine wakes, and wants one too. The drinks duly arrive, but a couple of sips is enough for Elaine. She sits back taking my hand in hers, and starts the conversation.

"You know darling, it seems like we've spent the last thirty years just keeping me alive."

"I guess we have to an extent, but it was worth it." I reply.

"It's been good, hasn't it, Mark." I know what she means, she means us, our lives together. She has used this phrase before.

"Yes, sweetheart, it's been more than good, it's been wonderful."

"I wouldn't change anything, Mark, not even the cancer if it meant we couldn't have been together."

"I wouldn't either, but that's easy for me to say, I'm not the one with cancer."

"I think it's worse for you, all I've got to do is die, you're the one who's going to be left behind to carry-on without me." She continues: "There's nothing more I can do for you now darling. There'll be people around who will help you, Julie, Mike, Bob, Stacy and others, but I can't do any more now."

There is a pause, I don't speak. The tears are running freely down my cheeks. Elaine is the captain of this exchange, and she speaks first again.

"Mark, I won't mind if you love somebody else."

I try to smile, but I can't. I just look at her, I don't know what to say. This has come right out of the blue at me.

I manage: "Are you sure about that?"

"Well, maybe just a little, but it would be an awful waste if you didn't."

I couldn't find an answer for her then, I still can't now.

"You're going to have to move on Mark, in everything I mean. You'll have to be strong, or you won't be able to live."

"Not sure I'll want to live."

"But you must. For me, for Sue and Ian (my sister and friend who both died young), you've got to carry on Mark. I know it won't be easy, but you must. I promise I'll be with you as much as I can."

"I know you will sweetheart, I know you will."

There is a slight pause, and I notice then just how tightly we are holding hands.

Elaine continues: "I'm not afraid you know, it's just a new adventure, like a new challenge, I've got to start out on my own this time, that's all. I know we'll see each other again, I just know it. We've done this before Mark, I've always felt that, you know I have, at some other time in the past, and we'll do it again."

"Well, I hope if there is a next time we can do it without the bloody cancer."

"Perhaps you'll have it next time, then I can look after you."

"That's cheered me up no end, thanks."

We manage to laugh. I don't remember many conversations, even serious ones, where we didn't laugh at some point. It was a strength in our marriage.

Though the tears have flowed freely from my eyes, Elaine's remain unclouded. As she looks at me, all that flows from them is love.

49 ALTERNATIVE CHRISTMAS

One year, 2006 I think, Elaine and myself had an alternative Christmas Day – on January 19th. It came about because of Elaine's nearly stepdad Leslie. I say nearly because Elaine's mum sadly died just before they were due to marry, but Les remained close, especially to Elaine.

He was a nice man but difficult to get to know. The phrase 'solitary as an oyster' could have been written for him. After mum's death he liked, on occasions, to take Elaine out for lunches, though she dreaded his driving. So, as we had no idea what to get him at Christmas we decided to take him out for Christmas dinner on the day itself.

First time was a place near Salisbury. Oh dear. They were grossly understaffed and over booked. The dining room was uncomfortably packed. No music at all, so we were all listening to each other talk. A strange burning smell announced the early demise of the Christmas puddings.

Service was sloooow, then seemed to stop altogether. The food when it came, being fair, wasn't too bad, except for the charred puds. We were trapped in there for six hours plus, Les seemed okay with it all, but Elaine and I hated every minute.

The following year we tried again at a place near Poole. Oh dear (again). They had jammed tables in wherever they could, it was heaving and hot as a Turkish bathhouse. Music was too loud and not even Christmassy, and people were talking too loud because of it. Kids, who obviously did not want to be there, were moving around, playing electronic games or jabbering on their bloody phones, as were many adults. Worst of all the food was unremarkable and easily forgotten.

All of this passed over Leslie's head completely. For a thin guy he shifted a lot of rations, then afterwards he wanted to walk it off, so we headed for Sandbanks and a walk along the shoreline. It was evilly cold and walking back, the wind bit right through us. Les didn't seem to notice.

By the time Elaine and I got home my nose was streaming, my throat was akin to a piece of raw meat, and I couldn't stop shivering. Elaine was frozen to the bone. Over whisky with honey and hot water, we decided that we deserved another Christmas, an alternative day to make amends.

January 19th was settled on to avoid our wedding anniversary (29th Dec'). Elaine's birthday (7th Jan') and the dates of my immediate families' deaths (Jan' 21-22 & 24). With the advent of what has since happened it's plain to see why I'm not a January person.

We had a tiny fir tree that I had rescued, which stood 15 inches high in its pot, so that became our Christmas tree for the day. We put some small baubles on it and tinsel too, but no lights as it wasn't man enough, but it served very well.

There was a small chicken with all the trimmings for the Christmas meal plus a saved pud, and a budget was set for presents at ten pounds each (though we did both cheat a little here). Christmas Carols came via CD.

Little presents stuffed in ankle socks were there to wake up to, then later we opened the 'bigger' presents over tea, coffee croissants and fizz. Due to our budget, they were mostly crap from cheap or charity shops though Elaine was quite taken with her coloured wooden set of clothes pegs.

The rest of the day we fooled around, read books, watched TV and then prepared the meal together for early evening. It was all great fun, and we always did agree it was one of our best Christmases ever.

December 25th Christmas Day 2020.

I was dreading waking up alone this morning and it was no better than expected.

In these later years, we always tried to spend Christmas day alone together. We'd do Christmas stockings for each other to open, in bed first thing, with tea and coffee.

Afterwards Elaine would go off to sort out Bruce while I would make a start on preparing the veg' etc. for dinner later on. Then, when Elaine returned things would go much as I have just described above as the alternative Christmas Day.

It was never any use trying to get her to wait and open some presents later on in the day. As I stated earlier, she was like a big kid at Christmas and couldn't contain herself where presents were concerned, whether giving or receiving.

We speak briefly on the phone; Elaine sounds sleepy but is cheerful and I tell her I'll be there around 1 o'clock.

Quite honestly, it's bloody miserable at home without her. I can't bear to listen to the carols on the radio, though I've always loved them in the past. So, I tidy up the house and prepare Christmas stockings to open with Elaine later. She has already told me where my stocking presents are, so I sort out his n' hers and am ready to leave home by 12.30.

At the last minute, I remember a box that arrived a while ago from Elaine's friend, Kimberly, who lives in the USA/Canada, and I take it with me as well.

When I arrive at Forest Holme, I find a genuine Christmas spirit is abroad at the hospice.

The staff have given presents to all the patients and Elaine has got a lovely deep green bed cover with a gold pattern on it and the Charlie Mackesy book, The Boy, The Mole, The Fox and The Horse, and though she already has a copy it is a wonderful gesture from them.

Elaine cannot concentrate too long on any one thing. Her co-ordination is becoming slightly clumsy and her eyes close frequently. I figure the drugs are on the increase.

She wants to open Kim's box first and my pocketknife makes short work of the packaging. It is full of fun and delights. It is as though Kim somehow knew there would not be another chance, another Christmas. There are cosmetics and perfume for Elaine and quirky toys etc. for us both plus four sets of toy antlers to wear on your head. Typical of my wife she loves these the best and with a little help pops on a set with small flashing lights, which she keeps on all day.

Her lunch arrives and she picks at bits and pieces of the meal. I help out a bit, but she does make a better job of the ice cream that follows.

We then have our stockings to open, though it's me doing most of the opening. It's fun, but bittersweet, isn't strong enough to describe it all for me.

One silly item Elaine loves is a LED battery-powered 'church candle' about four inches high. When switched on it has a soothing deep orange glow and it's placed on the chest at the end of her bed, where it stays.

The hospice has become quite noisy. Christmas seems to have cheered everyone. We keep the doors open so as not to be shut off from everything. There are visitors in relays for the other patients, and the old boy, Bill I think, whose room is further up the corridor has his TV on too loud, but no one seems to care.

The hospice staff constantly check-up on Elaine to make sure all is okay, I cannot praise them enough. They do their work without any real intrusion on our time together and all seem so pleased to be there.

Elaine's best pal Julie arrives to visit mid-afternoon, which gives me a chance to get out for a walk around and phone Colin, Elaine's brother, and others. Due to the lockdown visitors are not encouraged generally, and as Colin lives outside the area he cannot visit at all.

I walk around for an hour or so. The air is crisp and refreshing but it's all so surreal, like I'm playing out a part in a script and because I know the final act is imminent, I want to hit pause and hold it there forever.

Back at the hospice, Elaine is nodding off, then waking, then nodding again. Julie and I talk awhile, then struggle to hold back the tears as we hug our goodbyes. I will see her shortly as she and husband John have invited me to dinner at 5.30'ish. Elaine still has her antlers on though they keep slipping as she falls asleep. She is obviously tired, so I sit quietly beside her holding her hand and trying, unsuccessfully, to make sense of this day. Later I hug and kiss my darling goodbye and reluctantly leave around 5.30.

It is only a short drive to Julie and John's home, and I'm grateful for the company the wine (one glass) and the meal, in that order. Thank God for this couple, their kindness and friendship knows no boundaries.

I'm home by about 8 pm. I was tempted to call in at Forest Holme on my way back, but Elaine would most likely be settled for the night, and not wanting to disturb her, I decide to call it a day for Christmas with my wife.

The Lodge is dark and cold, everything just as I left it hours ago. The Christmas tree looks forlorn, forgotten and embarrassed in its traditional corner. As I sit on the settee and memories of so many warm and joyous Christmas times in the past, in this very room, come flooding back to me. I am simply overwhelmed.

I know this has been the last Christmas together for Elaine and I. I also know that it's this bastard I'll remember down through the years without her. Without Her.

How the hell will Christmas ever be without Elaine. The idea of a Merry Christmas without her infectious joy and happiness for it all is to me right now, utterly impossible to imagine. It's such a cruelty that this should all happen at this time of the year. The memories will flood back as constant as the season, and just as bitter.

Tears trickle down my cheeks and though I fight it, I can't stop the flood and weep uncontrollably.

How can such utter misery exist now, where such happiness lived before?

I cannot help but wonder where I'll be this time next year, what pain will I be feeling?

Starring at the blank TV screen I find no answer, a voice inside says, "Ask yourself next Christmas Eve."

50 ANNIVERSARIES

Not so many people know that Elaine and I married each other twice.

The first time was December 29th, 1995. The second time was July 18th 20??- we could always remember the day but later were never sure of the year.

Our original wedding came shortly after Elaine's divorce from her first husband was finalised. We hadn't been living together for very long, but I loved her fiercely, and over an evening meal of cod and chips at the kitchen table, I knelt and asked her to marry me.

She responded with a big YES, and then insisted we drive over to tell her parents, a phone call just wouldn't do, but we did finish the chips first.

We were not exactly very flush for money at the time, so a budget was set of £500 for our wedding and the reception which was to be held at home.

I think about sixty people were invited. This being quite a tight fit as the Lodge isn't all that big, but Elaine reckoned on some being in the garden, for a smoke, while at least two people would be in the toilets at any one time.

We married at Blandford register office, 3 pm on a freezing cold day. My wife-to-be looked stunning, and I fell in love all over again.

The reception went really well, but the cloud over it, that not many knew, was that the previous evening we had learned that Elaine had an aggressive form of cancer, and after our short honeymoon in Devon, she would be coming back to surgery and chemotherapy.

I can only imagine how this must have played on the mind of a newlywed woman. She must have worried so much. How was I going to view her after surgery then chemo', bald as well as scarred?

Elaine didn't do self-pity, at least not outwardly, and whatever her fears she kept them well hidden.

She hated the chemo' as much as the surgery. When it was over she threw out or burnt the clothes she'd worn to the sessions and even chucked the earrings she had worn as the association was too much to bear.

"Never again Mark, not even for you."

How those words were to come back to us in the coming years.

This was why she wanted a second wedding that would be happy, joyful and just for us. Cancer not invited.

We decided on July as both sets of parents had married then and the weather, hopefully, would be warmer.

Kingston Lacy Church, St Stephens, lies a short walk to the back of the Lodge. Elaine went to see the vicar in charge at home. I don't recall his name, but he was rumoured locally to be somewhat unconventional and mad as a box of frogs.

He didn't disappoint. When she arrived at the arranged time, Elaine found him sat at the kitchen table with most of his breakfast down the front of his cassock, paperwork piled on every surface and much of the floor, and too many cats and kittens running wild to count.

The stumbling block was that Elaine was Jewish, the church is C of E, as am I, if you want to put a handle on me, and she did not want some rather difficult to exclude parts of the Christian service to be included for us.

The vicar dug his heels in, so did Elaine, but after much 'consultation' and a little giving of ground, on both sides, the arrangements were settled.

Thus, on a beautiful summer's afternoon in July, we found ourselves walking up through the woods behind our home with Champagne and glasses in hand.

Elaine looked as though she had stepped from a Jane Austen novel.

She wore a gorgeous light summer dress and carried a posy of summer flowers, with her hair cut short, she looked stunning. If she hadn't been my wife, I would have married her again anyway (work that one out).

The vicar locked the three of us in the church and the ceremony went through beautifully, he even did part of it in Hebrew as a surprise for her.

We all drank Champagne, then we covered a glass and broke it underfoot at the altar (it's buried in our garden). The vicar took a couple of pictures, and then we walked back home, for scones, jam and tea, and a one-night honeymoon.

Out of our two weddings, Elaine much preferred to remember the last one. I'm just happy that she wanted to marry me at least once.

26th December 2020. Boxing Day.

I don't fear nightmares when I go to bed. I welcome the oblivion sleep defers on me. The nightmare begins when I wake from that mini-death into a new day.

It takes a split second for me to realise that I'm alone that she isn't beside me, reality floods in, my heart is made of lead and the weight drags at my spirit.

Elaine's not here at home, she's at the hospice, not dead still living, but I know she will not return. She is still alive though, is there not hope if life is present?

Fate is teasing me. Dangling useless threads of possibilities that can never be but wanting me to grab at them none the less, to make my suffering more and laugh at my impotent anger and tears.

Even though I know it's hopeless, I don't want to believe that this loneliness is to be my future, my waking reality.

I arrive at Forest Holme about 12.30 pm.

Elaine is sat up in bed, eyes closed. She still has her Christmas antlers on from yesterday. The batteries are nearly flat, so I guess they've been on all night. I never do find out for certain.

Her LED 'candle' is glowing on the end-of-bed chest, and I turn it out (the nurses switch it on at night for her until I take over. It is on every night for the rest of her life).

Elaine soon wakes and we have hugs, and kiss hello.

"How are you feeling, darling?" I ask her.

"Got very tired from yesterday, so I slept well."

"Any pain?"

"A bit uncomfortable earlier on. They altered the syringe driver, I'm okay now."

I glance down at the little machine in its 'sock' beside her. The people who invent these things are the ones who deserve the medals.

We chat for a while about the previous day. Her eyes close frequently and she 'drifts' but isn't actually falling into deep sleep at present.

Lunch soon arrives, and Elaine has some soup but only nibbles at the solid food. She sips at some fruit juice and the hiccups start again. Later she tries a few spoons of pudding, but really eats very little.

I'm silently willing her to eat more but my silence is not very effective.

Elaine dozes gently afterwards and I sit in the recliner by her side trying to read and holding her hand at the same time. Nurses pop in every so often to check all is okay with the driver and its patient.

The sounds of the hospice filter through to me.

That Christmas Spirit is still walking the corridors, and not far away some of the staff are singing Happy Birthday for one of the other patients.

Later Elaine wakes and gives me a big smile.

"Are you alright, Mark?"

"Yes, I'm fine," I lie.

She then continues; "You know it's good to have nice things in your life, our home, cars, all the material stuff that comes along. But at the end of the day none of it really matters that much. We own things for a while, then they just move on to someone else. All that really matters is what we are to each other, that's what counts the most."

I don't know if she's just thought of this now, or even if she's asking or telling me, but it did make me realise how deep her thoughts were running.

She interrupts my thinking. "I suppose, at the end it just boils down to love. How much you love and have been loved by others."

"Thank you for loving me, Mark" she says quietly, looking straight into my eyes.

"You don't have to thank me, darling. I love you and you love me, that's all there is to it."

"You won't forget me, will you Mark?"

"That's not possible love. Even if I get old and senile, I won't be forgetting you. I don't ever want to. You are my wife and always will be as far as I'm concerned. So, don't you go wandering off too far, my girl. I'm not wanting to spend half of eternity trying to find you cos' you've gone and gotten yourself lost somewhere."

"I'll be there for you, darling, I promise."

She closes her eyes and lies back against the pillows still holding on to my hand.

That short conversation seemed so bizarre, and still does even now.

The scaffold for the words was her impending death, what we both knew to be coming soon, yet we could just have easily been two people discussing a shopping list. There were tears playing close to the surface of my eyes, but Elaine remained unemotional.

The medication was taking more than just the pain away from her I'm sure. Yet the more I think about it the more I believe that she had come to terms with death a long time since, and had filed those terms away so she could bring them out now when needed, to ease the journey, the transition, from here to…

The next couple of days follow the same pattern.

I go to the hospice early afternoon and stay four to five hours. I read and Elaine sleeps mostly, we never really do have any long conversations again.

Tuesday 29th December.

I leave home in the morning today because it's a special day.

When I arrive at Forest Holme, I'm greeted by everyone with, "Happy Anniversary, Mark."

Elaine has proudly told them all it is our 25th today. I wasn't even sure she would be able to remember but she has told everyone who will listen.

I've brought a card for her and help her to open it as her co-ordination is not good and she isn't very strong. I notice a second syringe driver has now joined the first.

She bought a card for me, but it got left at home unwritten. It's on the mantelpiece anyway.

We agreed from the first never to do anniversary presents. At least that makes things easier.

I get a big smile with my kiss hello and my wife holds my hand tightly.

"Happy anniversary, darling."

I wish her the same and we kiss once more.

Looking into her eyes I see such love coming from them it is almost like a physical presence. I see them now as I write this, I don't think time will ever efface that memory from my heart or mind.

The impression I get now is that she has been holding on especially hard to get here.

It has been a personal challenge, a defiance against her illness to get to this date, twenty-five years together, nothing not even cancer, was going to get in her way to be alive for this day.

"Hello, Elaine."

A petite woman with short blond hair and wearing protective clothing, is framed in the doorway.

"Kathy it's you!"

The pleasure in my wife's voice is evident.

Kathy has been Elaine's councillor, on and off, for many years. She is based at the hospice but has been on leave over Christmas.

It's her first day back and she was shocked to see Elaine's name on the list of patients. Ironically, Elaine has a virtual appointment with her arranged for tomorrow morning (it's the last entry in her diary).

Kathy stays a short while and suggests having a face-to-face meeting in Elaine's room tomorrow, at the arranged time of 10 am, I'm invited to attend as well.

Kathy leaves and shortly afterwards nurses arrive with a bottle of Bucks Fizz and two glasses for my wife and I. After merrily wishing us "Happy Anniversary" they leave us alone, and I open the bottle and pour two half glasses.

We enjoy a short toast, "To Us," and Elaine manages one tiny sip and to be honest I don't want much more.

I know this is our ultimate 'fizz' together, there have been lots before, I can't even remember the first, what's the betting I never forget the last.

51 NEW YEAR OPERATIONS

One of the longest spells Elaine had in hospital was in late '96 to early '97, when she stayed in the Harbour Hospital at Poole for nearly two weeks.

This was when she had her second mastectomy and bi-lateral reconstruction. She was, I believe, the only patient in the hospital over the New Year period at the time.

As always, I stayed and worried at the hospital during her operation and went down to see her in recovery afterwards.

When she awoke, she became convinced there was a white pony running around between the beds and I was duly dispatched to capture it, and under her instruction tie it safely to the end of a bed close by.

(Strangely she 'saw' that pony again one evening in the hospice).

Later the drugs had worn off, and she screamed and swore as they tried to move her from trolley to bed. Elaine was their first patient to have had that particular surgery all in one go, and they were not sure how to handle her post-op.

I used to visit at different times, but often at late afternoon/evening when, as she healed, we would get her some exercise by walking around the mostly deserted hospital together.

We owned a blue Ford pick-up at the time and as I was often the only one in the car park, I would, for the sake of convenience, park next to the hospital entrance.

I don't believe that car park saw many pickup trucks. It was more used to Mercs' and BMW's, with the occasional Bentley thrown in, to make the others all feel inferior.

One evening, as I parked and was just getting out, a man appeared by the door next to me. A woman, who looked a bit like a nurse, was behind him.

Stupidly, my immediate thought was that Elaine had died, and they had rushed out to catch me before I got up to her room.

Without any intro' he fired into me. "WHY are you parking here!?"

"Eh, what's happened?"

"What do you mean by continually parking this truck here, this is a private hospital and so is the car park."

The penny dropped in my head, and an edge came into my voice.

"I'm-visiting-my-wife."

"What?"

"My wife is a patient here."

If ever a man wanted the earth to open at that moment and take him completely, this was it.

The woman stood behind him had developed a huge grin across her face.

"But you were parked here New Year's Eve all day."

"Yes, that is when she had her operation. I stayed all day."

"But as I rushed out to stop you last night, you just waved at me as you drove off."

"No, I waved to my wife her room is above the entrance and she was at the window."

"I was stood in the entrance."

"I couldn't see you, I've no rear-view mirror (it had fallen off a while back.) I just wave as I know she's there."

"Oh, God."

Poor Keith, for such was his name. He was the manager or assistant manager I believe, I'm not sure now, and he thought I was just using the car park because it was there.

It transpired he had become obsessed with catching the 'phantom truck driver', but he'd missed me every time. He even admitted to looking under the back cover of the truck on New Year's Eve, fearing there may have been a bomb hidden in it!

Ours must have been the only pickup he had ever seen parked there. Why he just didn't leave a note on the windscreen I do not know.

He couldn't apologise enough. Especially when I rubbed it in by telling him I thought that Elaine had died, and they had come out to tell me.

When I told her, Elaine laughed her head off.

Later, on one of our evening walks, we came across Keith locking his office door for the night. She teased him with, "We'll bring the Range Rover next time."

He managed a half-laugh and stole away quickly. We never did meet him again.

30th December 2020 (just).

I go up to bed later and later now. I do so as I hate going without Elaine there. She was usually in bed before me, and my being alone is torture. So, the light goes out moments before midnight and hopefully sleep will descend quickly over me.

Almost.

I seem to have just drifted off when a horrible 'clacking' noise, I don't immediately recognise, brings me back with a start.

The room is half-lit with an icy blue glare.

"Oh Christ, it's my mobile phone!"

I snatch it up, 12.18 am, and an unknown number.

"Hello?"

"Hi, is that Mark?"

"Yes."

"Hello, it's Clare here, at Forest Holme."

"Oh God no."

"It's okay, Mark, Elaine's alright."

"Christ."

"She's just woken up and got in a panic. She thought she'd missed seeing you and Kathy. I've explained that she hasn't, but she is a bit confused and wants to speak to you. Shall I put her on?"

"Yes, yes do, Clare, thanks."

My heart feels like a slumbering diesel motor recently fired-up after several decades neglect, and now is trying to make up for lost time.

"Mark?"

"Hello, darling."

"Oh Mark, I feel so stupid."

Her voice sounds frail, vulnerable even, I just want to hold her.

"Mark, I woke up suddenly. I thought I'd missed seeing you and Kathy, I felt angry, then afraid and I started to panic, I feel so stupid."

"You're not stupid darling, you just woke up suddenly, that's all."

"I know now, Mark, I didn't then; it was horrible. I wanted to speak to you, Clare said she'd call."

"Do you want me to come over now, Elaine?"

"No, stay there, I don't want you to drive now. I'll see you tomorrow."

"Actually, you'll see me today at about 10 o'clock, it's well gone midnight now."

"Oh, alright love, til later on then, goodnight, I love you."

"Love you too, darling, goodnight."

The phone falls silent. The blue glare from the screen briefly mocks my panic, before plunging me into darkness.

I flick on the bedside light, and head downstairs. I've not been drinking much in case of being called to the hospice at night. I figure I won't be called again tonight though. So now I pull out a bottle of Jim Beam, pour half a tumbler full, and down the lot. Then repeat.

I'm at Forest Holme just before 10 in the morning.

I've been thinking hard since last night. This situation with me on tenterhooks all the time just can't continue. As soon as I'm back from the hospice, I become a bundle of nerves, taking the phones with me everywhere in case I should miss a call THE call.

Many years ago, Elaine was recovering in bed from some cancer-related problem, when I took her some tea and we started talking about the possibility of her death.

We never did shy away from this type of conversation, but we didn't make it an everyday topic either. When the circumstances arose, the subject was discussed without embarrassment, and then left alone again.

While we were talking Elaine looked at me directly, and with her customary big smile said, "I won't be afraid Mark, as long as you're there to hold my hand."

So, I promised her I would be, and now I'm worrying.

What if she has a bad turn and I'm at home. It'll take me at least twenty minutes on clear roads to reach the hospice.

What if I drive like a twat, crash, injure or kill some poor bastard and/or myself? That's not going to help Elaine, no something has to change, and now.

I know what I need to do, just have to pick my moment.

As I walk along the side path to Elaine's room, I pass the window and can see she's lying back in bed, eyes closed.

She looks up as I enter the room. The ever-present smile appears and she greets me first.

"Hello, darling."

"Hello, sweetheart, you okay?" She sounds tired.

"I am now you're here. I'm sorry about last night Mark, I was silly for getting in a panic."

"Don't feel silly love, let's just blame it on the drugs."

"Alright, I feel better now."

I take off my coat then go over and kiss her and, as I gently squeeze her hand, I realise just how weak she is becoming.

Before we can say much more a knock at the door heralds the arrival of Kathy, Elaine's councillor. She's on time and kitted out in protective gear, which now seems so normal.

Elaine perks up now Kathy has arrived.

I met Kathy for the first time yesterday, and soon come to understand why Elaine likes and trusts her so much.

I find there is a genuineness about Kathy, coupled with an ability to connect and listen without any hint of condescension or indifference.

I don't think it is fair for me to say here what passed between the three of us. Much of the time it was just Kathy and I talking, with Elaine joining in now and then. But as it is Kathy's profession to council others, it is not for me to share anything, that was said, in case it causes difficulty for her.

Suffice to say, we passed 45 minutes together, and Elaine was all the happier for it, so was I.

After Kathy has gone the nurses come in to tidy both bed and patient, and check the syringe drivers.

I take the chance to walk the few minutes into Poole to buy a newspaper and get some air. When I return Elaine is lying down in bed, seemingly asleep.

I'm trying to keep quiet, but she hears me and asks; "Is that you, babe?"

"The one and only." I reply as I go to the side of the bed and kiss her.

The moment feels right.

"Elaine? Darling?"

"Hmmm."

"Do you want me to stay with you here from now on?"

With eyes still closed her answer is one clear word.

"Yes."

I'm hovering near the open door leading into the hospice. I can't go beyond because of the restrictions but a nurse soon comes along. It's Mandy and I ask her what the procedure is to allow me to stay.

"Wait here, Mark, I'll go and talk to Sister."

She's back in a couple of minutes.

"Mark, Sister says you can stay as long as you need to. We

can't let you use the relative's suite as it's all closed down at present, but you can use the facilities here and I'll show you how to work the recliner, they say it's very comfortable. We'll give you blankets and pillows to use and as Elaine isn't really eating now, we can feed you as well."

I'm so relieved, I can be here for however long, but there's things to do first.

I go outside and call best pal, Mike, he already has our spare keys and the codes for home, and he is more than happy to step in and look after things there.

Then I leave Forest Holme and head back to collect what I'll need for my stay at the hospice for at least the next few days.

At home, I pack up what I think I'll be needing, including alcohol and chocolate. It's all a bit rushed, like a last-minute military operation that's just got approval, but I'm all done in an hour or so and decide to have a cup of tea before I return.

The cats eye me suspiciously from their beds but make no move to come into the main house.

As I'm sitting at the kitchen table drinking my tea my eyes wander to the mirror on the wall opposite. Elaine bought that mirror at a scout jumble sale years before we met, it's been everywhere with her since.

For some years now we've pushed the Christmas cards we get around the inside of the frame, and every Christmas she drapes a large length of tinsel across the top.

It's all there now, but as I stare at it, it seems so pointless, Merry Christmas Happy New Year, fat fucking chance of that.

It's like everything I know, everything I have and love and believe in is slowly being sponged away before my eyes, and I can't do a damn thing to stop it. I'm powerless, trying to hold on to the handful of cold water that represents my life. I know and it's trickling out between my fingers, no matter how hard I press them together.

I can't lose Elaine, I just can't.
Please God, let me wake up.

How long ago it all seems since that operation at the Harbour 24 years back. So much of our happiness depended on its success and what we made of life, and each other, afterwards.

We've done a bloody sight better than many would, in the same circumstances, but thinking of what we have lived alongside all these years, the enormity of it can easily overwhelm.

As I finish my drink the thought strikes me, it's a quarter of a century since our honeymoon. We took the blue pick-up, it was the best vehicle we had at the time, we owned it for years. It's long since been scraped but the memories remain intact.

They'll live on as long as one of us does, one of us.

Memory lane is too costly an excursion right now, so I head for the door. I remember the credit card bill that needs paying at the last minute but decide to leave it for now, a decision I'll come to regret later. I just want to get out of here and back to Elaine.

Tomorrow I'll wake up in a hospice, on New Year's Eve.

The honeymoon is over.

52 PLOTS AND PLANS

September 2016.

Elaine had been on a new chemo' regime for a while now. It involved a hospital visit every three weeks and four main tablets to take twice a day in between, plus a few others as well.

She was struggling with the tablets and seemed depressed with this treatment in general, also she was developing some serious physical side effects. On top of this, she had stopped eating properly and was losing weight that she could not afford to.

I had become worried, as she was listless, vague and unlike her real self.

Things came to a head one Tuesday morning when she rang me at work to say that she had spoken to the oncology team at the Harbour Hospital, and they wanted her there NOW!

I rushed home and took her straight down.

When we got there, she was taken immediately to a private room and within minutes was in bed and hooked up to monitors and drips.

I will always remember her looking at me and whispering; "Is this it, Mark?"

"I don't think so," was my truthful reply, but it was plain to anyone that she was very ill, and things didn't look too good.

They feared sepsis, so pumped her full of powerful antibiotics which wiped out everything, and she was there for a week.

When she came out, she looked as though she'd just walked

from a refugee camp, she had lost so much weight and muscle tone. She was incredibly weak.

The chemo' had all been stopped, but the side effects continued for a time, and they were horrendous.

I had to coax her back to eating with tiny bowls of porridge and meals of half a small veggie burger with a couple of florets of broccoli and a spoonful of gravy, which was laced with some vitamin powder that I had gotten hold of, and she didn't know about.

She told me that in hospital she had felt so ill that she prepared herself to die, and had not expected to wake when she fell asleep.

Recovery was slow, and it was during this time that the decision was made to arrange and pay for her funeral.

This was because Elaine knew I would have enough to handle just dealing with her death, let alone trying to organise her send off.

Elaine was not keen on a traditional Jewish burial, or any of the local cemeteries either, nor did she wish to be cremated. But we have a local Woodland Burial Ground which she quite liked the idea of, and would I like to be buried there too, as she wanted us to be together.

I didn't mind as long as I was dead before 'moving in,' so we made an appointment to go for a viewing.

The man we met with was very nice, and decisions were made on type of coffin, service, wake and so on. Then as Elaine was too weak to walk far, he took us in a buggy to see two plots that were available together.

One was end of row, the other next to it. Elaine wanted me to have the end one as I would have more legroom so the inner one was marked down as hers.

We agreed to pay for everything there and then, and now we owned two plots of real estate. Elaine asked if we could plant some beans and potatoes on them until they were needed for us.

Our guide wasn't sure if she was joking, neither was I, as he had never been asked about vegetables before. But apparently others had asked if they could grow flowers in readiness for when they were buried, and he had to explain that they would all be lost when the grave was dug for the new tenant.

Though I had been back there on occasions since, it was Elaine's only visit, until the last.

30th December 2020, late pm.

I've been back at the hospice a few hours now. Elaine is lying down in bed, but even from earlier on, there is a change.

She seems not so much in a deep sleep but more just unable to wake up. She is also more restless, like someone living out a very vivid dream.

I have had some food, though it does feel strange, eating while she is lying so near to me, but there is little choice.

I read magazines and books from home, and I've got a few beers and some whisky also, to see me through.

As evening has turned to night so the 'voice' of the hospice has hushed, and I'm left pretty much to my own thoughts.

How long will I be here?

What happens after I leave?

How the hell am I going to face life after Elaine has gone?

I know the only way to get through this is to plan for one step at a time, but quite honestly, I could just run and run and keep running.

All that holds me here is Elaine, and she is everything.

The reclining chair turns out to be surprisingly comfortable, though the motors are fierce, and it squeaks like hell. I do sleep okay, but not for very long spells at a time.

I wake and check on my wife fairly frequently. I have been told to call for help if in any doubt whatsoever, and the staff are watching constantly.

It's an uneventful night and morning brings coffee and toast for me to start off New Year's Eve.

Elaine remains asleep but restless, and mid-morning the nurses come in to sort out the bed and its patient, so I take myself off and walk the few minutes into Poole, and the shops. I want a newspaper and need to revive the alcohol stocks.

It doesn't take long to do this and I'm soon on my way back, but I take a slightly longer route as it's so refreshing to walk in the crisp cold air.

My car is parked in front of the hospice, still covered in frost. It seems a good place to leave some cans of beer to keep cool, and as a makeshift fridge, it works very well over the coming days.

Back in her room and Elaine still seems asleep, but she obviously hears me come in and says my name, so I go to the bedside and greet her with a kiss.

She then surprises me by saying; "I want a cuddle."

It takes me several minutes to work out how to drop the rail on the side of the bed. When I've mastered this metal guardian, I squeeze myself onto the bed beside my wife and for a few precious, and as it turned out final, minutes we cuddled together, sharing the moment with two syringe drivers who were sworn to silence.

One of the doctors comes in just before lunchtime. I've not met her before and cannot now remember her name.

She checks Elaine over, who remains mostly asleep, and then says to me; "I've been reading Elaine's notes, is that right, she's been fighting cancer for thirty years?"

"Yes, it's all true, since 1991.

Then she said the strangest thing; "But she's so small."

"Yep, doc, that's my wife, petite, but with a big fighting spirit."

"She truly must have, what a battle, what strength."

The doctor leaves as lunch arrives for me.

After lunch I sit and read and hold Elaine's hand as she is now sitting up in bed, eyes closed. Later she wakes and has a few sips of tea, but the hiccups return and she stops drinking.

Her last ever food was around this time. It was three thin slices of a kiwi fruit which I cut for her from one which Julie had brought in for Elaine previously.

A fitting 'Last Supper' as she always did love fruit.

When Julie comes to visit Elaine, it is usually early to mid-afternoon and I use these opportunities to stretch my legs and get some fresh air by walking around and around the block.

I try to plan my day, develop my own routine, if you like, to try and avoid being entirely 'adopted' by that of the hospice.

A hospice is like any other institution in many ways. I realised quickly, that once you are captive within its walls you soon, albeit unconsciously, go with the general flow of life there. You are no longer part of the outside world. It is still there, but you are shut off from it, almost in a monastic sense.

Hospice is like a cog within a wheel, part of the whole, yet turning to its own decree and hurrying for no one.

I sense the need to counter this somehow, but do not want to push too hard against the walls which, to be fair, are not there to punish but to sustain.

I must be honest and say that before Elaine went into Forest Holme, I had always thought of a hospice as a house of death, a place where the Grim Reaper stalked the dimly lit corridors at night, searching out the next passenger for the ferry.

I could not have been more wrong.

If any 'spirit' stalks there it is more akin to the Christmas one than the hooded shadow.

There was no sense of dread or misery or suffering. Instead, I felt it had humour, laughter and fun with an uplifting feeling of optimism which, strangely enough, did not seem out of place.

Despite all this, I don't belong here.

I'm not a member of staff and I'm not a patient.

I'm not really a visitor either, as I am actually staying here now, briefly, but still indefinitely.

I have no real place here at all and feel a bit like the Cuckoo in a nest, accepted, welcomed even, but still not truly belonging to the environment in which it is living.

The afternoon drifts into evening and eventually the cloak of night spreads across the last hours of the year.

Elaine became quite restless earlier on and complained of pain. The nurses are quick to counter this with injections to back up the syringe drivers and now my darling is much more settled and sleeping peacefully.

A coldness creeps through my own veins as I think how these drugs are now taking over not just her life, but her death as well.

I have a notepad with me and it's now that I start to pen words that might be those that end up being read at her funeral.

It occurs to me just what a privilege it is to be with another human being, especially one whom you love so deeply, as their life slowly flickers out. Not everybody gets such a chance.

Many die away from their loves, victims of accident or sudden fate, with no opportunity on either side for goodbyes.

It is my lot in life to be here now, and even as the early fireworks begin to announce a new year, a new start, a new hope, I know that for me what's coming is a storm, a hell, the like of which I have never lived before.

But I would not be anywhere else but right here, right now, even if it were to cost me my life to do so.

53 HOLDING ON

"I don't want to linger. I want to go while someone still has something bad to say about me." -ELAINE KIRSCH EDSALL.

On a hot Friday afternoon in July 1990, whilst I was working on the cottage where she lived, Elaine came home and as we talked announced that she wanted to go for a walk by some water.

I suggested a local spot alongside the River Stour close to my home and she agreed that it sounded just right.

We drove over in my old Mini, and no one took any notice of us as we set out together on what was effectively, our first ever date.

Neither of us could have known then where that initial adventure was going to lead to. But since our first meeting some weeks previously, we both knew that the spark that existed between us had flared into a fire which was growing brighter and stronger all the time.

As we walked Elaine 'casually' held out her hand, and I just as 'casually', grasped it.

We walked and chatted quite naturally along the riverbank almost into town, then turned and headed back in the heat of the afternoon sun, towards the car.

With two fields left to cross, we again came to a huge Willow tree close on the riverbank where we both spontaneously stopped and turned to each other. I pulled her close and that was our first ever kiss.

All through our years since then, on or around the anniversary of that first walk, we have trod those fields once more, and stopped to re-kindle that kiss beside the Willow tree.

Nearly twenty years or so ago, we found the tree had fallen and were saddened to see our friend and witness lying on its side, seemingly a lost cause.

But nature had other ideas. The Willow held on and re-grew. The fallen trunk sprouted new life and it is once again a dominant feature on the riverbank.

The Lodge is surrounded by trees, they too have become like friends over so many years. One, a thick trunked Cedar of Lebanon, woke us as it fell at 3 am on the 19th of December 2019.

As the early morning darkness cleared to light, we discovered this old warrior almost at 45 degrees, and assumed it was the end for certain, but it too had other ideas. It is clinging to life, still being partly rooted in the earth.

When it fell Elaine would go over and talk to it, willing it to hold on and live.

Who would have thought then that it would out-live its encourager?

1st January 2021.

I've never been a New Year person. It always seems to me a sad time. More of a looking back to what you wanted that never happened, than a looking forward to what you hope is going to be.

January, even before I lost Elaine, was never a happy or hopeful month for me, and I doubt it ever will be now.

After all the fireworks of last night, the quiet that descended over the hospice in the early hours seemed more pronounced and thought-provoking than before. Elaine slept through it all.

I had a 'bitsa' night. 'Bitsasleep' 'bitsawake', but around 6.30 in the morning the hospice begins to stir into life, and I bleakly think to myself for how much of this year is Elaine going to be able to, or want to, hold on for.

I'm not blind, or a fool. She is not eating and is hardly taking any moisture, and she is on some seriously strong painkillers. Regardless of the cancer, no one can survive this way for long.

One of the nurses brings me coffee and toast and, as I sit and watch the staff going up and down the corridor, I suddenly feel like screaming at them.

"LOOK she's in here, why aren't you doing something to make her better? Why don't you treat her; she's your patient, your responsibility?"

I, of course, already know the answer. I just need to say it to myself.

"This is a hospice, not a hospital. There is no treatment left that can save her life. She's here to be spared the pain and misery that her condition will bring if they do not intervene. The price is her silence, her unconsciousness, her deep slumber just as predicted, and a hastening of the inevitable."

"Would you rather hear her screams if she were awake and aware?"

I feel foolish, chastised by my inner self and despite the coffee, the toast remains dry in my mouth.

As the morning progresses more visitors come and go for the other patients, and the voices of life beyond our room, steal in to remind me of an outside world. Nurses come to check on Elaine at regular intervals and Julie arrives in the afternoon giving me a chance of some exercise and welcome fresh air outside of the hospice environment.

The day ends much as it began, I'm left alone with my thoughts and my still-sleeping wife.

Saturday 2nd January 2021.

Doctor Kevin and a companion visit in the morning. While Kevin and I talk the other doctor uses some of the small sponges on sticks which, when dipped in water are used to moisten the patient's mouth and lips.

Her eyes are closed but at one point she playfully bites the sponge and refuses to let go. The game seems to amuse her and her smile tells that Elaine is still with us, despite the ever-increasing drugs.

Taking me aside, Doctor Kevin confirms that she only has a short time left, days at most, and as he has been correct about everything else to date, I've no reason to doubt his predictions.

It is so very strange to stand and talk about her impending death while she lies, eyes closed and smiling, just a few feet from us. Mostly in her own world, but partially at least, still in ours.

The doctors leave and shortly after I am given lunch. Then I sit holding Elaine's hand, talking to her and trying unsuccessfully to stifle my tears and imploring God to wake me from this hell.

There are fewer visitors today, and after a while the only sound is Bill's TV from along the corridor.

Now, Bill's TV was always a bit too loud, but it never seemed to bother Elaine and I soon got used to it, but this particular afternoon the volume started to creep up and up, until, quite frankly, it got to '*Spinal Taps*' number 11 on the scale.

It was simply deafening. I never would have thought that a TV could get so loud. I quickly shut our door, but it makes little difference, and none of the staff are around. Being restricted to the room, I can't go and investigate, and it occurs to me that maybe he's died and fallen onto the TV remote. It doesn't seem very likely, but surely no one could be conscious in a room with such a horrendous sound.

Looking out into the corridor there's nobody about, the noise is awesome, so I retreat back and decide to ring for help. As I've got the bell push in my hand, I hear a door slam and hurried footsteps outside.

"BILL, BILL TURN THE TELLY DOWN."

Again; "BILL, TURN IT DOWN, oh for God's sake!"

"TURN IT DOWN BILL."

"WHAT?"

"TURN IT DOWN."

"I CAN'T HEAR YOU. MY HEARING AIDS AREN'T WORKING."

"I REALISE THAT, WHERE'S THE CONTROL?"

In a few seconds came blessed silence.

"MY HEARING AIDS AREN'T WORKING."

"It's okay Bill, don't shout, I understand."

It turned out that the batteries in both of his hearing aids had failed, and so he was near stone deaf.

The nurses had a meeting on at the other end of the hospice, and then they couldn't work out just what the noise was for a few minutes.

As for Elaine, she slept through it all. If she had been awake and capable of writing, this would have been just the sort of bizarre incident to be included into her blog, she would have loved it. Another observation on the quirky side of life that she wrote about so well.

Sunday 3rd January 2021.

Elaine became quite restless during the night. I called for help when at one point she said the word "Pain." And the night staff gave her some extra injections to counter this.

I haven't really talked much about the hospice staff, but I do truly believe that all of the warm and generous atmosphere that prevails throughout the building is down to them.

Early on, it was apparent to me, that those working there wanted to be there.

Doctor Kevin, who comes from up-country, told me he had waited until a place was available at Forest Holme before he moved down, as this was where he wanted to work.

Talking to one of the nurses one night, it transpired she had jacked in a good job in the banking sector, to re-train as a nurse in later life, because she wanted to work at the hospice.

Let's face it, they aren't there for the money. They are there because they want to be there, to help, to make a difference and they certainly do succeed in that.

I simply cannot fault the care and attention they gave to Elaine. It was second to none. I can understand now why she felt she would be safe there.

I noticed when they came to check the meds or change the bed and make Elaine more comfortable, they constantly talked to her, even though, later on, she rarely replied or possibly could not even hear them.

They would talk as if she were part of the conversation and 'include' her at all times. Whether it was one nurse or more, they always told her what they were doing and why and talked her through it. She was never ignored.

For me to single out any one person here would be, to do all of them a disservice. But there is one incident that has stuck in my mind that I just must mention.

Late each afternoon the yellow bin-bag in the room would be changed and it was nearly always the same man who did it. He would come quietly into the room, hold up the replacement bag and nod towards the bin, which was close by Elaine's bed. I don't remember him ever speaking.

When the bag had been changed, he would look over to me, on the other side of the bed, smile and without a backward look, leave.

As I got more used to him appearing I started to just say" Thank you" as he left and this was acknowledged by a slight incline of his head.

He obviously knew why I was there, and Elaine too, and I'm pretty sure he witnessed my frequent tears.

God alone knows how many times he must have been a spectator to this type of scene.

The last time I saw him was, I believe, somewhat later than usual on this Sunday afternoon.

He came in as before, and nodded to me, but he hesitated as his gaze fell on Elaine. He seemed slightly embarrassed, like someone caught out by something totally unexpected chanced upon in familiar surroundings.

He changed the bag, then as he turned, he again looked at Elaine on the bed, then he looked up directly over at me. Our eyes, almost in guilty fashion, caught each other's and I instantly felt his sympathy.

There was between us, for a fleeting moment, a shared humanity, a solidarity if you like.

I felt in that glance that he had shouted ten thousand words of silent support across the room to me, then he was gone. I swear as long as I live I will never forget that man, or that moment.

Julie comes in today shortly after lunch and I take the opportunity to get out for a while.

As the car has not been moved lately, I decide to take it for a drive around the local area. Later I ring Mike to find he's at his house which isn't far away, so I go over to see him and have real coffee.

Talking to Mike, I become aware that I am nervous and jittery. There is something inside that is trying to talk to me, but I don't want to listen.

Mike confirms that all is okay back at home, it's then that I remember the bloody credit card bill that's got to be paid. I could have gone back and done it this afternoon, but I forgot. It's too late now, perhaps in the morning?

Back at Forest Holme, Julie is about ready to leave when I return, she says she'll be back on Tuesday. She has known Elaine for 30 years plus, and I know her feelings are on a level with my own.

After supper I sit and read and hold my wife's hand frequently. I prepare for sleep around 11 o'clock but before I settle, I feel the need to sit close to Elaine, which I do and stroke her hair and face.

Her sleep seems deeper, in fact I know it is, then out of nowhere the words come to me, and I speak softly to her.

"We've got to get out of here, both of us my love. You've got to leave one way, me another, but we've both got to get out soon. There's no need to hold on Elaine, I know it's just your body that won't give in, I know your spirit wants to soar and make the break."

"Go my sweetheart, because I can't leave before you."

She, of course, didn't reply, and I'll never know in this life if she heard me, but I still like to think, that she did.

54 YOU'LL BE ALRIGHT

"Elaine, no matter what where or who, I will simply love you forever." - Mark.

I guess we all have strange or weird experiences throughout our lives. Random and unexpected events which occur without any explanation or any known reason, but just happen out of the blue often during the most ordinary of days.

Some hit hard at the time and aren't easily forgotten, others by their nature are so mild and brief that they pass into memory fairly quickly and are then only resurrected when something in the present trips that memory within us.

This doesn't mean that their impact at the time was any the less real.

What I'm starting with here is not dramatic or supernatural at all, but coming as it did under the circumstances at the time, it had a marked effect on both Elaine and myself, but we rarely talked of it afterwards.

It came to mind because the words "you'll be alright" always bring it back to me.

We were at the Harbour Hospital in Poole (yet again!) and were there because Elaine had come to the end of a chemotherapy course involving new-for-her drugs. She had recently had a scan to determine if the new regime was affecting the spreading cancer within her, and we were here this afternoon to be told the results.

Results days were always a bastard.

There is usually a week or more between the scan and getting the result, and we would both start getting a bit uptight as the day drew nearer. It was a few years ago now, and the appointments then were always late on a Friday afternoon, so you had nearly all the day itself to sweat as well.

We arrived spot on time as Elaine hated being there any longer than was necessary and were a bit dismayed to find the waiting area almost full.

The waiting area consists of easy chairs and little sofas, arranged around small coffee tables, so you often have to sit opposite complete strangers, something I personally dislike.

The only seat available for us this afternoon, was one of the sofas, so we sat down together with Elaine on my right. In the seats across from us were two older women.

Across from Elaine was a woman of late middle age, with short dark hair, wearing tinted glasses, she was engrossed in a magazine. Opposite me, a much older lady who looked to be into her eighties.

She was immaculately dressed in a long grey skirt, black woolen cardigan with a white blouse beneath, and an expensive looking necklace around her neck. It was obvious she was no stranger to money, but it was her face which commanded the most attention.

It was thin, but not gaunt, with very pale almost translucent skin and a straight lipped ungenerous mouth. She had light grey, nearly white hair, well cut and shaped, and the brightest grey eyes I have ever seen.

What struck me most though was that since we had come in she had not taken those eyes off Elaine.

She wasn't exactly staring at her but more studying her, as of someone with a personal interest. She didn't even appear to blink.

Elaine was aware of this and when we sat, she gave the lady her usual big smile as a way of saying "Hello." But it had no visible effect.

The woman wearing glasses carried on reading her magazine and did not look up at us at all.

Elaine looked at me and raised her eyes slightly as if to say, "What the?" and then she turned back to the woman who was still studying her with no hint of embarrassment whatsoever.

We spoke between ourselves, though I don't recall what we said and then we fell silent, there was something unnerving and bizarre in this situation, she was still intensely watching Elaine, and I noticed now that my wife was returning her gaze.

Then, with no warning, or attempt at any introduction the elderly woman leaned towards Elaine and said in a clear toneless voice, "You'll be alright, don't worry, you'll be alright."

Just those eight words, and that was it.

Elaine's eyes widened and she opened her mouth to speak but only managed a whispered, hesitant, "Thank you."

The other woman then spoke to her companion and was showing her something in the magazine when we heard Elaine's name being called to go through.

As we followed the nurse Elaine said to me in hushed tones;" What was all that about? Why was she so interested in me?

"I don't know," was all I could say, as we had now reached the office of Doctor Chakrabarti and were shown in.

It was good news, very good news. The cancer had taken a hammer blow and receded right back. Elaine did not need any further treatment at present, we were ecstatic.

(Indeed, she did not need more treatment for over a year, a long time for us.)

We were walking back towards the waiting area when Elaine suddenly grabbed my arm and said, "That lady, how did she know?"

We hurried on through but the seats they had occupied were empty. As we got out to the car Elaine stopped and looked at me.

"Mark, she was real, wasn't she?"

"What do you mean, do you think she was an angel or something?"

"No, not exactly, but it was weird wasn't it? Why would you say that to a complete stranger, in there of all places? She never spoke to anyone else and thinking of it, nobody else seemed to notice them."

Looking back that was true, but I guess Elaine knows the answer by now.

Monday 4th January 2021.

My wife is dying in this room before my eyes. She is hanging on to life by the thinnest of threads, and when it breaks, which must be soon, she will be free. She has been at Forest Holme hospice for two weeks now. I know this is the last stage of her life and our lives together.

I cannot conceive of a world without my darling, it is too great a thing to take in. We have been together thirty years, twenty-five years and six days married. I would not exchange one second of that time for a lifetime with any other, it would be too high a price to pay.

I know she would rather have left by now. Never afraid of dying she would want to spare me, and others, this hovering around deaths anti-room that has many entrances but only one exit.

I'm sure that once we got to our twenty-fifth, she would have been happy to call it a day and stepped through to begin her next adventure.

It's a dull morning outside, and for the first time since I've been here, there is a heaviness in the atmosphere of this room.

Elaine is asleep, or is she unconscious? I'm not sure of the difference now. I have it in my mind to shoot home this morning and sort that damn credit card bill, but I'm nervous about leaving her.

Thinking back now, I don't understand just why an outstanding bill took on such importance. Elaine was always insistent that bills were all paid up on time to avoid any penalties, which she viewed as wasting money. But given the situation did it really matter.

I can only assume that I needed something else to focus on, something I could control, but other than that I can't explain it.

One of the nurses looked at Elaine around 9 am and stated that my wife is not in immediate danger, so I get ready to leave and even say goodbye to her, but I just can't go. I don't want to leave her alone, so it's coat off and I sit and think.

The solution comes to me later and I call Julie who agrees to come in this afternoon, instead of tomorrow, so I can go home for an hour or so. I pass the morning reading and chatting to the nurses who come and go at regular intervals. Elaine remains seemingly oblivious to all.

Julie is with me bang on two o'clock, and after hugs and hellos, I'm on my way.

Back home I find the cats sharing one of their beds together, whether for warmth or companionship I'm not sure. They look at me, but I get no greeting.

I go through to the lounge and switch on the computer, then dig out the bill. Never have been keen on internet banking. Impersonal at best, and a balls-up waiting to pounce nearly always.

Sure enough, they require a raft of new security measures to be put in place and I could happily launch the pc through the window, but this has to be done, so I take a few deep breaths, and get on with it.

After the longest twenty minutes of my life, it's all sorted, and I'm on my way back out to the car.

I remember stopping outside and thinking is this really happening? I feel stuck between two worlds. Everything around me here I've known for decades, yet I don't feel I belong here. The hospice feels to me right now, more like home, I assume this is because Elaine is there, and I need to be by her side.

There is no time to think, just act, so I start the journey 'home' to my wife.

After parking in the same space I left earlier, I walk around the hospice to the outside entrance to Elaine's room.

Julie is stood outside.

A glance through the window reveals three nurses fussing around Elaine and my guts go into an instant knot.

"She's okay, Mark, they asked me to wait out here while they change the bed and replace the syringe driver batteries."

"Oh, Christ, Julie, I thought she'd died and I'd missed her."

"No, she's about the same as when you left, I've been talking to her but there are no replies."

They soon call us back in, and after briefly warming up, Julie takes her leave. I am once again alone with my wife.

So, I sit and read, have supper, a drink or two, then later shower and read some more, holding on to Elaine's hand between turning pages.

Night descends fully, and with it comes that creeping silence that seems so particular to this place.

I turn on Elaine's glowing Christmas 'candle' at the foot of her bed and sit close, stroking her hair and making no attempt to halt the tears on their familiar route down my cheeks.

Once again, I feel the need to speak to her and I do so loud enough that she can hear if that's possible.

"We have to leave Elaine; we've got to get out of this bloody room. We need to go, both of us, there's no reason to hang on like this, love."

"You'll be alright, I'm sure of it, you can let go now you've done enough. I'll never forget, I promise, and I'll never stop loving you, just be there for me when my time comes. I'm so sorry I can't go with you."

The tears choked any more words, and it's back to the shower room to wash my eyes and try to compose myself. Then I settle into my now familiar recliner bed by her side.

Tuesday 5th January 2021.

Its 3 am, I'm awake. Elaine is in the same position on her left side, facing me. She's breathing okay but it's slower. I know it is. I drift back to whatever it is that passes for sleep and am awake again at 5.30.

Her breathing has changed, more laboured. I'm up, wash and change my clothes and am back beside her before 6 o'clock.

Somehow, I know that which we have dodged for the past thirty years has, at last, found this room.

One of the nurses hears me moving and brings coffee. She checks-out Elaine then leaves without comment, which says more than words to me.

I sit and whisper to my wife and hold her hand.

Another coffee and more nurses. They look over Elaine, then leave us alone.

About 7.30 I realise that Elaine's breathing has become shorter and quicker. I know what is happening, there is no point calling for assistance, she is beyond any help now anyway.

I keep repeating how much I love her and saying thanks for the wonderful life we have shared together.

It is my tears that run down her cheeks and eyelids. Her right eye is slightly open, but I don't know if I have caused that brushing away the tears or if she somehow did it herself.

Just on 8 am the door opens slightly, its Clare, one of the nurses, just come on duty.

"Morning Mark, how are y..."

The look on my face must have said it all. She darts out, puts on her protective gear, and is back in the room in record time.

She bends close to Elaine, whose breathing is now erratic and very shallow, then straightens up and looking over at me shakes her head, answering my unsaid question.

I cry, not like a child, but like a man. A child could not comprehend the depth and measure of this emotion, but I know it only too well. I cry because of love and loss, but mostly of love.

I will her to die, not live, but die, as it is now the only door open to her as that to life has all but closed. I know one way or another, she will be free, the struggle over at last. I want her to know peace because I love her more deeply and intensely than I would ever have thought was possible before I met her.

The lights are going out in my world with her. They, I know, will never shine out so bright again, if ever at all. My darling. My wife. My love.

Her breathing is now so shallow. She is still on her left side, right eye slightly open, I am holding her hand.

There's one longer breath in, then out, then a short breath in and then…

I look up at Clare and she leans forward and then looks at me. The small shake of her head has the biggest meaning ever in my life.

MARK'S WORDS AT ELAINE'S FUNERAL

Life was one long adventure with Elaine. There was laughter and tears, hope and despair, humour- mostly black- and tons of love.

I have been blessed beyond words to have had such a partner to love and be loved by, and with whom to face life's challenges head on.

Elaine promised me that she will be there when it's my time to go. Sitting in the stillness of the hospice at night, I pondered on how this reunion might take place:

I think I'll 'wake up' by the large copper beech tree in our driveway and I'll walk down towards The Lodge. The truck will be parked outside and fully loaded- in fact it will be overloaded. Elaine will be sat in the passenger seat. She'll wind down the window and say:

"Come on, Ted, where the Hell have you been, we've got a fair to go and do"

I'll look at the back of the truck and as always, there's enough to fill several stall pitches... But I'll just sigh inwardly and walk round to the driver's side, all the time hoping that she's remembered the cold beer and Indian takeaway for later on.

I'll climb in beside her, start the engine, beep the horn twice, and we'll say, "All aboard the Skylark." A silly ritual we shared and I will look over towards her. And that sunshine smile will come and light up my world once again.

Then we will be off and it's the start of a new adventure together, only this time it'll last forever. I can honestly say that I can hardly wait for it to begin.

Goodnight my beloved darling, don't wander far without me."

ELAINE'S WORDS FOR HER FUNERAL

Despite the cancer trying to kill me at annoyingly frequent intervals, I've had a lovely life.

I only ever wanted to be with Mark, see my friends, spend time with my horse and do my work…and that's exactly what I did.

Without the depth and strength of Mark's love I couldn't have lived so long; I didn't know it was possible to love and be loved so much and feel so utterly content in his arms.

My wonderfully loyal inspirational friends who carried me over bad times, rejoiced with me in the good, cried, laughed, giggled, healed, and have always known the best answer to any problem was cake. My life became so much richer because of you, so much better.

Generous horses found me in unexpected ways. They taught me to reach inside myself and find a simpler way of communicating. To listen. To feel. To find my Quiet Place. They showed me joy in small achievements and that no matter how often you start over, it's where you end that counts.

I nearly became a horsewoman; I ended in exactly the right place to start again next time around.

Work was never really work. I loved the excitement of buying stock, even when doing so meant getting up at some ungodly hour. I loved setting up stalls and selling, but most of all I loved organising the vintage fairs. All the people coming together to create a wonderland, and all the people coming to buy and saying how much they enjoyed it.

I've had the pleasure of indulging my passions throughout my life, I've made the best of what landed at my feet, and now I fully intend to make the most of dying.

I'll leave you to carry on living for me.

Make sure it's good.

EDITOR'S NOTE:

Elaine and I met online. Isn't that the way, living continents apart? I was so drawn to her that I invited myself for a visit, but when the train pulled into Wimbourne, I felt awkward stumbling down the narrow steps, bags bumping along behind, scanning the platform for a face I didn't know. Then I saw a hand-lettered sign: *Gray Mare*. Just above it was a broad toothy smile and a nearly bald head. She said she was so happy I'd believed her scam about having cancer.

We were entwined in the passion of horses and writing and friendship. We sent secret messages back and forth in our blogs; we wrote each other poems instead of notes. There is a freedom that comes with falling in love with someone who has cancer. There is no need for artifice. We said what we felt, both favoring blunt honesty, and declared our commitment on the spot.

Of course, we talked about her book often. Then covid hit and my summer visit was cancelled by travel restrictions. Toward the latter part of 2020, Elaine told me I might have to finish the book for her, and I said I would.

Written in the last year of her life, the manuscript was completed but not fully organized. I arranged the chapters, added some stray writing from Elaine's blog, and the photos. She had asked Mark to contribute, but according to him, she'd never seen him write more than a postcard. Mark did continue the story in a vulnerable, eloquent way, telling their unique love story while sharing his heartfelt loss courageously. He is every bit her match.

I've kept my promise; it was a labor of love. If Elaine's memoir has shortcomings, know that they are mine and not hers.

Anna Blake
Infinity Farm, Colorado
September 2021